CONTENTS

4

Introduction

With 500 recipes designed to get your weekly menu out of the routine you will quickly get a taste of healthy, hearty, nutritive meals for every day! Prepare your most favorite traditional Indian dishes even faster with the help of your pressure cooker. As many recipes are vegan or can be easily changed this book is suitable for the most demanding cook.

Dive into 500 amazingly fun and diverse recipes. Indulge in Sugary Coconut Parfait or Cardamom Shrikhand, enjoy simple street classics like Chicken and Cumin Rice. Rich fulfilling flavors are what Indian cooking is about. Discover new sure-to-be favorites within snacks and appetizers, learn how to deal with the most intricate Indian spices and sauces.

The ultimate simplicity and recipes designed for Instant Pot are what makes this cookbook the only one you will ever need on Indian cooking at home. Indian Instant Pot Cookbook is going to become a true game-changer for those seeking approachable, fast and simple recipes. Make Indian cuisine one of your best cooking pleasures!

Indian Instant Pot Breakfast Recipes

Mustard Potato Curry
Preparation time: 10 minutes
Cooking time: 20 minutes
Servings: 4
Ingredients:
- 4 gold potatoes, peeled and cubed
- ½ teaspoon mustard seeds
- 1 tablespoon chana dal, soaked in ¼ cup hot water for 30 minutes and drained
- 2 big yellow onions, chopped,
- 1 teaspoon ginger, grated
- 10 curry leaves
- 2 green chilies, chopped
- A pinch of asafetida powder
- ¼ teaspoon turmeric powder
- ½ cup water
- 4 tablespoons coriander, chopped
- Salt and black pepper to the taste

Directions:
1. Set the Instant pot on Sauté mode, add the mustard seeds and brown them for 2 minutes.
2. Add the potatoes, onions, ginger and the other ingredients, toss, put the lid on and cook on High for 18 minutes.
3. Release the pressure naturally for 10 minutes, divide the masala into bowls and serve.
Nutrition: calories 100, fat 0.6, fiber 4.7, carbs 22.3, protein 2.8

Cashew Rava Upma
Preparation time: 10 minutes
Cooking time: 15 minutes
Servings: 3
Ingredients:
- 1 cup fine rava(cream of wheat)
- 1 green chili, chopped
- 1 yellow onion, chopped
- 1 teaspoon chana dal
- 1 teaspoon urad dal
- 2 and ½ cups water
- 1 teaspoon ginger, grated
- ½ teaspoon cumin seeds
- 1 teaspoon mustard seeds
- 10 curry leaves
- 12 cashews, chopped
- 2 tablespoons coriander
- 2 teaspoon sugar
- 2 tablespoons ghee, melted
- Salt and black pepper to the taste

Directions:
1. Set the Instant pot on Sauté mode, add the rava, and heat up for 2 minutes.
2. Add the ghee and whisk well.
3. Add the chana dal and urad dal, stir and cook for 2 minutes.
4. Add the cumin, mustard seeds, cashews and curry leaves, stir and cook for 2 minutes more.

5. Add the chili and the remaining ingredients, toss, put the lid on and cook on High for 9 minutes.
6. Release the pressure naturally for 10 minutes, divide the mix between plates and serve.
Nutrition: calories 200, fat 12, fiber 2.6, carbs 20.8, protein 3.6

Punjabi Potato Paratha
Preparation time: 40 minutes
Cooking time: 30 minutes
Servings: 9
Ingredients:
For the stuffing:
- 4 potatoes, peeled and cubed
- ½ cup water
- 2 green chilies, chopped
- ½ teaspoon Punjabi garam masala
- ½ teaspoon red chili powder
- 1 teaspoon dry mango powder
- 2 teaspoons coriander, chopped
- Salt and black pepper to the taste
- 2 tablespoons ghee, melted
- Cooking spray
For the paratha dough:
- 2 cups whole wheat flour
- A pinch of salt
- 2 teaspoons vegetable oil
- Water as required
- Yogurt for serving

Directions:
1. Set the instant pot on Sauté mode, add 2 tablespoons ghee, heat it up, add the chilies, garam masala and chili powder and sauté for 2 minutes.
2. Add the potatoes and the other ingredients for the stuffing except the cooking spray, stir, put the lid on and cook on High for 15 minutes.
3. Release the pressure naturally for 10 minutes, cool the mix down and mash it a bit with a potato masher.
4. In a bowl, combine the flour with the vegetable oil and the other ingredients for the dough, stir, knead well and leave aside for 30 minutes.
5. Shape 2 balls out of this dough, flatten them well on a working surface in round shapes.
6. Add the potato mix in the center of one circle, put the other one on top, press well and seal the edges.
7. Heat up a pan with cooking spray over medium high heat, add the paratha, cook for 6 minutes on each side, transfer to a platter and serve with yogurt on top.
Nutrition: calories 203, fat 4.4, fiber 3.3, carbs 36.6, protein 4.6

Buttermilk Rice Dosa

Preparation time: 20 minutes
Cooking time: 20 minutes
Servings: 6
Ingredients:

- ½ cup semolina
- ½ cup rice flour
- 2 tablespoons whole wheat flour
- 1 green chili, minced
- 1 yellow onions, chopped
- 6 curry leaves, chopped
- 1 teaspoon ginger, grated
- 2 cups buttermilk
- 10 black peppercorns, crushed
- 1 tablespoon coriander, chopped
- Salt to the taste

For tempering the dosa:

- 1 teaspoon cumin seeds, ground
- ½ teaspoons mustard seeds
- 1 teaspoon vegetable oil
- 2 tablespoons ghee, melted

Directions:

1. Heat up a pan with 1 teaspoon oil over medium-high heat, add cumin and mustard seeds and toast for 3 minutes.
2. In a bowl, combine the seeds mix with the semolina, rice flour and the other ingredients except the melted ghee, stir well, cover the bowl and leave aside for 20 minutes.
3. Set the instant pot on Sauté mode, add the ghee and heat it up.
4. Pour the dosa batter, spread into the pot, put the lid on and cook on High for 15 minutes.
5. Release the pressure naturally for 10 minutes, divide the dosa between plates and serve for breakfast.

Nutrition: calories 200, fat 6.4, fiber 1.7, carbs 29.6, protein 6

Rice Poha

Preparation time: 10 minutes
Cooking time: 20 minutes
Servings: 6
Ingredients:

- 1 and ½ cups parched rice
- 2 green chilies, chopped
- ½ teaspoon turmeric powder
- 2 tablespoons peanuts, chopped
- 1 yellow onion, chopped
- 1 potato, peeled and cubed
- 1 teaspoon mustard seeds
- 1 teaspoon cumin seeds
- 8 curry leaves, chopped
- 2 tablespoons coconut, grated
- 1 tablespoons coriander, chopped
- 2 tablespoons vegetable oil
- 1 teaspoon sugar
- Salt to the taste

Directions:

1. Set the Instant pot on Sauté mode, add the oil, heat it up, add the mustard, cumin seeds and curry leaves, stir and toast for 3 minutes.

2. Add the rice, turmeric and peanuts, toss and brown for 3 minutes more.
3. Add the chilies and the other ingredients, put the lid on and cook on High for 14 minutes.
4. Release the pressure naturally for 10 minutes, divide everything between plates and serve.

Nutrition: calories 327, fat 7.4, fiber 2.7, carbs 58.4, protein 6.3

Rice Kanda Poha

Preparation time: 10 minutes
Cooking time: 10 minutes
Servings: 2
Ingredients:

- 1 and ½ cups red beaten rice
- 1 yellow onion, chopped
- ½ teaspoon turmeric powder
- 1 teaspoon mustard seeds
- 2 and ½ tablespoons peanuts, chopped
- 12 curry leaves, chopped
- 1 green chili, chopped
- 1 teaspoon sugar
- 2 tablespoons vegetable oil
- Salt to the taste

Directions:

1. Set the Instant pot on Sauté mode, add the oil, heat it up, add the mustard seeds and the rice and brown for 3 minutes.
2. Add the turmeric and the onion and brown for 2 minutes more.
3. Add the rest of the ingredients, put the lid on and cook on Low for 5 minutes.
4. Release the pressure naturally for 10 minutes, divide the mix between plates and serve for breakfast.

Nutrition: calories 899, fat 20.5, fiber 6.1, carbs 56.7, protein 17.1

Fenugreek Wheat Paratha

Preparation time: 10 minutes
Cooking time: 10 minutes
Servings: 8
Ingredients:

- 2 cups whole wheat flour
- 1 cup fenugreek leaves, chopped
- 2 green chilies, chopped
- 8 garlic cloves, minced
- 1 cup water
- 2 teaspoons vegetable oil
- 2 tablespoons ghee, melted

Directions:

1. In a bowl, combine the flour with the fenugreek and the other ingredients except the ghee, and knead a smooth dough.
2. Shape medium balls out of this mix and flatten them on a working surface.
3. Set the Instant pot on Sauté mode, add the ghee, heat it up, add the parathas, cook for 4 minutes on each side, divide between plates and serve for breakfast.

Nutrition: calories 228, fat 6.1, fiber 6.4, carbs 37.9, protein 8.6

Gold Potato Masala

Preparation time: 10 minutes
Cooking time: 23 minutes
Servings: 4
Ingredients:

- 2 big gold potatoes, peeled and cubed
- 1 yellow onion, chopped
- 2 tomatoes, chopped
- 2 teaspoons ginger, grated
- 2 green chilies, chopped
- 10 curry leaves, chopped
- 1 teaspoon cumin seeds
- 1 teaspoon mustard seeds
- 2 teaspoons chana dal
- 1 teaspoon urad dal
- ½ teaspoon turmeric powder
- 10 cashews, chopped
- 2 teaspoons gram flour
- 1 and ½ cusp water
- 2 tablespoons coriander, chopped
- 2 tablespoons vegetable oil
- Salt to the taste

Directions:
1. Set the Instant pot on Sauté mode, add the oil, heat it up, add the chilies, curry leaves, cumin, mustard seeds, chana dal, urad dal and turmeric and cook for 5 minutes.
2. Add the cashews and brown them for 3 minutes more.
3. Add the potatoes and the other ingredients, put the lid on and cook on High for 15 minutes.
4. Release the pressure naturally for 10 minutes, divide everything between plates and serve.

Nutrition: calories 167, fat 10.7, fiber 3.9, carbs 16.6, protein 3.4

French-styled Oats Upma

Preparation time: 10 minutes
Cooking time: 20 minutes
Servings: 4
Ingredients:

- 1 cup quick oats
- ¼ cup onions, chopped
- ¼ cup French beans, chopped
- ¼ cup carrots, chopped
- ¼ cup green peas
- 8 curry leaves, chopped
- 1 teaspoon cumin seeds
- 1 teaspoon mustard seeds
- 1 teaspoon chana dal
- 10 peanuts, chopped
- ½ teaspoon ginger, grated
- 2 tablespoons coriander, chopped
- 2 green chilies, chopped
- 1 and ½ cups water
- Salt to the taste
- 1 and ½ tablespoons ghee, melted

Directions:
1. Set the instant pot on Sauté mode, add the ghee, heat it up, add the oats, curry leaves, cumin seeds, mustard seeds, chana dal and peanuts and cook for 5 minutes.
2. Add the other ingredients, put the lid on and cook on High for 15 minutes.
3. Release the pressure naturally for 10 minutes, divide everything between plates and serve.

Nutrition: calories 247, fat 12.4, fiber 8, carbs 28.2, protein 8.2

Creamy Wheat Upma

Preparation time: 10 minutes
Cooking time: 20 minutes
Servings: 2
Ingredients:

- 1 cup cream of wheat
- 2 tablespoons ghee, melted
- 1 teaspoon cumin seeds
- 1 teaspoon urad dal
- 1 teaspoon mustard seeds
- 1 teaspoon chana dal
- 2 red chilies, minced
- 1 yellow onion, chopped
- A pinch of asafetida powder
- 2 large tomatoes, roughly chopped
- 1 teaspoon ginger, grated
- 6 curry leaves, chopped
- ½ teaspoon red chili powder
- ¼ teaspoon turmeric powder
- 2 and ½ cups water
- Salt to the taste

Directions:
1. Set the instant pot on Sauté mode, add the ghee, heat it up, add the cream of wheat, cumin, urad dal, mustard seed, chana dal and chilies, stir and cook for 5 minutes.
2. Add the onion and the other ingredients, put the lid on and cook on High for 15 minutes.
3. Release the pressure naturally for 10 minutes, divide the mix between plates and serve.

Nutrition: calories 269, fat 14.8, fiber 6.5, carbs 31.7, protein 5.9

Wheat Vermicelli Upma

Preparation time: 10 minutes
Cooking time: 15 minutes
Servings: 3
Ingredients:

- 1 cup whole wheat vermicelli
- 2 tablespoons vegetable oil
- ½ teaspoon mustard seeds
- ½ teaspoon cumin seeds
- 1 yellow onion, chopped
- ½ teaspoon ginger, grated
- 1 green chili, chopped
- 1 red chili, chopped
- 8 curry leaves, chopped
- 2 cups water
- ½ teaspoon sugar
- 2 tablespoons coriander, chopped
- Salt to the taste

Directions:
1. Set the instant pot on Sauté mode, add the oil, heat it up, add the mustard and cumin seeds and brown for 2 minutes.
2. Add the onion, ginger and the chilies, stir and sauté for 2 minutes more.
3. Add the vermicelli and the other ingredients, put the lid on and cook on High for 11 minutes.
4. Release the pressure naturally for 10 minutes, divide everything between plates and serve for breakfast.

Nutrition: calories 136, fat 10, fiber 2.3, carbs 10.5, protein 2.1

Flattened Rice Poha

Preparation time: 10 minutes
Cooking time: 15 minutes
Servings: 2
Ingredients:
- 1 and ½ cups flattened rice
- ½ cup green peas
- 1 teaspoon cumin seeds
- 1 tablespoon vegetable oil
- 2 green chilies, chopped
- 1 teaspoon ginger, grated
- 1 cup water
- ½ teaspoon black pepper
- ½ teaspoon garam masala
- ½ cup coriander, chopped
- 1 teaspoon lemon juice
- 12 cashews, chopped

Directions:
1. Set the instant pot on Sauté mode, add the oil, heat it up, add the cumin, chilies and ginger and cook for 2 minutes
2. Add the rice and cook for 2 minutes more.
3. Add the rest of the ingredients, put the lid on and cook on High for 11 minutes more.
4. Release the pressure naturally for 10 minutes, divide everything between plates and serve for breakfast.

Nutrition: calories 285, fat 16, fiber 4, carbs 30.4, protein 7.1

Mung Pongal

Preparation time: 5 minutes
Cooking time: 15 minutes
Servings: 4
Ingredients:
- ½ cup white rice
- ½ cup split mung lentils
- 3 cups water
- ½ cup jaggery, grated mixed with ½ cup water
- 12 cashews, chopped
- 5 tablespoons ghee, melted
- ½ teaspoon cardamom powder

Directions:
1. In your Instant pot, combine the rice with the lentils and the other ingredients, toss, put the lid on and cook on High for 15 minutes.
2. Release the pressure fast for 5 minutes, divide everything into bowls and serve for breakfast.

Nutrition: calories 293, fat 19.2, fiber 2.5, carbs 26.1, protein 4.9

Milky Cardamom Dalia

Preparation time: 15 minutes
Cooking time: 20 minutes
Servings: 4
Ingredients:
- 1 tablespoon ghee, melted
- ½ cup dalia
- 2 cups water
- 1 and ½ cups milk
- 1/3 cup sugar
- ½ teaspoon cardamom
- 1 tablespoon almonds, chopped
- 1 tablespoon cashews

Directions:
1. Set the instant pot on Sauté mode, add the ghee, heat it up, add the dalia and roast for 4 minutes.
2. Add the water, put the lid on and cook on High for 6 minutes.
3. Release the pressure naturally for 10 minutes, add the rest of the ingredients, put the lid back on and cook on High for 10 minutes more.
4. Release the pressure fast for 5 minutes, divide the mix between plates and serve.

Nutrition: calories 364, fat 12.3, fiber 3.4, carbs 7, protein 3.4

Black Chickpeas Shallot Curry

Preparation time: 10 minutes
Cooking time: 25 minutes
Servings: 4
Ingredients:
- 1 cup black chickpeas, soaked in water overnight and drained
- 2 cups water
- ½ teaspoon fennel seeds
- 1-inch cinnamon, crushed
- 4 cloves, crushed
- 1 teaspoon nutmeg, ground
- ½ cup coconut, grated mixed with ½ cup water
- 1/3 cup shallots, chopped
- 1 teaspoon ginger, grated
- 2 green chilies, chopped
- 12 curry leaves, chopped
- ½ teaspoon mustard seeds
- 1 teaspoon red chili powder
- ¼ teaspoon turmeric powder
- 1 teaspoon coriander powder
- 2 tablespoons coconut oil
- Salt to the taste

Directions:
1. Set the instant pot on Sauté mode, add the oil, heat it up, add the fennel cinnamon, cloves and nutmeg, stir and cook for 2 minutes.
2. Add the coconut, shallots, ginger, chilies and the curry leaves, stir and cook for 2 minutes more.
3. Add the chickpeas and the other ingredients, toss, put the lid on and cook on High for 20 minutes.
4. Release the pressure naturally for 10 minutes, divide everything into bowls and serve.

Nutrition: calories 342, fat 11.4 fiber 3.4, carbs 15.5, protein 6.6

Paneer Cashew Cheese Masala

Preparation time: 10 minutes
Cooking time: 30 minutes
Servings: 4
Ingredients:
- 20 cashews, chopped
- 4 tomatoes, chopped
- 2 tablespoons butter
- 4 garlic cloves, mined
- 1-inch ginger, grated
- 1 Indian bay leaf
- 1 teaspoon red chili powder
- 1 and ½ cups water
- 2 green chilies, chopped
- 1 teaspoon garam masala
- 1 cup cottage cheese, diced
- 2 tablespoons whipping cream
- 1 teaspoon sugar
- Salt to the taste
- 2 tablespoons coriander, chopped

Directions:
1. Set the instant pot on sauté mode, add the butter, heat it up, add the garlic, ginger, bay leaf, garam masala and the chili powder, stir and cook for 5 minutes.
2. Add the cashews and the other ingredients, toss, put the lid on and cook on High for 25 minutes.
3. Release the pressure naturally for 10 minutes, divide everything into bowls and serve for breakfast.
Nutrition: calories 208, fat 13.6, fiber 2.2, carbs 12.8, protein 10.8

Milky Oats Porridge

Preparation time: 5 minutes
Cooking time: 20 minutes
Servings: 4
Ingredients:
- 1 cup rolled oats
- 2 cups water
- 1 cup milk
- 2 tablespoons sugar

Directions:
1. In your instant pot, combine the water with the oats and the other ingredients, put the lid on and cook on High for 20 minutes.
2. Release the pressure fast for 5 minutes, stir the mix, divide it into bowls and serve.
Nutrition: calories 131, fat 2.6, fiber 2.1, carbs 22.8, protein 4.7

Mung Khichdi

Preparation time: 10 minutes
Cooking time: 15 minutes
Servings: 2
Ingredients:
- 2 tablespoons ghee, melted
- 1 yellow onion, chopped
- 1 teaspoon cumin seeds
- ½ teaspoon ginger, grated
- 1/3 cup tomatoes, chopped
- 1 green chili, chopped
- 1/3 cup potatoes, peeled and chopped
- 1/3 cup carrots, chopped
- ¼ cup green peas
- 1/3 cup rolled oats
- 1/3 cup mung lentils
- ¼ teaspoon red chili powder
- ¼ teaspoon turmeric powder
- 2 and ½ cups water
- Salt to the taste

Directions:
1. Set the instant pot on Sauté mode, add the ghee, heat it up, add the cumin, ginger, chili, chili powder and turmeric, stir and cook for 5 minutes.
2. Add the onion and the other ingredients, toss, put the lid on and cook on High for 10 minutes.
3. Release the pressure naturally for 10 minutes, divide everything into bowls and serve.
Nutrition: calories 253, fat 6.7, fiber 3.5, carbs 22.4, protein 6.7

Okra Masala

Preparation time: 10 minutes
Cooking time: 20 minutes
Servings: 2
Ingredients:
- 2 tablespoons vegetable oil
- 10 ounces bhindi (okra)
- 1 yellow onion, chopped
- 1 teaspoon ginger and garlic paste
- 2 tomatoes, chopped
- 1 teaspoon coriander powder
- ½ teaspoon red chili powder
- ½ teaspoon fennel powder
- ½ teaspoon turmeric powder
- ½ teaspoon garam masala
- ½ teaspoon dry mango powder
- Salt to the taste
- 2 tablespoons coriander, chopped

Directions:
1. Set the instant pot on Sauté mode, add the oil, heat it up, add the ginger and garlic paste, coriander powder, chili powder, fennel, turmeric, mango powder and garam masala, toss and cook for 5 minutes.
2. Add the rest of the ingredients, put the lid on and cook on High for 15 minutes.
3. Release the pressure naturally for 10 minutes, divide everything into bowls and serve for breakfast.
Nutrition: calories 245, fat 7.8, fiber 2.4, carbs 22.5, protein 2.5

Chili Peas Matar

Preparation time: 5 minutes
Cooking time: 25 minutes
Servings: 4
Ingredients:

- 4 carrots, sliced
- 1 cup green peas
- 1 teaspoon cumin, ground
- 1-inch ginger, grated
- 2 chili peppers, chopped
- ¼ teaspoon garam masala
- ½ teaspoon red chili powder
- 2 tablespoons vegetable oil
- ½ cup water
- 1 tablespoon coriander, chopped
- Salt to the taste

Directions:

1. Set the Instant pot on Sauté mode, add the cumin, ginger, chilies, garam masala and chili powder, stir and cook for 5 minutes.
2. Add the carrots and the other ingredients, toss, put the lid on and cook on High for 20 minutes.
3. Release the pressure fast for 5 minutes, divide the mix into bowls and serve for breakfast.

Nutrition: calories 300, fat 7.7, fiber 3.4, carbs 15.6, protein 5.7

Garam Masala Capsicum

Preparation time: 10 minutes
Cooking time: 20 minutes
Servings: 3
Ingredients:

- 4 capsicums, chopped
- 3 potatoes, peeled and cubed
- ½ teaspoon turmeric powder
- ½ teaspoon red chili powder
- 1 teaspoon mango powder
- 1 teaspoon garam masala
- 2 tablespoons vegetable oil
- Salt to the taste

Directions:

1. Set the instant pot on Sauté mode, add the oil, heat it up, add the turmeric, chili powder, mango powder and garam masala, toss and cook for 5 minutes.
2. Add the rest of the ingredients, put the lid on and cook on High for 15 minutes.
3. Release the pressure naturally for 10 minutes, divide the mix between plates and serve.

Nutrition: calories 254, fat 9.7, fiber 6.2, carbs 39.2, protein 4.8

Jeera Potatoes

Preparation time: 10 minutes
Cooking time: 12 minutes
Servings: 5
Ingredients:

- 6 potatoes, peeled and cubed
- Salt to the taste
- 3 tablespoons vegetable oil
- 2 teaspoons cumin seeds
- 3 green chilies, chopped
- ½ teaspoon turmeric powder

- ½ teaspoon red chili powder
- ¼ cup coriander, chopped
- 4 teaspoons lemon juice

Directions:

1. Set the Instant pot on Sauté mode, add the oil, heat it up, add the cumin, chilies, turmeric and chili powder, stir and cook for 2 minutes.
2. Add the rest of the ingredients, put the lid on and cook on High for 10 minutes.
3. Release the pressure naturally for 10 minutes, divide everything between plates and serve.

Nutrition: calories 245, fat 11.4, fiber 3.5, carbs 15.5, protein 3.6

Potato Radish Pods Ki Sabzi

Preparation time: 10 minutes
Cooking time: 20 minutes
Servings: 4
Ingredients:

- ¼ pound radish pods
- 2 potatoes, peeled and cubed
- ½ teaspoon chili powder
- 1 teaspoon turmeric powder
- ¼ teaspoon garam masala powder
- 3 tablespoons mustard oil
- Salt to the taste
- 1 teaspoon mango powder

Directions:

1. Set the Instant pot on Sauté mode, add the oil, heat it up, add the chili powder, turmeric, and garam masala, stir and cook for 5 minutes.
2. Add the potatoes and the other ingredients, put the lid on and cook on High for 15 minutes.
3. Release the pressure naturally for 10 minutes, divide everything into bowls and serve.

Nutrition: calories 245, fat 11.3, fiber 5.4, carbs 13.2, protein 3.4

Stuffed Bitter Melon

Preparation time: 10 minutes
Cooking time: 20 minutes
Servings: 4
Ingredients:

- 1 teaspoon turmeric powder
- 1 teaspoon red chili powder
- ¼ teaspoon punjam garam masala
- 1 teaspoon mango powder
- 1 teaspoon fennel powder
- 2 yellow onions, chopped
- 3 tablespoons vegetable oil
- 1 tablespoon coriander, chopped
- Salt to the taste
- 12 small karela

Directions:

1. Set the instant pot on Sauté mode, add the oil, heat it up, add the turmeric, chili powder, garam masala, mango powder and fennel powder, stir and cook for 5 minutes.
2. Add the rest of the ingredients , put the lid on and cook on High for 15 minutes.
3. Release the pressure naturally for 10 minutes, divide everything into bowls and serve for breakfast.

Nutrition: calories 300, fat 14.6, fiber 3.5, carbs 12.5, protein 4.6

Spicy Okra Fry

Preparation time: 10 minutes
Cooking time: 20 minutes
Servings: 4
Ingredients:

- 1 pound okra (bhindi), sliced
- 1 teaspoon coriander powder
- ½ teaspoon turmeric powder
- 1 teaspoon cumin powder
- 1 teaspoon chili powder
- 1 teaspoon mango powder
- 1 teaspoon garam masala powder
- 1 teaspoon chaat masala
- 2 tablespoons vegetable oil
- ½ cup water
- Salt to the taste

Directions:
1. In your instant pot, combine the okra with the coriander, turmeric and the other ingredients, put the lid on and cook on High for 20 minutes.
2. Release the pressure naturally for 10 minutes, divide everything into bowls and serve for breakfast.
Nutrition: calories 245, fat 9.8, fiber 3.4, carbs 15.6, protein 7.6

Banana Beans Daal

Preparation time: 10 minutes
Cooking time: 10 minutes
Servings: 4
Ingredients:

- 8 bananas, peeled and sliced
- ½ cup yellow mung dal
- 1 yellow onion, chopped
- 5 garlic cloves, minced
- ½ teaspoon ginger, grated
- 2 green chilies, chopped
- ¼ tablespoon turmeric powder
- 1 tablespoon cumin seeds
- 1 tablespoon coconut spice powder
- ½ tablespoon coriander, chopped
- ½ tablespoon red chili powder
- 1 tablespoon curry powder
- 3 tablespoons vegetable oil
- Juice of 1 lime
- ¼ cup water

Directions:
1. Set the instant pot on Sauté mode, add the mung dal, ginger, chilies, turmeric, cumin, coconut powder, coriander, chili and curry powder, stir and cook for 5 minutes.
2. Add the bananas and the other ingredients, put the lid on and cook on High for 5 minutes.
3. Release the pressure naturally for 10 minutes, divide the mix into bowls and serve for breakfast.
Nutrition: calories 470, fat 20.8, fiber 7.9, carbs 72.2, protein 6

Mango Beans Dal

Preparation time: 5 minutes

Cooking time: 20 minutes
Servings: 4
Ingredients:

- ¼ cup mung dal
- 1 teaspoon chili powder
- 1 teaspoon turmeric powder
- 1 green mango, peeled and cubed
- Salt to the taste
- 1 teaspoon nigella seeds
- 2 tablespoons ghee, melted
- 1 teaspoon mustard seeds
- 2 red chilies, minced
- 1 shallot, chopped

Directions:
1. Set the Instant pot on Sauté mode, add the mung dal, chili and turmeric powder and cook for 2 minutes.
2. Add the mango and the other ingredients, put the lid on and cook on High for 18 minutes.
3. Release the pressure fast for 5 minutes, divide the dal into bowls and serve for breakfast.
Nutrition: calories 300, fat 15.4, fiber 3.4, carbs 17.6, protein 11.2

Sweet Potato Cream Soup

Preparation time: 10 minutes
Cooking time: 17 minutes
Servings: 4
Ingredients:

- 2 garlic cloves, minced
- 1 red onion, chopped
- 1 tablespoon sesame oil
- 1 teaspoon ginger, grated
- 1 red chili, chopped
- 2 teaspoons turmeric powder
- 1 teaspoon cumin, ground
- 2 sweet potatoes, peeled and cut into chunks
- 1 cup red lentils
- 2 cups veggie stock
- ½ tablespoon basil, chopped

Directions:
1. Set the instant pot on Sauté mode, add the oil, heat it up, add the garlic, onion, ginger, chili, turmeric and the cumin and sauté for 2 minutes.
2. Add the sweet potatoes and the other ingredients, put the lid on and cook on High for 15 minutes.
3. Release the pressure naturally for 10 minutes, divide everything into bowls and serve for breakfast.
Nutrition: calories 314, fat 12.5, fiber 5.4, carbs 22, protein 1.9

Carrot Rasam and Mung Dal

Preparation time: 10 minutes
Cooking time: 10 minutes
Servings: 4
Ingredients:
- 14 baby carrots, peeled and sliced
- 2 tomatoes, chopped
- 2 tablespoons yellow mung dal
- 1 tablespoon ghee, melted
- ¼ tablespoon turmeric powder
- Salt to the taste
- Juice of ½ lime
- 2 cups water
- 4 garlic cloves, mined
- 1-inch ginger, grated

Directions:
1. Set the instant pot on sauté mode, add the ghee, heat it up, add the mung dal, turmeric, garlic and ginger and sauté for 2 minutes.
2. Add the carrots and the other ingredients, put the lid on and cook on High for 8 minutes.
3. Release the pressure naturally for 10 minutes, divide the mix into bowls and serve for breakfast.

Nutrition: calories 344, fat 15.5, fiber 3.5, carbs 23.4, protein 5.67

Tomato Rice

Preparation time: 10 minutes
Cooking time: 20 minutes
Servings: 4
Ingredients:
- 1 cup basmati rice, soaked in 1 and ½ cups water
- ½ cup yellow mung dal, soaked for 30 minutes and drained
- 2 tomatoes, chopped
- 1 potato, peeled and cubed
- 2 green chilies, chopped
- 1 tablespoon garlic and ginger paste
- 1 shallot, chopped
- 4 cloves, ground
- 3 cardamom, crushed
- 2 bay leaves
- ½ tablespoon cumin seeds
- 3 tablespoons vegetable oil
- ½ tablespoon sambar powder
- Salt to the taste

Directions:
1. Set the instant pot on Sauté mode, add the oil, heat it up, add the chilies, garlic paste, shallot, cloves, cardamom, bay leaves and cumin seeds, stir and sauté for 5 minutes.
2. Add the rice and the other ingredients, put the lid on and cook on High for 15 minutes.
3. Release the pressure naturally for 10 minutes, divide the mix into bowls and serve for breakfast.

Nutrition: calories 244, fat 11.7, fiber 4.5, carbs 18.9, protein 3.4

Milky Grated Paneer Spread

Preparation time: 10 minutes
Cooking time: 15 minutes
Servings: 4
Ingredients:
- 1 cup grated paneer
- 1 cup milk
- ½ cup jaggery
- ¼ tablespoon pistachios, chopped
- 3 tablespoons semolina
- 1 tablespoon ghee, melted
- 4 cardamom, ground
- 2 cups water

Directions:
1. Grease a steel bowl with the ghee, add all the ingredients except the water inside and whisk well.
2. Put the water in the instant pot, add the trivet inside, add the bowls, put the lid on and cook on High for 15 minutes.
3. Release the pressure naturally for 10 minutes, whisk the mix, cool down and serve as a breakfast spread.

Nutrition: calories 300, fat 14.5, fiber 4.5, carbs 17.4, protein 4.9

Green Cauliflower Dosa

Preparation time: 10 minutes
Cooking time: 12 minutes
Servings: 6
Ingredients:
- 3 cups cauliflower florets
- 2 potatoes, peeled and cubed
- ½ cup green peas
- 1 carrot, chopped
- 1 yellow onion, chopped
- 1 tablespoon green chili paste
- 4 garlic cloves, minced
- 1 tablespoon ginger, grated
- 1 tablespoon red chili powder
- 1 tablespoon coriander, chopped
- 1 tablespoon cumin powder
- 1 tablespoon dry mango powder
- 2 tablespoons vegetable oil
- ¼ tablespoon turmeric powder
- Salt to the taste
- ½ tablespoons mustard seeds
- 1 tablespoon cumin, ground

Directions:
1. Set the instant pot on Sauté mode, add the oil, heat it up, add the chili paste, garlic, ginger, chili powder, coriander, cumin, mango and turmeric powder, mustard seeds and cumin and sauté for 3 minutes.
2. Add the rest of the ingredients, put the lid on and cook on High for 9 minutes.
3. Release the pressure naturally for 10 minutes, divide everything into bowls and serve for breakfast.

Nutrition: calories 355, fat 16.5, fiber 3.5, carbs 18.2, protein 3.4

Basmati Rice Masala
Preparation time: 10 minutes
Cooking time: 20 minutes
Servings: 4
Ingredients:
- 1 cup basmati rice
- 2 tablespoons masala paste
- 1 and ½ cups water
- Salt to the taste
- 2 tablespoons ghee, melted
- 1 yellow onion, chopped
- 1 cup cauliflower florets
- 1 cup green beans, trimmed and halved
- 2 carrots, sliced
- 1 red bell pepper, chopped
- 2 potatoes, peeled and cubed
- 2 tomatoes, chopped
- 1 tablespoon mint, chopped
- 24 soya granules, toasted

Directions:
1. Set the instant pot on Sauté mode, add the ghee, heat it up, add the masala paste, onion, cauliflower and the other ingredients except the rice and water, stir and sauté for 4 minutes.
2. Add the remaining ingredients, put the lid on and cook on High for 16 minutes.
3. Release the pressure naturally for 10 minutes, divide everything between plates and serve.

Nutrition: calories 288, fat 11.2, fiber 4.65, carbs 12.4, protein 5.4

Green Peas Basmati Rice
Preparation time: 10 minutes
Cooking time: 20 minutes
Servings: 4
Ingredients:
- 1 and ¼ cups basmati rice, soaked for 30 minutes and drained
- 2 and ½ cups water
- ½ cup green peas
- 2 green chilies, chopped
- ½ cup yellow onion, chopped
- ½ cup tomatoes, chopped
- 4 garlic cloves, minced
- 2 teaspoons coriander seeds
- 3 cloves, crushed
- 1-inch cinnamon stick
- ½ teaspoon fennel seeds, ground
- ¼ teaspoon turmeric powder
- 1 teaspoon cumin seeds
- 2 tablespoons vegetable oil
- Salt to the taste

Directions:
1. Set the instant pot on Sauté mode, add the oil, heat it up, add the garlic, coriander, cloves, cinnamon , fennel, turmeric and cumin seeds, stir and cook for 4 minutes.
2. Add the rest of the ingredients, put the lid on and cook on High for 16 minutes.
3. Release the pressure naturally for 10 minutes, divide the mix between plates and serve.

Nutrition: calories 436, fat 8.1, fiber 3.6, carbs 81.4, protein 8.4

Spinach and Chana Dal Rice
Preparation time: 10 minutes
Cooking time: 20 minutes
Servings: 4
Ingredients:
- 1 cup basmati rice
- 1 and ½ cups water
- ½ cup chana dal
- 4 handfuls spinach, chopped
- 1 tablespoon coriander, chopped
- 1 tablespoon mint, chopped
- 2 tomatoes, cubed
- 1 yellow onion, sliced
- 1 potato, peeled and cubed
- ½ tablespoon ginger, grated
- 1 tablespoon biryani masala
- Salt to the taste
- 1 tablespoon garam masala
- 2 tablespoons vegetable oil

Directions:
1. Set the instant pot on Sauté mode, add the oil, heat it up, add the ginger, onion, biryani masala, salt and garam masala, stir and cook for 4 minutes.
2. Add the rice and the other ingredients, put the lid on and cook on High for 16 minutes.
3. Release the pressure naturally for 10 minutes, divide everything into bowls and serve for breakfast.

Nutrition: calories 355, fat 11.4, fiber 3.5, carbs 25.4, protein 4.6

Curry Rava Upma
Preparation time: 10 minutes
Cooking time: 20 minutes
Servings: 4
Ingredients:
- 1 cup broken wheat rava
- ¼ cup water
- ¼ cup yellow onion, chopped
- ¼ cup carrot, chopped
- ¼ cup green beans, trimmed and chopped
- ¼ cup cauliflower florets
- ½ teaspoon mustard seeds
- ½ teaspoon cumin seeds
- 6 curry leaves, chopped
- 1 teaspoon ginger, grated
- 2 teaspoons green chilies, minced
- ¼ teaspoon turmeric powder
- 1 teaspoon vegetable oil
- 1 teaspoon ghee, melted
- 2 tablespoons coriander, chopped
- Salt to the taste

Directions:
1. Set the instant pot on Sauté mode, add the oil and the ghee, heat them up, add the mustard seeds, cumin seeds, curry leaves, ginger, chilies, and the turmeric, stir and sauté for 5 minutes.
2. Ad the wheat rava and the other ingredients, put the lid on and cook on High for 15 minutes.
3. Release the pressure naturally for 10 minutes, divide the mix into bowls and serve for breakfast.

Nutrition: calories 400, fat 13.54, fiber 4.5, carbs 22.4, protein 4.9

Millet Uppittu

Preparation time: 10 minutes
Cooking time: 20 minutes
Servings: 4
Ingredients:

- 1 cup mixed millet
- ¼ cup carrot, chopped
- 1 yellow onion, chopped
- ¼ cup water
- ¼ cup French beans, chopped
- ¼ cup cauliflower florets
- ½ teaspoon mustard seeds
- 5 curry leaves, chopped
- ½ teaspoon cumin seeds
- 2 green chilies, chopped
- 1 teaspoon ginger, grated
- ¼ teaspoon turmeric powder
- 1 tablespoon ghee, melted
- 2 tablespoons coriander, chopped
- Salt to the taste

Directions:
1. Set the instant pot on Sauté mode, add the ghee, heat it up, add mustard seeds, curry leaves, cumin, chilies, ginger, and turmeric, stir and cook for 5 minutes.
2. Add the millet and the remaining ingredients, put the lid on and cook on High for 15 minutes.
3. Release the pressure naturally for 10 minutes, divide the mix into bowls and serve for breakfast.

Nutrition: calories 299, fat 11.2, fiber 4.5, carbs 16.7, protein 5.6

Tapioca Pearls Knichdi

Preparation time: 10 minutes
Cooking time: 25 minutes
Servings: 4
Ingredients:

- 1 cup water
- 1 cup sabudana (tapioca pearls)
- 1 potato, peeled and cubed
- ½ teaspoons mustard seeds
- ½ teaspoon cumin seeds
- 1 yellow onion, chopped
- 2 green chilies, chopped
- 1 teaspoon ginger, grated
- ¼ teaspoon turmeric powder
- Juice of 1 lemon
- ¼ cup peanuts, roasted and chopped
- 2 tablespoons vegetable oil
- 2 tablespoons coriander, chopped
- Salt to the taste

Directions:
1. Set the instant pot on Sauté mode, add the oil, heat it up, add the mustard seeds, cumin seeds, chilies, ginger, turmeric and the peanuts and cook for 5 minutes.
2. Add the rest of the ingredients, put the lid on and cook on High for 20 minutes.
3. Release the pressure naturally for 10 minutes, divide the mix into bowls and serve for breakfast.

Nutrition: calories 388, fat 11.9, fiber 3.5, carbs 22, protein 6.7

Toast Chili Upumavu

Preparation time: 5 minutes
Cooking time: 20 minutes
Servings: 4
Ingredients:

- 10 bread slices, toasted and cubed
- ¼ cup vegetable stock
- 2 yellow onions, chopped
- 3 tomatoes, chopped
- 1 teaspoon sambar powder
- 2 green chilies, chopped
- 1 teaspoon turmeric powder
- 4 curry springs, chopped
- 1 teaspoon mustard seeds
- Salt to the taste
- 2 tablespoons butter
- 1 tablespoon coriander, chopped

Directions:
1. Set the instant pot on Sauté mode, add the butter, heat it up, add the sambar powder, turmeric, curry springs, mustard seeds and salt, stir and cook for 5 minutes.
2. Add the bread and the other ingredients, put the lid on and cook on High for 15 minutes.
3. Release the pressure fast for 5 minutes, divide everything into bowls and serve.

Nutrition: calories 399, fat 11, fiber 6.7, carbs 15.6, protein 5.6

Farro Corn Masala

Preparation time: 10 minutes
Cooking time: 25 minutes
Servings: 4
Ingredients:

- 2 cups water
- 2 cups farro
- 1 cup corn
- 1 cup cauliflower florets
- 1 tablespoon vegetable oil
- 2 tablespoons chaat masala
- 2 yellow onions, chopped
- 6 garlic cloves, minced
- 1 tablespoon cumin, ground
- 2 tablespoons coriander, ground
- ½ tablespoon turmeric powder
- Juice of ½ lemon
- 1 tablespoon sugar
- 1 tablespoon cilantro, chopped
- 1 tablespoon chili powder

Directions:
1. Set the instant pot on Sauté mode, add the oil, heat it up, add the onions, garlic, masala, cumin, coriander, turmeric, and chili powder, stir and cook for 5 minutes.
2. Add the farro and the other ingredients, toss, put the lid on and cook on High for 20 minutes.
3. Release the pressure naturally for 10 minutes, divide the mix into bowls and serve for breakfast.

Nutrition: calories 165, fat 5, fiber 5, carbs 7, protein 10

Cardamom Oats Kheer

Preparation time: 10 minutes
Cooking time: 15 minutes
Servings: 4
Ingredients:
- ½ cup rolled oats
- 1 and ½ cups water
- 3 tablespoons almonds, chopped
- A pinch of cardamom, ground
- 3 teaspoons flax seed, ground
- A pinch of nutmeg, ground
- 1 teaspoon sugar
- 2/3 cup milk

Directions:
1. In your instant pot, combine the oats with the water and the other ingredients, put the lid on and cook on High for 15 minutes.
2. Release the pressure naturally for 10 minutes, divide into bowls and serve for breakfast.

Nutrition: calories 188, fat 6, fiber 4, carbs 6, protein 9

Peach and Mango Lassi

Preparation time: 5 minutes
Cooking time: 5 minutes
Servings: 4
Ingredients:
- 2 mangoes, peeled, seeded and cubed
- 2 peaches, stones removed and cubed
- 1 cup yogurt
- ½ cup skim milk
- 1 teaspoon ginger, grated
- 4 mint leaves, chopped
- ½ cup water

Directions:
1. In your instant pot, combine the mangoes with the peaches and the other ingredients, put the lid on and cook on High for 5 minutes
2. Release the pressure fast for 5 minutes, blend the mix using an immersion blender, divide into bowls and serve for breakfast.

Nutrition: calories 171, fat 8, fiber 4, carbs 6, protein 5

Potato Egg Curry

Preparation time: 10 minutes
Cooking time: 25 minutes
Servings: 4
Ingredients:
- 4 eggs
- 1 and ½ tablespoons ghee, melted
- 3 green cardamoms
- ½ teaspoon cumin, ground
- 2 cups yellow onions, chopped
- 1 tomato cubed
- 2 teaspoons ginger garlic paste
- A pinch of turmeric powder
- Salt to the taste
- 1 teaspoon garam masala

- 1 teaspoon red chili powder
- 4 potatoes, peeled and cubed
- 2 tablespoons coriander, chopped

Directions:
1. Set the instant pot on Sauté mode, add the ghee, heat it up, add the cardamom, cumin, onion, ginger paste, turmeric, salt, garam masala, and chili powder and cook for 5 minutes.
2. Add the rest of the ingredients, toss, put the lid on and cook on High for 20 minutes.
3. Release the pressure naturally for 10 minutes, divide into bowls and serve for breakfast.

Nutrition: calories 200, fat 8, fiber 4, carbs 6, protein 8

Curry Quinoa

Preparation time: 10 minutes
Cooking time: 15 minute
Servings: 3
Ingredients:
- ½ cup quinoa, rinsed
- 1 teaspoon mustard seeds
- 1 tablespoon vegetable oil
- 2 teaspoons ginger, grated
- 1 potato, peeled and cubed
- 1 yellow onion, chopped
- 2 green chilies, chopped
- 6 curry leaves, chopped
- Salt to the taste
- ½ cup water
- ½ cup peas
- 1 teaspoon coriander powder
- ½ teaspoon chili powder
- 1 teaspoon turmeric powder
- 2 tablespoons cilantro, chopped
- 1 teaspoon lime juice

Directions:
1. Set the instant pot on Sauté mode, add the oil, heat it up, add the mustard seeds, ginger, chilies, curry leaves, salt, coriander, chili powder and turmeric powder, stir and cook for 3 minutes.
2. Add the quinoa and the other ingredients, toss, put the lid on and cook on High for 12 minute.
3. Release the pressure naturally for 10 minutes, stir the quinoa mix, divide into bowls, and serve.

Nutrition: calories 250, fat 4.8, fiber 4.5, carbs 11.6, protein 10

Creamy Potato Mushrooms
Preparation time: 10 minutes
Cooking time: 20 minutes
Servings: 3
Ingredients:
- ½ cup yellow onions, chopped
- 1 potato, peeled and cubed
- 1 cup mushrooms, sliced
- 1 tablespoon mint, chopped
- 1 green chili, chopped
- 1 teaspoon ginger garlic paste
- 1 teaspoon garam masala
- 1 teaspoon turmeric powder
- ½ teaspoon red chili powder
- ¼ cup yogurt
- 1 tablespoon coriander, chopped
- 2 tablespoons vegetable oil

Directions:
1. Set the instant pot on Sauté mode, add the oil, heat it up, add the mushrooms, chili, ginger paste, garam masala, turmeric and red chili powder, stir and cook for 3 minutes.
2. Add rest of the ingredients, put the lid on and cook on High for 17 minutes.
3. Release the pressure naturally for 10 minutes, divide the mix between plates and serve for breakfast.
Nutrition: calories 200, fat 12, fiber 6, carbs 7.7, protein 9

Rice Bowls with Masala Sprouts
Preparation time: 10 minutes
Cooking time: 20 minutes
Servings: 2
Ingredients:
- 1 cup flattened rice
- Salt to the taste
- 1 teaspoon sugar
- 1 teaspoon lemon juice
- 1 tablespoon ghee, melted
- ½ teaspoon mustard seeds
- 4 curry leaves, chopped
- 2 green chilies, minced
- ½ cup potato, peeled and cubed
- ¼ cup veggie stock
- 1 teaspoon turmeric powder
- ½ cup yellow onion, chopped
- 1 tablespoon coriander, chopped
- ½ cup peanuts, chopped
- ½ teaspoon chaat masala
- A pinch of black pepper
- ¼ cup cumin powder
- 1 cup green mung sprouts
- ¼ cup tomato, cubed

Directions:
1. Set the instant pot on Sauté mode, add the ghee, heat it up, add mustard seeds, curry leaves, chili, turmeric, coriander, peanuts, chaat masala, black pepper and cumin powder, stir and cook for 5 minutes.
2. Add the rest of the ingredients, toss, put the lid on and cook on High for 15 minutes.

3. Release the pressure naturally for 10 minutes, divide the mix into bowls and serve.
Nutrition: calories 263, fat 11.8, fiber 5.5, carbs 9.7, protein 1.1

Ragi and Urad Dal Idli
Preparation time: 30 minutes
Cooking time: 12 minutes
Servings: 3
Ingredients:
- 1 cup urad dal, soaked in ½ cup water for 30 minutes
- ¼ cup poha
- 2 cups ragi flour
- 4 methi seeds
- 8 kale leaves, chopped
- Salt to the taste
- Cooking spray

Directions:
1. In a bowl, combine the urad dal with the poha and the other ingredients except the cooking spray, stir well and shape medium cakes out of this mix.
2. Grease the instant pot with the cooking spray, add the cakes inside, put the lid on and cook on High for 12 minutes.
3. Release the pressure naturally for 10 minutes, divide the cakes between plates and serve for breakfast.
Nutrition: calories 260, fat 12, fiber 5, carbs 6.6, protein 8.3

Beans Masala
Preparation time: 10 minutes
Cooking time: 20 minutes
Servings: 4
Ingredients:
- 1 teaspoon mustard seeds
- 2 teaspoons urad dal
- 1 curry leaf, chopped
- 2 cups French beans, trimmed
- ½ cup yellow onion, chopped
- ½ teaspoon turmeric powder
- 1 tablespoon vegetable oil
- Salt to the taste
- 4 shallots, chopped
- 3 garlic cloves, minced
- 3 tablespoons coconut, shredded
- 1 tablespoon coriander seeds
- 1 teaspoon jeera
- 2 red chilies, chopped
- 2 tablespoons coriander, chopped

Directions:
1. In your instant pot, combine the mustard seeds with the oil, curry leaf and the other ingredients, toss, put the lid on and cook on High for 20 minutes.
2. Release the pressure naturally for 10 minutes, stir the mix, divide it into bowls and serve.
Nutrition: calories 480, fat 9.8, fiber 3.5, carbs 16.8, protein 6

Pineapple Masala

Preparation time: 5 minutes
Cooking time: 10 minutes
Servings: 4
Ingredients:
- 1 teaspoon black peppercorns
- 2 teaspoons coriander seeds
- 1 teaspoon pomegranate seeds, dried
- ½ teaspoon ajowan seeds
- ¼ teaspoon chili powder
- 1 papaya, peeled and cubed
- Juice for 2 limes
- 1 pineapple, peeled and cubed
- 4 bananas, peeled and cubed
- A handful mint, chopped

Directions:
1. In your instant pot, combine the peppercorns with the coriander and the other ingredients, put the lid on and cook on High for 10 minutes.
2. Release the pressure fast for 5 minutes, divide everything into bowls and serve for breakfast.

Nutrition: calories 173, fat 4.3, fiber 2, carbs 7.5, protein 5

Banana Curd Salad

Preparation time: 5 minutes
Cooking time: 6 minutes
Servings: 2
Ingredients:
- 2 green chilies, chopped
- 2 bananas, peeled and sliced
- 2 cups curd
- ¼ teaspoon red chili powder
- ½ tablespoon sugar
- 1 tablespoon coriander

Directions:
1. In your instant pot, combine the bananas with the chilies and the other ingredients, put the lid on and cook on High for 6 minutes.
2. Release the pressure fast for 5 minutes, divide into bowls and serve for breakfast.

Nutrition: calories 257, fat 4,8, fiber 4, carbs 11.6, protein 8.10

Milky Rice Bowls

Preparation time: 10 minutes
Cooking time: 20 minutes
Servings: 4
Ingredients:
- 1 and ½ cups basmati rice
- 1 teaspoon cardamom, ground
- 3 cups milk
- 1 teaspoon rosewater
- 2 tablespoons sugar
- 3 tablespoons pistachios

Directions:
1. In your instant pot, combine the rice with the cardamom and the other ingredients, toss, put the lid on and cook on High for 20 minutes.

2. Release the pressure naturally for 10 minutes, divide the mix into bowls and serve for breakfast.

Nutrition: calories 180, fat 11, fiber 5.4, carbs 8.4, protein 7

Rice Salad

Preparation time: 10 minutes
Cooking time: 30 minutes
Servings: 6
Ingredients:
- 2 cups basmati rice
- 4 cups water
- Salt to the taste
- ½ cup vegetable oil
- 1/3 cup rice vinegar
- 1 tablespoon sesame oil
- 2 tablespoons ginger, grated
- 1 and ¼ cups mango, peeled and cubed
- 1 cup cucumber, cubed
- ½ cup scallions, chopped
- ¼ cup cilantro, chopped

Directions:
1. Set your instant pot on Sauté mode, add the oil, heat it up, add the scallions and sauté for 5 minutes.
2. Add the rice, water and the other ingredients, toss, put the lid on and cook on High for 25 minutes.
3. Release the pressure naturally for 10 minutes, divide the mix into bowls and serve for breakfast.

Nutrition: calories 320, fat 14, fiber 1, carbs 45, protein 4

Apricot Rava Pudding

Preparation time: 10 minutes
Cooking time: 20 minutes
Servings: 3
Ingredients:
- 1 and ½ cups milk
- ½ cup sugar
- 4 tablespoons semolina (rava)
- ½ cup strawberries, chopped
- 4 apricot, stones removed and cubed
- 2 tablespoons pecans, chopped

Directions:
1. In your instant pot, combine the sugar with the milk and the other ingredients, toss, put the lid on and coo on High for 20 minutes.
2. Release the pressure naturally for 10 minutes, divide the mix into bowls and serve for breakfast.

Nutrition: calories 190, fat 5.4, fiber 4.2, carbs 8.6, protein 10

Tomato Omelet

Preparation time: 10 minutes
Cooking time: 10 minutes
Servings: 2
Ingredients:
- 2 eggs, whisked
- 1 tomato, cubed
- 1 yellow onion , chopped
- 1 green bell pepper, chopped
- Salt and the black pepper to the taste
- 1 cup water
- Cooking spray

Directions:
1.   In a bowl, mix the eggs with the other ingredients except the cooking spray and the water and whisk well
2.   Grease a pan that fits your instant pot with cooking spray and pour the omelet mix inside.
3.   Add the water to your instant pot, add the trivet inside, add the pan with the omelet mix, put the lid on and cook on High for 10 minutes.
4.   Release the pressure naturally for 10 minutes, divide the omelet between plates and serve.
Nutrition: calories 271, fat 12, fiber 5, carbs 5.6, protein 7.8

Turmeric Omelet

Preparation time: 10 minutes
Cooking time: 12 minutes
Servings: 4
Ingredients:
- 4 eggs, whisked
- 2 tablespoons milk
- A pinch of turmeric powder
- 2 tablespoons butter, melted
- 1 green bell pepper, chopped
- 1 tomato, cubed
- 1 potato, boiled, peeled and cubed
- 12 coriander stems, chopped
- 1 green chili pepper, chopped
- Salt and black pepper to the taste

Directions:
1.   Set the instant pot on Sauté mode, add the butter, melt it, add the bell pepper, tomato, potato, coriander and chili pepper, stir and sauté for 2 minutes.
2.   Add the rest of the ingredients, toss, spread, put the lid on and cook on High for 10 minutes.
3.   Release the pressure naturally for 10 minutes, divide the omelet between plates and serve for breakfast.
Nutrition: calories 342, fat 6.4, fiber 5.3, carbs 9.6, protein 9

Figs and Spinach Salad

Preparation time: 5 minutes
Cooking time: 8 minutes
Servings: 4
Ingredients:
- 1 cup spinach, torn
- 5 figs, cut into quarters
- 10 cherry tomatoes, halved
- 1 cucumber, sliced
- ¼ cup red wine vinegar
- 1 teaspoon mustard
- ¼ cup vegetable oil
- Salt and black pepper to the taste

Directions:
1.   In your instant pot, combine the spinach with the figs and the other ingredients, toss, put the lid on and cook on Low for 8 minutes.
2.   Release the pressure fast for 5 minutes, divide into bowls and serve for breakfast.
Nutrition: calories 161, fat 7, fiber 3.3, carbs 6.5, protein 5

Mung Dal Pongal

Preparation time: 10 minutes
Cooking time: 20 minutes
Servings: 2
Ingredients:
- ¼ cup mung dal, soaked for 2 hours and drained
- ¼ cup millet, soaked for 2 hours and drained
- 1 and ½ cups water
- 2 tablespoons brown rice
- 4 peppercorns
- 4 cashews, chopped
- ¼ teaspoon cumin, ground
- 1 green chili, chopped
- Salt to the taste
- 1 teaspoon ginger, grated
- 1 teaspoon turmeric powder
- 2 teaspoons ghee, melted

Directions:
1.   In your instant pot, combine the mung dal with the millet and the other ingredients, toss, put the lid on and cook on High for 20 minutes.
2.   Release the pressure naturally for 10 minutes, stir the mix, divide it into bowls and serve for breakfast.
Nutrition: calories 370, fat 11.6, fiber 4, carbs 9.8, protein 6.5

Ragi Halwa

Preparation time: 10 minutes
Cooking time: 10 minutes
Servings: 2
Ingredients:

- 4 tablespoons ragi flour
- 1 cup water
- 1 big apple, cored and cubed
- 1 teaspoon ghee, melted
- 2 teaspoons jaggery

Directions:

1. In your instant pot, combine the apple with the ghee and the other ingredients, toss, put the lid on and cook on High for 10 minutes.
2. Release the pressure naturally for 10 minutes, blend the mix using an immersion blender, divide into bowls and serve for breakfast.

Nutrition: calories 128, fat 2.4, fiber 9.1, carbs 33.6, protein 1.1

Millet Malt Java

Preparation time: 10 minutes
Cooking time: 10 minutes
Servings: 2
Ingredients:

- ¼ cup ragi flour (millet flour)
- 1 and ½ cups water
- 1 and ½ tablespoons sugar
- 1 and ½ cups milk
- 2 teaspoons ghee, melted
- A pinch of cardamom powder
- 1 tablespoon almonds, chopped

Directions:

1. In your instant pot, mix the ragi flour with the water and the other ingredients, put the lid on and cook on High for 10 minutes.
2. Release the pressure naturally for 10 minutes, stir the mix, divide it into bowls and serve.

Nutrition: calories 272, fat 8.5, fiber 4, carbs 11.7, protein 6

Broccoli Bhurji

Preparation time: 10 minutes
Cooking time: 20 minutes
Servings: 4
Ingredients:

- 3 eggs, whisked
- 1 cup broccoli florets, chopped
- Salt to the taste
- 2 yellow onions, chopped
- 2 tomatoes, cubed
- 1 teaspoon turmeric powder
- 5 garlic cloves, minced
- 2 teaspoons red chili powder
- 2 tablespoons coriander, chopped
- 2 tablespoons vegetable oil

Directions:

1. Set the instant pot on Sauté mode, add the oil, heat it up, add the onions, garlic, chili powder and turmeric, stir and cook for 5 minutes.
2. Add the whisked eggs and the other ingredients, toss, put the lid on and cook on High for 15 minutes.
3. Release the pressure naturally for 10 minutes, divide the mix between plates and serve for breakfast.

Nutrition: calories 290, fat 7.2, fiber 2, carbs 5.8, protein 7

Indian Instant Pot Lunch Recipes

Paneer Fenugreek Masala
Preparation time: 10 minutes
Cooking time: 20 minutes
Servings: 4
Ingredients:
- 1 pound paneer, cut into chunks
- 1 teaspoon cumin seeds
- 2 tablespoons butter
- 1 yellow onions, chopped
- 1 tablespoon ginger, grated
- 1 tablespoon garlic, minced
- 4 tomatoes, cubed
- ¼ cup cashews, chopped
- 2 tablespoons fenugreek leaves, chopped
- ¼ cup water
- ¼ cup coconut cream
- 1 tablespoon honey
- Salt to the taste
- 1 teaspoon red chili powder
- ½ teaspoon turmeric powder

Directions:
1. In your instant pot, combine the butter with the cumin and all the other ingredients except the paneer, cream and honey, toss, put the lid on and cook on High for 15 minutes.
2. Release the pressure naturally for 10 minutes, add the paneer, cream and honey, toss, set the machine on Sauté mode again, cook for 5 minutes more, divide into bowls and serve for lunch.
Nutrition: calories 387, fat 22.7, fiber 5.9, carbs 38.5

Potato Baingan Masala
Preparation time: 10 minutes
Cooking time: 20 minutes
Servings: 6
Ingredients:
- 2 and ½ tablespoons mustard oil
- 1 cup red bell peppers, chopped
- 1 cup yellow onion, chopped
- 1 cup green chilies, chopped
- 1-inch ginger, grated
- 5 garlic cloves, minced
- 4 tomatoes, cubed
- 10 cashews, chopped
- 8 baby eggplants, halved
- 3 potatoes, peeled and cubed
- ½ cup veggie stock
- 1 teaspoon cumin seeds
- 1 teaspoon coriander powder
- 1 teaspoon turmeric powder
- 2 teaspoons cayenne pepper
- 1 teaspoon garam masala
- Salt to the taste
- 1 tablespoons mint, chopped

Directions:
1. Set the instant pot on Sauté mode, add the oil, heat it up, add the onion, chilies, ginger, garlic, cumin, coriander, turmeric, cayenne and garam masala, toss and cook for 5 minutes.
2. Add the remaining ingredients, put the lid on and cook on High for 15 minutes.
3. Release the pressure naturally for 10 minutes, divide the mix into bowls and serve for lunch.
Nutrition: calories 392, fat 9.8, fiber 32.5, carbs 74.8, protein 12.1

Spinach Paneer
Preparation time: 10 minutes
Cooking time: 15 minutes
Servings: 4
Ingredients:
- 1 pound spinach, torn
- 1 teaspoon cumin seeds
- 1 tablespoon ghee, melted
- 2 cups paneer, cubed
- 1 yellow onion, chopped
- 1 green chili pepper, minced
- 1-inch ginger, grated
- 5 garlic cloves, minced
- 1 tomato, cubed
- ¼ cup water
- 1 teaspoon garam masala
- ½ teaspoon turmeric powder
- 1 teaspoon coriander powder
- Salt to the taste

Directions:
1. Set the instant pot on Sauté mode, add the ghee, heat it up, add the onion, chili pepper, ginger, garlic, garam masala, turmeric, coriander and cumin seeds, stir and cook for 4 minutes.
2. Add the rest of the ingredients, put the lid on and cook on High for 11 minutes.
3. Release the pressure naturally for 10 minutes, divide the mix into bowls and serve.
Nutrition: calories 337, fat 16.4, fiber 5.7, carbs 36, protein 14.2

Dum Potatoes
Preparation time: 10 minutes
Cooking time: 20 minutes
Servings: 4
Ingredients:
- 10 baby potatoes, peeled and halved
- 1 yellow onion, chopped
- 2 tablespoons ghee, melted
- 2 teaspoons ginger, grated
- 2 teaspoons garlic, minced
- 2 tomatoes, crushed
- 1 teaspoon garam masala
- 1 tablespoon red chili powder
- ½ teaspoon turmeric powder
- 10 cashews, chopped
- ¼ cup milk
- Salt to the taste
- 1 tablespoon cilantro, chopped

Directions:
1. In a blender, combine the cashews with the milk, pulse well and transfer to a bowl.
2. Set the instant pot on Sauté mode, add the ghee, heat it up, add the onion, garlic, ginger, garam masala, chili powder, turmeric powder and cashew paste, stir and cook for 5 minutes.
3. Add the remaining ingredients, put the lid on and cook on High for 15 minutes.
4. Release the pressure naturally for 10 minutes, divide into bowls and serve.
Nutrition: calories 202, fat 11.3, fiber 4.8, carbs 52, protein 5.7

Mung and Potato Khichuri

Preparation time: 10 minutes
Cooking time: 20 minutes
Servings: 4
Ingredients:

- ½ cup mung lentils
- ½ cup white rice
- 3 cups water
- 1 tablespoon ghee, melted
- ½ teaspoon cumin seeds
- ½ tablespoon ginger, grated
- 1 yellow onion, chopped
- 1 tomato cubed
- 1 tablespoon cilantro, chopped
- 1 potato, peeled and cubed
- ½ cup carrot, chopped
- ½ cup green peas
- ¼ teaspoon turmeric powder
- ½ teaspoon cayenne pepper

Directions:
1. Set the instant pot on Sauté mode, add the ghee, heat it up, add the cumin, ginger, turmeric and cayenne, stir and cook for 3 minutes.
2. Add the lentils and the other ingredients, toss, put the lid on and cook on High for 17 minutes more.
3. Release the pressure naturally for 10 minutes, divide everything between plates and serve for lunch.
Nutrition: calories 208, fat 5.2, fiber 7.6, carbs 12, protein 8.2

Carrot Rice One Pot

Preparation time: 10 minutes
Cooking time: 20 minutes
Servings: 4
Ingredients:

- 1 cup basmati rice
- 1 green chili pepper, chopped
- 1 tablespoon ghee, melted
- ½ tablespoon ginger, grated
- ½ cup yellow onion, chopped
- ½ tablespoon garlic, minced
- Salt to the taste
- ½ cup tomato, cubed
- 1 potato, peeled and cubed
- 2 cups mixed carrots and green beans, roughly chopped
- 1 and ½ cups water
- ½ teaspoon turmeric powder
- ½ teaspoon garam masala
- 1 bay leaf
- 1 teaspoon cumin seeds

Directions:
1. Set the instant pot on Sauté mode, add the ghee, heat it up, add the ginger, chili pepper, garlic, turmeric, garam masala, bay leaf and cumin seeds, stir and cook for 5 minutes.
2. Add the rice and the other ingredients, stir, put the lid on and cook on High for 15 minutes.
3. Release the pressure naturally fro 10 minutes, divide the mix into bowls and serve.
Nutrition: calories 344, fat 12.5, fiber 4.5, carbs 16.5, protein 3.5

Buttery Spiced Tomato Chicken

Preparation time: 10 minutes
Cooking time: 20 minutes

Servings: 4
Ingredients:

- 14 ounces canned tomatoes, cubed
- 5 garlic cloves, minced
- 2 teaspoons ginger, grated
- ½ teaspoon cayenne pepper
- 1 teaspoon turmeric powder
- 1 teaspoon smoked paprika
- Salt to the taste
- 1 teaspoon cumin, ground
- 1 teaspoon garam masala
- 1 pound chicken thighs, boneless, skinless
- 4 ounces butter, soft
- 4 ounces coconut cream
- ½ cup cilantro, chopped

Directions:
1. Set the instant pot on Sauté mode, add the butter, melt it, add the garlic, ginger, cayenne, turmeric, paprika, cumin and garam masala, stir and cook for 3 minutes.
2. Add the chicken and the rest of the ingredients, put the lid on and cook on High for 17 minutes.
3. Release the pressure naturally for 10 minutes, divide everything between plates and serve.
Nutrition: calories 340, fat 20, fiber 1, carbs 16.3, protein 25

Rice Chicken Biryani

Preparation time: 30 minutes
Cooking time: 30 minutes
Servings: 4
Ingredients:
For the marinade:

- 2 teaspoons garam masala
- 1 tablespoon ginger, grated
- 1 tablespoon garlic, grated
- 1 tablespoon red chili powder
- ½ teaspoon turmeric powder
- ¼ cup cilantro, chopped
- ¼ cup mint, chopped
- 2 tablespoons lemon juice
- 1 cup yogurt
- Salt to the taste
- 2 pounds chicken thighs, skinless and boneless

For the remaining ingredients:

- 3 cups basmati rice
- 3 tablespoons ghee, melted
- 2 yellow onions, chopped
- 2 bay leaves
- 1 teaspoon saffron powder

Directions:
1. In a bowl, combine the ingredients for the marinade with the chicken, toss and keep in the fridge for 30 minutes.
2. Set the instant pot on Sauté mode, add the ghee, heat it up, add the chicken mix, rice, bay leaves, onions and the saffron, put the lid on and cook on High for 30 minutes.
3. Release the pressure naturally for 10 minutes, divide the mix into bowls and serve.
Nutrition: calories 383, fat 16.7, fiber 4.5, carbs 66, protein 7.5

Chicken Chili Masala

Preparation time: 10 minutes
Cooking time: 20 minutes
Servings: 4
Ingredients:
- 1 pound chicken breast, skinless, boneless and halved
- ¼ cup yogurt
- 2 teaspoons red chili powder
- 1 tablespoon lime juice
- 1 tablespoon garlic, minced
- 1 tablespoon ginger, grated
- ½ teaspoon turmeric powder
- 1 teaspoon garam masala
- 2 tablespoons ghee, melted
- 1 cup yellow onion, chopped
- 1 cup tomato puree
- ½ cup water
- ½ cup heavy cream
- 1 tablespoon fenugreek leaves, dried
- 1 tablespoon cilantro, chopped

Directions:
1.   In a bowl, mix the chicken with the yogurt, chili powder, lime juice, garlic, ginger, turmeric and garam masala, toss and keep in the fridge for 10 minutes.
2.   Set the instant pot on Sauté mode, add the ghee, heat it up, add the chicken breasts and the onion and cook for 5 minutes.
3.   Add the rest of the ingredients, put the lid on and cook on High for 15 minutes.
4.   Release the pressure naturally for 10 minutes, divide the mix into bowls and serve.

Nutrition: calories 305, fat 15.6 fiber 3.2, carbs 14, protein 27.7

Goat Peppercorn Curry

Preparation time: 10 minutes
Cooking time: 30 minutes
Servings: 4
Ingredients:
- 1 pound goat meat, bone-in
- ½ tablespoon garlic, minced
- ½ tablespoon ginger, grated
- 1 green chili pepper, chopped
- 3 tablespoons ghee, melted
- 1 tomato, cubed
- 1 tablespoon lemon juice
- ½ teaspoon cumin seeds
- 6 cloves
- 6 black peppercorns
- 1 bay leaf
- 1 black peppercorns
- ¼ teaspoon turmeric powder
- 1 teaspoon cayenne pepper
- ¼ cup water

Directions:
1.   Set the instant pot on Sauté mode, add the ghee, heat it up, add the garlic, ginger, chili pepper, cumin, peppercorns, cloves, bay leaf, turmeric and cayenne, toss and cook for 5 minutes.
2.   Add the meat and brown it for 5 minutes more.
3.   Add the rest of the ingredients, put the lid on and cook on High for 20 minutes.
4.   Release the pressure naturally for 10 minutes, divide the curry into bowls and serve for lunch.

Nutrition: calories 253, fat 13.5, fiber 2, carbs 8.34, protein 24.65

Lamb Roghan Ghosht

Preparation time: 30 minutes
Cooking time: 20 minutes
Servings: 4
Ingredients:
- 1 pound leg of lamb, cubed
- 1 red onion, chopped
- 4 garlic cloves, minced
- 2 teaspoons ginger, grated
- ¼ cup yogurt
- 1 tablespoon tomato paste
- 2 teaspoons garam masala
- ¼ cup cilantro, chopped
- Salt to the taste
- ½ teaspoon cinnamon powder
- 1 teaspoon turmeric powder
- ¼ cup water

Directions:
1.   In a bowl, combine the lamb meat with the onion and the other ingredients, toss and keep in the fridge for 30 minutes.
2.   Transfer the whole mix to your instant pot, put the lid on and cook on High for 20 minutes.
3.   Release the pressure naturally for 10 minutes, divide everything into bowls and serve for lunch.

Nutrition: calories 327, fat 12.4, fiber 2.3, carbs 15.6, protein 17

Vindalho Pork Curry Pot

Preparation time: 10 minutes
Cooking time: 35 minutes
Servings: 6
Ingredients:
- 5 red chilies, chopped
- 1 teaspoon turmeric powder
- 2 teaspoons cumin seeds
- 1 teaspoon black pepper
- 6 cardamom pods
- 8 cloves
- ½ teaspoon mustard seeds
- 1 tablespoon ginger, grated
- 1 tablespoon garlic, minced
- 2 teaspoons tamarind paste
- 1 teaspoon brown sugar
- ¼ cup apple cider vinegar
- 1 and ½ pounds pork ribs, cut into medium pieces
- 1 cup water
- 2 cups yellow onion, chopped
- 3 tablespoons vegetable oil

Directions:
1.   Set the instant pot on Sauté mode, add the oil, heat it up, add the onion, chilies, turmeric, cumin, black pepper, cardamom, cloves, mustard seeds and tamarind paste, stir and cook for 5 minutes.
2.   Add the meat and brown it for 5 minutes more.
3.   Add the rest of the ingredients, put the lid on and cook on High for 25 minutes.
4.   Release the pressure naturally for 10 minutes, divide everything into bowls and serve.

Nutrition: calories 374, fat 22.2, fiber 3, carbs 18.3, protein 26

Shrimp Tomato Chili Curry

Preparation time: 5 minutes
Cooking time: 15 minutes
Servings: 4
Ingredients:

- 1 pound shrimp, peeled and deveined
- 1 green chili pepper, chopped
- 1 teaspoon mustard seeds
- 1 tablespoon vegetable oil
- 1 cup yellow onion, chopped
- ½ tablespoon ginger, grated
- ½ tablespoon garlic, minced
- 1 cup tomato, chopped
- 4 ounces coconut milk
- 1 tablespoon lime juice
- ½ teaspoon turmeric powder
- ½ teaspoon garam masala
- ½ teaspoon red chili powder
- ¼ cup cilantro, chopped

Directions:
1.   Set the instant pot on Sauté mode, add the oil, heat it up, add the onion, ginger, garlic, turmeric, garam masala, and chili powder, stir and cook for 3 minutes.
2.   Add the shrimp and the rest of the ingredients, put the lid on and cook on High for 12 minutes.
3.   Release the pressure fast for 5 minutes, divide the mix into bowls and serve for lunch.
Nutrition: calories 226, fat 10, fiber 5.4, carbs 8.5, protein 12.4

Channay Chickpeas Masala

Preparation time: 10 minutes
Cooking time: 40 minutes
Servings: 4
Ingredients:

- 2 cups chickpeas
- 2 tablespoons vegetable oil
- 1 bay leaf
- 1 yellow onion, chopped
- 2 teaspoons garlic, minced
- 2 teaspoons ginger, grated
- 2 tomatoes, chopped
- 2 teaspoons coriander powder
- 2 teaspoons dried mango powder
- 2 teaspoons cumin powder
- Salt to the taste
- 1 teaspoon garam masala
- 1 teaspoon turmeric powder
- 2 cups water

Directions:
1.   Set the instant pot on Sauté mode, add the oil, heat it up, add the onion, garlic and ginger and sauté for 5 minutes.
2.   Add the coriander, mango powder, cumin, garam masala and turmeric and cook for 5 minutes more.
3.   Add the rest of the ingredients, put the lid on and cook on High for 30 minutes.
4.   Release the pressure naturally for 10 minutes, divide the mix into bowls and serve.

Nutrition: calories 300, fat 13.45, fiber 4.5, carbs 16.5, protein 3.6

Keema Beef Peas

Preparation time: 10 minutes
Cooking time: 20 minutes
Servings: 4
Ingredients:

- 2 tablespoons ghee, melted
- 1 yellow onion, chopped
- 4 teaspoons garlic, minced
- 1 green chili, minced
- 1 teaspoon ginger, grated
- 1 tablespoon coriander powder
- 1 teaspoon sweet paprika
- ½ teaspoon cumin, ground
- ½ teaspoon garam masala
- ½ teaspoon turmeric powder
- ¼ teaspoon cardamom, ground
- 1 pound beef meat, ground
- 14 ounces canned tomatoes, chopped
- 2 cup peas
- 1 tablespoon cilantro, chopped

Directions:
1.   Set the instant pot on Sauté mode, add the ghee, heat it up, add the garlic, chili and ginger, stir and cook for 5 minutes.
2.   Add the coriander, cumin, garam masala, turmeric and cardamom, stir and cook for 5 minutes more.
3.   Add the rest of the ingredients, put the lid on and cook on High for 10 minutes.
4.   Release the pressure naturally for 10 minutes, divide the mix into bowls and serve.
Nutrition: calories 320, fat 13.5, fiber 4.6, carbs 16.5, protein 3.5

Yellow Peas Toor Dal

Preparation time: 10 minutes
Cooking time: 15 minutes
Servings: 4
Ingredients:

- 1 cup split peas, soaked in water for 20 minutes and drained
- 1 tablespoon vegetable oil
- 1 teaspoon cumin seeds
- 1 Serrano pepper, chopped
- Salt to the taste
- ½ cup onion masala
- ½ teaspoon garam masala
- 1 tablespoon cilantro, chopped
- 3 cups water

Directions:
1.   Set the instant pot on Sauté mode, add the oil, heat it up, add the cumin, Serrano pepper, onion masala and garam masala, stir and cook for 3 minutes.
2.   Add the rest of the ingredients, put the lid on and cook on High for 12 minutes.
3.   Release the pressure naturally for 10 minutes, divide the mix into bowls and serve for lunch.
Nutrition: calories 320, fat 11.3, fiber 4.6, carbs 18.4, protein 4.5

Brown Cardamom Rice with Lamb
Preparation time: 10 minutes
Cooking time: 30 minutes
Servings: 4
Ingredients:
- 1 cup brown rice, soaked in water for 10 minutes and drained
- 2 tablespoons vegetable oil
- 5 cardamom pods
- 4 cloves
- ½ teaspoon cinnamon powder
- 2 bay leaves
- ½ teaspoon fennel seeds
- ½ teaspoon cumin seeds
- 1 pound lamb stew meat, cubed
- 4 teaspoons garlic, minced
- 1 yellow onion, chopped
- 2 teaspoons ginger, grated
- 2 teaspoons coriander powder
- Salt to the taste
- 1 teaspoon garam masala
- 2 teaspoons sweet paprika
- ¼ teaspoon turmeric powder
- 1 cup water
- 1 tablespoon mint, chopped

Directions:
1. Set the instant pot on Sauté mode, add the oil, heat it up, add the cardamom, cloves, cinnamon, bay leaves, fennel and cumin, stir and cook for 2 minutes.
2. Add the garlic, onion, ginger, coriander, garam masala, paprika and turmeric and sauté for 3 minutes more.
3. Add the meat and brown it for 5 minutes more.
4. Add the rest of the ingredients, put the lid on and cook on High for 20 minutes more.
5. Release the pressure naturally for 10 minutes, divide the mix into bowls and serve.
Nutrition: calories 338, fat 16.7, fiber 3.5, carbs 20.4, protein 14.3

Serrano Potato and Pea Curry
Preparation time: 10 minutes
Cooking time: 15 minutes
Servings: 4
Ingredients:
- 1 teaspoon cumin seeds
- 2 tablespoons vegetable oil
- ½ cup onion masala
- 1 Serrano pepper, minced
- Salt to the taste
- 1 pound potatoes, peeled and cubed
- ½ teaspoon garam masala
- 2 cups peas
- 1 and ½ cups water

Directions:
1. Set the instant pot on Sauté mode, add the oil, heat it up, add the onion masala, Serrano pepper and garam masala, stir and cook for 2 minutes.

2. Add the potatoes and the other ingredients, toss, put the lid on and cook on High for 13 minutes.
3. Release the pressure naturally for 10 minutes, divide the mix into bowls and serve.
Nutrition: calories 300, fat 11.2, fiber 4.5, carbs 18.4, protein 6.6

Curry Shrimp Biryani
Preparation time: 10 minutes
Cooking time: 26 minutes
Servings: 4
Ingredients:
- 1 cup basmati rice, soaked in water and drained
- 2 tablespoons ghee, melted
- 1 tablespoon cashews, chopped
- 1 tablespoon raisins
- 2 red onions, chopped
- 3 cloves
- 4 cardamom pods
- ½ teaspoon cumin seeds
- 2 teaspoons ginger, grated
- 2 teaspoons garlic, minced
- 1 green chili, chopped
- 20 curry leaves
- 1 tomato, chopped
- 1 teaspoon garam masala
- 1 teaspoon sweet paprika
- Salt to the taste
- ½ teaspoon turmeric powder
- 1 cup water
- 1 pound shrimp, peeled and deveined
- 1 tablespoon cilantro, chopped
- 1 tablespoon mint, chopped

Directions:
1. Set the instant pot on Sauté mode, add the ghee, heat it up, add the cloves, cardamom, cumin, ginger, garlic, chili, curry leaves, garam masala, paprika and turmeric, stir and cook for 6 minutes.
2. Add the onion, stir and cook for 10 minutes more.
3. Add the rest of the ingredients, except the cilantro and the mint, put the lid on and cook on High for 10 minutes.
4. Release the pressure naturally for 10 minutes, add the cilantro and the mint, stir, divide into bowls and serve for lunch.
Nutrition: calories 311, fat 11.3, fiber 5.6, carbs 16.4, protein 13.4

Chickpeas Kana Chana

Preparation time: 10 minutes
Cooking time: 35 minutes
Servings: 4
Ingredients:
- 2 cups brown chickpeas, soaked overnight and drained
- ½ teaspoon cumin seeds
- 2 tablespoons ghee, melted
- ½ teaspoon black mustard seeds
- 1 black cardamom
- ½ teaspoon coriander powder
- Salt to the taste
- ½ teaspoon dried mango powder
- ½ teaspoon turmeric powder
- ½ teaspoon garam masala
- 1/3 teaspoon sweet paprika
- ¼ teaspoon black salt
- 1 cup water
- 1 tablespoon cilantro, chopped

Directions:
1. Set the instant pot on Sauté mode, add the ghee, heat it up, add the cumin, mustard seeds, cardamom, coriander, mango powder, turmeric, garam masala, paprika and black salt, stir and cook for 5 minutes.
2. Add the rest of the ingredients, put the lid on and cook on High for 30 minutes.
3. Release the pressure naturally for 10 minutes, divide the mix into bowls and serve for lunch.
Nutrition: calories 300, fat 12.4, fiber 4.5, carbs 15.5, protein 5.6

Onion Langar Dal

Preparation time: 10 minutes
Cooking time: 30 minutes
Servings: 4
Ingredients:
- 2 tablespoons ghee, melted
- 1 cup urad dal, soaked overnight in cold water and drained
- 1 teaspoon cumin seeds
- ¼ cup chana dal, rinsed
- 1 cup onion masala
- 3 cups water
- Salt to the taste
- A pinch of cayenne pepper
- 1 and ½ teaspoon garam masala
- 1 tablespoon cilantro

Directions:
1. Set the instant pot on Sauté mode, add the ghee, heat it up, add the urad dal, cumin and chana dal, stir and cook for 2 minutes.
2. Add the rest of the ingredients, put the lid on and cook on High for 28 minutes.
3. Release the pressure naturally for 10 minutes, divide into bowls and serve.
Nutrition: calories 300, fat 11.2, fiber 3.4, carbs 14.5, protein 4.5

Masala Macaroni

Preparation time: 10 minutes
Cooking time: 10 minutes
Servings: 3
Ingredients:
- 2 cups elbow macaroni
- ½ cup bell pepper, chopped
- ½ cup carrots, chopped
- ½ cup red onion, chopped
- 1 and ¾ cups water
- 1 cup onion, masala
- ½ teaspoon garam masala
- 2 tablespoons ghee, melted
- Salt to the taste
- 1 tablespoon cilantro, chopped

Directions:
1. In your instant pot, mix the macaroni with the bell pepper and the other ingredients except the cilantro, put the lid on and cook on High for 10 minutes.
2. Release the pressure naturally for 10 minutes, divide the mix between plates, sprinkle the cilantro on top and serve for lunch.
Nutrition: calories 355, fat 15.4, fiber 4.5, carbs 17.4, protein 3.5

Masala Tomato Beans Curry

Preparation time: 10 minutes
Cooking time: 45 minutes
Servings: 4
Ingredients:
- 2 cups red kidney beans, soaked overnight and drained
- 1 Serrano pepper, chopped
- 1 yellow onion , chopped
- 3 tablespoons ghee, melted
- 2 teaspoons garlic, minced
- 1 bay leaf
- 2 teaspoons ginger, grated
- 1 teaspoon garam masala
- 1 teaspoon coriander powder
- Salt to the taste
- ½ teaspoon turmeric powder
- 1 teaspoon sweet paprika
- A pinch of cayenne pepper
- 2 cup tomato puree
- 2 cups water
- 1 tablespoon cilantro, chopped

Directions:
1. Set the instant pot on Sauté mode, add the ghee, heat it up, add the pepper, onion, garlic, bay leaf, ginger, garam masala, coriander, turmeric, paprika and cayenne, stir and cook for 10 minutes.
2. Add the rest of the ingredients, put the lid on and cook on High for 35 minutes.
3. Release the pressure naturally for 10 minutes, divide the mix into bowls and serve for lunch.
Nutrition: calories 400, fat 13.4, fiber 4.5, carbs 22.3, protein 4.5

Cardamom Chicken Masala
Preparation time: 10 minutes
Cooking time: 20 minutes
Servings: 4
Ingredients:
- ¼ cup vegetable oil
- 4 cloves
- 3 green cardamom
- 1 black cardamom
- ½ star anise
- ½ teaspoon cumin seeds
- 2 pounds chicken thighs, skinless, boneless and cut into quarters
- 1 teaspoon coriander powder
- Salt to the taste
- 1 and ¼ cup onion masala
- 1 yellow onion, chopped
- 1 teaspoon garam masala
- 1 tablespoon cilantro, chopped

Directions:
1. Set the instant pot on Sauté mode, add the oil, heat it up, add the cloves, cardamom, star anise, cumin seeds, coriander and the chicken, stir and cook for 5 minutes.
2. Add the rest of the ingredients, put the lid on and cook on High for 15 minutes.
3. Release the pressure naturally for 10 minutes, divide the mix into bowls and serve.

Nutrition: calories 563, fat 30.5, fiber 0.6, carbs 2.7, protein 66

Coconut Peas Curry
Preparation time: 10 minutes
Cooking time: 10 minutes
Servings: 4
Ingredients:
- ½ teaspoon black mustard seeds
- 1 tablespoon coconut oil, melted
- 30 curry leaves
- ½ cup carrots, sliced
- ½ cup peas
- ½ cup corn
- ½ cup okra, trimmed and halved
- ½ cup coconut, grated
- 2/3 cup water
- 1 green chili pepper, chopped
- Salt to the taste
- ½ teaspoon cumin, ground
- ¼ teaspoon turmeric powder
- ½ cup yogurt

Directions:
1. Set the instant pot on Sauté mode, add the oil, heat it up, add the mustard seeds and curry leaves, stir and cook for 2 minutes.
2. Add the rest of the ingredients, put the lid on and cook on High for 8 minutes.
3. Release the pressure naturally for 10 minutes, divide the mix between plates and serve for lunch.

Nutrition: calories 322, fat 12.3, fiber 4.5, carbs 19.8, protein 5.6

Ginger Carrots Chicken Soup
Preparation time: 10 minutes
Cooking time: 30 minutes
Servings: 4
Ingredients:
- 1 pound chicken breast, skinless, boneless and cubed
- 1 cup mixed carrots, peas and potatoes, peeled and cubed
- 1 tablespoon ginger, grated
- ½ cup corn
- 2 tablespoons lemon juice
- 1 teaspoon ghee, melted
- 4 peppercorns
- 1 bay leaf
- 4 cloves

Directions:
1. Set your instant pot on sauté mode, add the ghee, heat it up, add the peppercorns, bay leaf, ginger and cloves, stir and cook for 5 minutes.
2. Add the meat, stir and brown for 5 minutes more.
3. Add the other ingredients, toss, put the lid on and cook on High for 20 minutes.
4. Release the pressure naturally for 10 minutes, divide into bowls and serve.

Nutrition: calories 373, fat 14, fiber 4, carbs 13.4, protein 18

Potato and Broccoli Cream
Preparation time: 10 minutes
Cooking time: 15 minutes
Servings: 4
Ingredients:
- 2 cups broccoli florets
- 1 potato, peeled and cubed
- 1 yellow onion, chopped
- 4 garlic cloves, minced
- ½ cup milk
- Salt to the taste
- 1 tablespoon cream
- 1 tablespoon ghee, melted
- ¼ teaspoon oregano, dried
- 1 teaspoon turmeric powder
- ½ teaspoon garam masala

Directions:
1. Set your instant pot on sauté mode, add the ghee, heat it up, add the onion, garlic, oregano, turmeric and garam masala, stir and cook for 2 minutes.
2. Add the rest of the ingredients, put the lid on and cook on High for 13 minutes.
3. Release the pressure naturally for 10 minutes, blend the soup using an immersion blender, divide into bowls and serve.

Nutrition: calories 311, fat 12, fiber 4.5, carbs 11.7, protein 9

Mulligatawny Tomato Soup
Preparation time: 10 minutes
Cooking time: 35 minutes
Servings: 6
Ingredients:
- 1 yellow onion, chopped
- ¼ cup ghee, melted
- 1 red chili pepper, minced
- 1 carrot, peeled and cubed
- 2 teaspoons ginger, grated
- 3 garlic cloves, minced
- 2 apples, peeled, cored and cubed
- 1 tablespoon curry powder
- 14 ounces canned tomatoes, chopped
- Salt to the taste
- 1 teaspoon cumin, ground
- ½ teaspoon cinnamon powder
- ½ teaspoon sweet paprika
- ¼ teaspoon cardamom, ground
- ½ teaspoon turmeric powder
- ½ teaspoon thyme, dried
- ½ cup red lentils, soaked overnight and drained
- 4 cups chicken stock
- 1 cup coconut milk
- 1 tablespoon cilantro, chopped

Directions:
1. Set your instant pot on sauté mode, add the ghee, heat it up, add the onion, chili pepper, ginger and garlic, stir and sauté for 5 minutes.
2. Add the curry powder, cumin, cinnamon, paprika, cardamom, turmeric, thyme and salt, stir and cook for 5 minutes more.
3. Add the rest of the ingredients, put the lid on and cook on High for 25 minutes.
4. Release the pressure naturally for 10 minutes, divide the soup into bowls, and serve.
Nutrition: calories 383, fat 12, fiber 5.4, carbs 11.7, protein 10

Coconut Cauliflower Soup
Preparation time: 10 minutes
Cooking time: 25 minutes
Servings: 4
Ingredients:
- 1 pound cauliflower florets
- 2 cups broccoli florets
- 3 garlic cloves, minced
- 1 yellow onion, chopped
- 14 ounces coconut cream
- 2 cups chicken stock
- 1 tablespoon red curry paste
- 2 tablespoons chives, chopped

Directions:
1. In your instant pot, combine the cauliflower with the broccoli and all the other ingredients, toss, put the lid on and cook on High for 25 minutes.
2. Release the pressure naturally for 10 minutes, blend using an immersion blender, ladle into bowls and serve.
Nutrition: calories 291, fat 4.6, fiber 4, carbs 9.7, protein 6.7

Spinach Soup
Preparation time: 10 minutes
Cooking time: 20 minutes
Servings: 2
Ingredients:
- 2 cups spinach, chopped
- 3 garlic cloves, minced
- 1 tablespoon gram flour
- ¼ cup yellow onion, chopped
- ¼ teaspoon cumin powder
- 1 bay leaf
- 2 cups water
- 1 tablespoon olive oil
- Salt to the taste
- A pinch of black pepper

Directions:
1. Set your instant pot on sauté mode, add the oil, heat it up, add the onion, garlic, cumin and bay leaf, stir and cook for 5 minutes.
2. Add the rest of the ingredients, put the lid on and cook on High or 15 minutes.
3. Release the pressure naturally for 10 minutes, blend the soup with an immersion blender, ladle into bowls and serve.
Nutrition: calories 199, fat 4.5, fiber 4, carbs 9.6, protein 11

Indian Coconut Soup
Preparation time: 10 minutes
Cooking time: 25 minutes
Servings: 4
Ingredients:
- 1 tablespoon sunflower oil
- 2 teaspoons black mustard seeds
- 1 tablespoon curry powder
- 10 curry leaves, chopped
- 1 teaspoon turmeric powder
- 2 red chilies, chopped
- 1-inch ginger, grated
- 2 garlic cloves, minced
- 1 yellow onion, chopped
- ½ cup basmati rice
- 1 tablespoon mango chutney
- 3 cups chicken stock
- 1 pound white fish fillets, boneless, skinless and cubed
- 15 ounces coconut milk
- Salt and black pepper to the taste
- Juice of 2 limes
- 1 teaspoon garam masala
- 1 tablespoon coriander, chopped

Directions:
1. Set your instant pot on sauté mode, add oil, heat it up, add the mustard seeds, curry powder, curry leaves, turmeric, chilies, ginger, garlic and onion, stir and sauté for 10 minutes.
2. Add the fish and the rest of the ingredients except the coriander, put the lid on and cook on High for 15 minutes.
3. Release the pressure naturally for 10 minutes, ladle into bowls and serve with the coriander sprinkled on top.
Nutrition: calories 291, fat 8.3, fiber 2, carbs 8.5, protein 9

Potato Ki Kadhi

Preparation time: 10 minutes
Cooking time: 20 minutes
Servings: 4
Ingredients:

- 6 cups gold potatoes, peeled and cubed
- 2 tablespoons ghee, melted
- ½ cup yogurt
- 1 teaspoon cumin seeds
- ¼ teaspoon fenugreek seeds
- Salt and black pepper to the taste
- 1 bay leaf
- 2 teaspoons ginger paste
- 1 red chili, chopped
- 2 tablespoons cilantro, chopped
- ¼ teaspoon garam masala

Directions:
1. Set your instant pot on Sauté mode, add the oil, heat it up, add the cumin seeds, fenugreek seeds, bay leaf, ginger paste, chili and garam masala, stir and cook for 5 minutes.
2. Add the potatoes and the rest of the ingredients, put the lid on and cook on High for 15 minutes.
3. Release the pressure naturally for 10 minutes, blend the soup using an immersion blender, divide into bowls and serve.
Nutrition: calories 310, fat 7.4, fiber 4, carbs 11.6, protein 11

Beans and Hominy Soup

Preparation time: 10 minutes
Cooking time: 20 minutes
Servings: 4
Ingredients:

- 1 tablespoon ghee, melted
- 2 cups carrots, peeled and cubed
- 2 cups celery, chopped
- 30 ounces hominy, drained
- 6 cups water
- 15 ounces kidney beans, rinsed and drained
- 4 cups rutabaga, cubed
- Salt to the taste

Directions:
1. Set your instant pot on Sauté mode, add the ghee, heat it up, add the carrots and the celery, stir and sauté for 2 minutes.
2. Add the rest of the ingredients, stir, put the lid on and cook on High for 18 minutes.
3. Release the pressure naturally for 10 minutes, divide the soup into bowls and serve.
Nutrition: calories 385, fat 9.6, fiber 4, carbs 14.8, protein 10

Indian Tomato Soup

Preparation time: 10 minutes
Cooking time: 20 minutes
Servings: 2
Ingredients:

- 4 tomatoes, peeled and chopped
- 3 garlic cloves, minced
- 1 Indian bay leaf
- 1 yellow onion, chopped
- 1 tablespoon butter
- 1 cup water
- 1 tablespoon cream
- ½ tablespoon sugar
- Salt and black pepper to the taste

Directions:
1. Set the instant pot on Sauté mode, add the butter, heat it up, add the garlic and the onion, stir and sauté for 5 minutes.
2. Add the tomatoes and the other ingredients, put the lid on and cook on High for 15 minutes.
3. Release the pressure naturally for 10 minutes, blend everything using an immersion blender, divide the soup into bowls and serve.
Nutrition: calories 280, fat 5.7, fiber 3, carbs 11.6, protein 7.4

Coriander Cabbage Soup

Preparation time: 10 minutes
Cooking time: 25 minutes
Servings: 6
Ingredients:

- 2 pounds green cabbage, shredded
- Salt and black pepper to the taste
- 1 cup tomatoes, chopped
- 1 yellow onion, chopped
- 4 garlic cloves, minced
- 2 tablespoons parsley, chopped
- 1 quart water
- 4 tablespoons lemon juice
- 1 teaspoon turmeric powder
- 1 tablespoon coriander powder

Directions:
1. In your instant pot, combine the cabbage with the tomatoes and all the other ingredients, put the lid on and cook on High for 25 minutes.
2. Release the pressure naturally for 10 minutes, ladle the soup into bowls and serve.
Nutrition: calories 272, fat 6.4, fiber 4, carbs 11.7, protein 9

Celery Turkey Soup

Preparation time: 10 minutes
Cooking time: 25 minutes
Servings: 4
Ingredients:

- 2 tablespoons butter
- 1 cup celery, chopped
- 1 cup carrot, chopped
- 2 cups yellow onion, chopped
- 4 teaspoons yellow curry powder
- 4 cups chicken stock
- ¼ cup white rice
- 2 green apples, cored, peeled and cubed
- 2 bay leaves
- Salt to the taste
- 2 cups turkey meat, cooked, skinless, boneless and shredded
- ¼ cup heavy cream

Directions:
1. Set your instant pot on Sauté mode, add the butter, heat it up, add the onion, curry powder and bay leaves, stir and cook for 5 minutes.
2. Add the rest of the ingredients, put the lid on and cook on High for 20 minutes.
3. Release the pressure naturally for 10 minutes, divide the soup into bowls and serve.
Nutrition: calories 320, fat 15.4, fiber 4, carbs 16.7, protein 12.2

Coconut Turkey Soup

Preparation time: 10 minutes
Cooking time: 25 minutes
Servings: 6
Ingredients:
- 3 cups turkey meat, cooked, skinless, boneless and shredded
- 1 quart water
- 2 garlic cloves, minced
- 1-inch ginger, grated
- 2 tablespoons curry powder
- 2 tablespoons vegetable oil
- 1 teaspoon cumin, ground
- 2 potatoes, peeled and cubed
- 3 carrots, sliced
- 1 cup coconut milk
- ¼ cup lime juice
- 1 tablespoon coriander, chopped

Directions:
1. Set your instant pot on Sauté mode, add the oil, heat it up, add the garlic, ginger, cumin, and curry powder, stir and sauté for 5 minutes.
2. Add the rest of the ingredients except the coriander, put the lid on and cook on High for 20 minutes.
3. Release the pressure naturally for 10 minutes, ladle the soup into bowls, sprinkle the coriander on top and serve.

Nutrition: calories 290, fat 7.5, fiber 4, carbs 11.8, protein 11

Turmeric Shrimp Stew

Preparation time: 5 minutes
Cooking time: 15 minutes
Servings: 4
Ingredients:
- 1 pound shrimp, peeled and deveined
- 1 tablespoon vegetable oil
- 1 yellow onion, chopped
- 1 teaspoon ginger, grated
- 2 teaspoons turmeric powder
- 1 teaspoon coriander, ground
- 1 teaspoon cumin, ground
- 1 teaspoon sweet paprika
- 1 teaspoon curry powder
- ½ teaspoon chili powder
- 2 garlic cloves, mined
- 15 ounces coconut milk
- Salt to the taste
- 14 ounces tomato sauce

Directions:
1. Set the instant pot on Sauté mode, add the oil, heat it up, add the onion, ginger, turmeric, coriander, cumin, paprika, curry powder, chili powder and garlic, stir and sauté for 5-6 minutes.
2. Add the rest of the ingredients, put the lid on and cook on High for 10 minutes.
3. Release the pressure fast for 5 minutes, divide the stew into bowls and serve.

Nutrition: calories 376, fat 8.3, fiber 3, carbs 8, protein 11.3

Herbed Beef Stew

Preparation time: 10 minutes
Cooking time: 35 minutes
Servings: 4
Ingredients:
- 1 teaspoon mustard seeds
- 1 cup tomatoes, chopped
- 2 green chilies, minced
- 1 cup red onions, chopped
- 1 tablespoon chili powder
- 1 teaspoon fenugreek seeds
- 1 tablespoon garam masala
- 1 tablespoon coriander powder
- 2 teaspoons fennel powder
- 2 teaspoons cumin powder
- 1 teaspoon turmeric powder
- 1 tablespoon ginger garlic paste
- Salt to the taste
- 2 tablespoons coconut oil
- 2 pounds beef stew meat, cubed
- 1 carrot, sliced
- 1 plantain, peeled and cubed
- 8 curry leaves
- 1 and ½ cups water

Directions:
1. Set your instant pot on Sauté mode, add the oil, heat it up, add the meat, onion, chilies and curry leaves, stir and brown for 5 minutes.
2. Add the tomatoes, chili powder, fenugreek seeds and the rest of the ingredients, put the lid on and cook on High for 30 minutes.
3. Release the pressure naturally for 10 minutes, divide the stew into bowls and serve.

Nutrition: calories 371, fat 13, fiber 4, carbs 22.8, protein 14

Masala Potato Stew

Preparation time: 10 minutes
Cooking time: 25 minutes
Servings: 4
Ingredients:
- 1 potato, peeled and cubed
- 1 carrot, peeled and cubed
- 1 yellow onion, chopped
- 1-inch ginger, grated
- 2 garlic cloves, minced
- 2 green chilies, chopped
- 2 curry leaves
- 2 tablespoons coconut oil
- Salt and black pepper to the taste
- ½ teaspoon erachii masala
- 1 cup water
- 1 cup milk

Directions:
1. Set your instant pot on Sauté mode, add the oil, heat it up, add the onion, garlic, ginger and the curry leaves, stir and cook for 5 minutes.
2. Add the rest of the ingredients, put the lid on and cook on High for 20 minutes.
3. Release the pressure naturally for 10 minutes, divide the stew into bowls and serve.

Nutrition: calories 264, fat 12, fiber 4, carbs 9, protein 18

Ghee Carrot Pudding

Preparation time: 10 minutes
Cooking time: 20 minutes
Servings: 4
Ingredients:
- 5 carrots, peeled and roughly grated
- 1 and ½ cups almond milk
- 1 cup coconut milk
- 1 tablespoon ghee, melted
- 2 tablespoons honey
- ½ teaspoon cardamom, ground
- ½ teaspoon ginger, grated
- ½ teaspoon cinnamon powder
- ½ teaspoon cloves, ground
- A pinch of salt
- 1 star anise
- ¼ cup cashews, chopped
- ¼ cup raisins

Directions:
1. Set your instant pot on Sauté mode, add the ghee, heat it up, add the carrots and ginger and sauté for 5 minutes.
2. Add the rest of the ingredients, put the lid on and cook on High for 15 minutes.
3. Release the pressure naturally for 10 minutes, divide the mix into bowls and serve.

Nutrition: calories 280, fat 12, fiber 5.5, carbs 9, protein 5.6

Chickpeas and Oregano Masala

Preparation time: 10 minutes
Cooking time: 25 minutes
Servings: 4
Ingredients:
- 1 yellow onion, chopped
- 1 pound chickpeas, rinsed and drained
- 20 ounces canned tomatoes, chopped
- 1 teaspoon oregano, dried
- ½ teaspoon turmeric powder
- ½ teaspoon garam masala
- ½ teaspoon coriander, ground
- 2 tablespoons ghee, melted
- A pinch of salt and black pepper
- ½ teaspoon red pepper flakes

Directions:
1. Set the instant pot on Sauté mode, add the ghee, heat it up, add the onion, oregano, turmeric garam masala and the coriander, stir and sauté for 5 minutes.
2. Add all the other ingredients, put the lid on and cook on High for 20 minutes.
3. Release the pressure naturally for 10 minutes, divide the mix into bowls and serve.

Nutrition: calories 280, fat 12, fiber 4.5, carbs 14.5, protein 7.8

Nutmeg Mutton Stew

Preparation time: 10 minutes
Cooking time: 30 minutes
Servings: 4
Ingredients:
- 1 pound mutton, cubed
- 4 cups water
- 1 tablespoon butter, melted
- 1 and ½ cups yellow onion, chopped
- 1 carrots, chopped
- ¼ cup potato, cubed
- 1 teaspoon nutmeg, ground
- 2 teaspoons turmeric powder
- ½ teaspoon chili powder

Directions:
1. Set your instant pot on Sauté mode, add the oil, heat it up, add onion, the meat, nutmeg, turmeric and chili powder, stir and cook for 5 minutes.
2. Add the rest of the ingredients, put the lid on and cook on High for 25 minutes.
3. Release the pressure naturally for 10 minutes, divide the mix into bowls and serve.

Nutrition: calories 382, fat 8.5, fiber 3, carbs 23.0, protein 15.4

1

Garlicky Broccoli Junka

Preparation time: 5 minutes
Cooking time: 15 minutes
Servings: 4
Ingredients:
- 1 yellow onion, chopped
- 2 tablespoons vegetable oil
- ½ teaspoon mustard seeds
- 1 tablespoon garlic-ginger paste
- ½ teaspoon cumin seeds
- 1 teaspoon turmeric powder
- 1 teaspoon chili powder
- 1 pound broccoli florets
- 2 teaspoons water
- Salt to the taste
- 3 tablespoons gram flour

Directions:
1. Set your instant pot on Sauté mode, add the oil, heat it up, add the onion, garlic paste, mustard and cumin seeds, stir and cook for 5 minutes.
2. Add the broccoli and the rest of the ingredients, put the lid on and cook on High for 10 minutes.
3. Release the pressure fast for 5 minutes, divide the stew into bowls and serve.

Nutrition: calories 272, fat 5.4, fiber 4, carbs 11.7, protein 8

Zucchini Chili Curry

Preparation time: 10 minutes
Cooking time: 20 minutes
Servings: 2
Ingredients:

- 2 zucchinis, cubed
- 1 tablespoon coconut oil
- ½ teaspoon mustard seeds
- ¼ teaspoon asafetida powder
- 2 garlic cloves, minced
- ½ teaspoon turmeric powder
- 1 teaspoon red chili powder
- 1 teaspoon cumin powder
- ½ teaspoon garam masala
- Salt to the taste
- ½ cup veggie stock

Directions:
1. Set your instant pot on Sauté mode, add the oil, heat it up, the mustard seeds and the garlic, stir and cook for 3 minutes.
2. Add the zucchinis and the rest of the ingredients, put the lid on and cook on High for 17 minutes.
3. Release the pressure naturally for 10 minutes, divide the stew into bowls and serve.
Nutrition: calories 265, fat 5.67, fiber 3, carbs 9, protein 5.1

Sweet Paprika and Peas Curry

Preparation time: 10 minutes
Cooking time: 20 minutes
Servings: 4
Ingredients:

- 1 tablespoon coconut oil
- 1 yellow onion, chopped
- 2 garlic cloves, minced
- 1 teaspoon ginger, grated
- 2 zucchinis, cubed
- ½ teaspoon sweet paprika
- 2 tablespoons curry powder
- ½ teaspoon cumin, ground
- ½ teaspoon thyme, dried
- 1 cup green peas
- 14 ounces coconut milk
- ½ cup vegetable stock
- Salt to the taste
- ¼ cup cilantro, chopped

Directions:
1. Set your instant pot on Sauté mode, add the oil, heat it up, add the garlic, onion and the ginger, stir and sauté for 5 minutes.
2. Add the zucchinis and the rest of the ingredients, put the lid on and cook on High for 15 minutes..
3. Release the pressure naturally for 10 minutes, divide the stew into bowls and serve.
Nutrition: calories 280, fat 12, fiber 4, carbs 11.8, protein 12

Coconut Lentils Stew

Preparation time: 10 minutes
Cooking time: 25 minutes
Servings: 8
Ingredients:

- 1 cup split pigeon peas
- 1 pound butternut squash, peeled and cubed
- 1 tomato, cubed
- 1 cup coconut, shredded
- ½ teaspoon turmeric powder
- ½ teaspoon cumin, ground
- 2 cups veggie stock
- 2 tablespoons vegetable oil
- 1 teaspoon mustard seeds
- ½ teaspoon red pepper flakes
- 1 garlic clove, minced
- Juice of 1 lime
- 1 tablespoon honey
- 1 tablespoon coriander, chopped

Directions:
1. Set your instant pot on Sauté mode, add the oil, heat it up, add the coconut, turmeric, cumin, mustard sees, pepper flakes and garlic, stir and cook for 5 minutes.
2. Add the peas, squash and the remaining ingredients, put the lid on and cook on High for 20 minutes.
3. Release the pressure naturally for 10 minutes, divide the stew into bowls and serve.
Nutrition: calories 282, fat 11.4, fiber 5.4, carbs 8, protein 12

Zucchini and Turnips Soup

Preparation time: 10 minutes
Cooking time: 20 minutes
Servings: 4
Ingredients:

- 2 cups zucchinis, cubed
- 2 cups turnips, cubed
- ½ cup water
- 1 tablespoon coconut oil
- ½ cup yellow onion, chopped
- 5 cups veggie stock
- 2 handfuls spinach, chopped
- 1 teaspoon lemon juice
- 1 tablespoon ginger, grated
- 2 tablespoons garlic, minced
- Salt to the taste

Directions:
1. Set the instant pot on Sauté mode, add the oil, heat it up, add the onion, ginger and the garlic, stir and sauté for 5 minutes.
2. Add the turnips and the rest of the ingredients except the parsley, put the lid on and cook on High for 15 minutes.
3. Release the pressure naturally for 10 minutes, divide the soup into bowls and serve.
Nutrition: calories 231, fat 13, fiber 3, carbs 8, protein 11.1

Paprika Bean Stew

Preparation time: 10 minutes
Cooking time: 30 minutes
Servings: 4
Ingredients:

- 2 tablespoons vegetable oil
- 2 garlic cloves, minced
- 1 yellow onion, chopped
- 2 teaspoons sweet paprika
- 2 bay leaves
- Salt and black pepper to the taste
- 1 cup mushrooms, sliced
- 7 ounces seitan, chopped
- 2 cups canned beans, drained
- 1 cup water
- 1 tablespoon parsley, chopped

Directions:
1.   Set the pot on Sauté mode, add the oil, heat it up, add the onion, garlic, paprika and bay leaves, stir and sauté for 5 minutes.
2.   Add the beans and the rest of the ingredients except the parsley, put the lid on and cook on High for 25 minutes.
3.   Release the pressure naturally for 10 minutes, add the parsley, divide the stew into bowls and serve.
Nutrition: calories 272, fat 12, fiber 4, carbs 9, protein 11.3

Green Beans Cumin Curry

Preparation time: 10 minutes
Cooking time: 20 minutes
Servings: 4
Ingredients:

- 4 cups green beans, trimmed and halved
- 2 teaspoons vegetable oil
- 2 potatoes, cubed
- 3 garlic cloves, mined
- ½ teaspoon turmeric powder
- ¼ teaspoon asafetida powder
- Salt to the taste
- ½ teaspoon cumin, ground
- ¼ cup water
- 1 tablespoon lemon juice
- 1 tablespoon cilantro, chopped

Directions:
1.   In your instant pot, combine the green beans with the oil and the all the other ingredients except the cilantro, put the lid on and cook on High for 20 minutes.
2.   Release the pressure naturally for 10 minutes, divide the stew into bowls and serve with the cilantro sprinkled on top.
Nutrition: calories 251, fat 13, fiber 5, carbs 9.8, protein 7.6

Indian Instant Pot Side Dish Recipes

Chili Button Mushrooms
Preparation time: 5 minutes
Cooking time: 20 minutes
Servings: 4
Ingredients:
- 1 pound button mushrooms, halved
- 1 tablespoon ginger, grated
- 2 tablespoons vegetable oil
- 3 garlic cloves, minced
- 1 green chili, chopped
- 3 tablespoons yogurt
- 2 teaspoons coriander seeds
- 1 teaspoon tomato puree
- ½ teaspoon turmeric powder
- ½ teaspoon chili powder
- Salt to the taste

Directions:
1. Set the instant pot on Sauté mode, add the oil, heat it up, add the garlic, ginger and the chili, stir and sauté for 5 minutes.
2. Add the rest of the ingredients, put the lid on and cook on High for 15 minutes more.
3. Release the pressure fast for 5 minutes, divide the mix between plates and serve.

Nutrition: calories 103, fat 7.4, fiber 1.5, carbs 6.7, protein 4.6

Coriander Okra Mix
Preparation time: 5 minutes
Cooking time: 20 minutes
Servings: 4
Ingredients:
- 1 pound okra, trimmed and halved
- 1 teaspoon chili flakes
- 1 yellow onion, chopped
- 2 teaspoons coriander seeds
- 3 tablespoons mustard oil
- 1 teaspoon turmeric powder
- 1 teaspoon garam masala
- Salt to the taste
- 2 teaspoons dried mango powder

Directions:
1. Set the instant pot on Sauté mode, add the oil, heat it up, add the onion and sauté for 5 minutes.
2. Add the okra and the other ingredients, put the lid on and cook on High for 15 minutes.
3. Release the pressure fast for 5 minutes, divide the mix between plates and serve.

Nutrition: calories 151, fat 10.8, fiber 4.4, carbs 11.4, protein 2.6

Masala Potato
Preparation time: 10 minutes
Cooking time: 20 minutes
Servings: 4
Ingredients:
- 1 teaspoon mustard seeds
- 1 tablespoon vegetable oil
- 1 yellow onion, chopped
- 5 curry leaves
- 1 teaspoon cumin seeds
- 2 green chilies, chopped
- ½ teaspoon red chili powder
- 1 teaspoon coriander seeds
- ½ teaspoon turmeric powder
- 2 potatoes, peeled and cut into chunks
- 1 teaspoon garam masala
- 1 tablespoon coriander, chopped

Directions:
1. Set the instant pot on Sauté mode, add the oil, heat it up, add the mustard seeds and the onion and sauté for 5 minutes.
2. Add the curry leaves, cumin and the other ingredients, toss, put the lid on and cook on High for 15 minutes.
3. Release the pressure naturally for 10 minutes, divide the mix between plates and serve.

Nutrition: calories 123, fat 4, fiber 3.5, carbs 20.2, protein 2.5

Coconut Beans and Peppers
Preparation time: 10 minutes
Cooking time: 20 minutes
Servings: 4
Ingredients:
- 1 red bell pepper, cut into chunks
- 1 green bell pepper, cut into chunks
- 1 tablespoon vegetable oil
- 10 mushrooms, halved
- 1 cup green beans, trimmed and halved
- 1 tablespoon cumin seeds
- 2 yellow onions, chopped
- 2 cups tomatoes, chopped
- Salt to the taste
- 1 teaspoon turmeric powder
- ½ tablespoon chili powder
- 2 green chilies, chopped
- 1 cup coconut cream
- 1 tablespoon garam masala

Directions:
1. Set the instant pot on Sauté mode, add the oil, heat it up, add the onions, cumin, turmeric, chili powder and green chilies, stir and cook for 5 minutes.
2. Add the rest of the ingredients, put the lid on and cook on High for 15 minutes.
3. Release the pressure naturally for 10 minutes, divide the mix between plates and serve.

Nutrition: calories 254, fat 18.8, fiber 6.4, carbs 21.4, protein 5.7

Ginger Potato

Preparation time: 10 minutes
Cooking time: 20 minutes
Servings: 4
Ingredients:
- 4 potatoes, peeled and roughly cubed
- 1 tablespoon coriander seeds
- 2 tablespoons vegetable oil
- 2 teaspoons cumin seeds
- 2 green chilies, chopped
- 1 teaspoon red chili powder
- 1 tablespoon ginger, grated
- ½ teaspoon turmeric powder
- Salt to the taste
- 2 teaspoons mango powder
- ¼ cup veggie stock

Directions:
1. In your instant pot, combine the potatoes with the oil and the other ingredients, put the lid on and cook on High for 20 minutes.
2. Release the pressure naturally for 10 minutes, divide everything between plates and serve.

Nutrition: calories 300, fat 6.23, fiber 3.4, carbs 11.5, protein 5.5

Curry Cabbage Thoran

Preparation time: 10 minutes
Cooking time: 15 minutes
Servings: 4
Ingredients:
- 2 red chilies, chopped
- 1 teaspoon cumin seeds
- 3 tablespoons coconut oil
- 2 tablespoons curry leaves, chopped
- 2 teaspoons black mustard seeds
- 1 tablespoon ginger, grated
- 1 pound green cabbage, shredded
- Salt to the taste
- ½ cup coconut, grated

Directions:
1. Set the instant pot on Sauté mode, add the oil, heat it up, add the chilies, cumin, curry leaves and mustard seeds, toss and cook for 2 minutes.
2. Add the cabbage and the other ingredients, put the lid on and cook on High for 13 minutes.
3. Release the pressure naturally for 10 minutes, divide everything between plates and serve.

Nutrition: calories 166, fat 14.3, fiber 4.1, carbs 9.9, protein 2.4

Potato Sabjee

Preparation time: 10 minutes
Cooking time: 15 minutes
Servings: 4
Ingredients:
- 1 yellow bell pepper, roughly cubed
- 1 potato, peeled and roughly cubed
- 1 carrot, sliced
- ½ cup peas

- 2 tablespoons mustard oil
- 1 teaspoon cumin seeds
- 1 teaspoon mustard seeds
- 1 yellow onion, chopped
- 6 ounces canned tomatoes, chopped
- 2 garlic cloves, minced
- 1 tablespoon ginger, grated
- 1 teaspoon fenugreek leaves, dried
- 1 teaspoon turmeric powder
- Salt to the taste
- 1 teaspoon garam masala
- 1 tablespoon coriander, chopped

Directions:
1. Set the instant pot on Sauté mode, add the oil, heat it up, add cumin seeds, mustard seeds, onion, garlic, ginger, turmeric and garam masala, stir and cook for 3 minutes.
2. Add the rest of the ingredients, put the lid on and cook on High for 12 minutes.
3. Release the pressure naturally for 10 minutes, divide everything between plats and serve.

Nutrition: calories 200, fat 3.4, fiber 3.45, carbs 6.7, protein 3.4

Aromatic Rice Mix

Preparation time: 10 minutes
Cooking time: 30 minutes
Servings: 4
Ingredients:
- 2 cups basmati rice
- 6 cups water
- Salt to the taste
- 2 cardamom pods
- 2 cloves
- 3 tablespoons vegetable oil
- ½ teaspoon black mustard seeds
- ¼ teaspoon chili flakes
- ½ teaspoon cumin seeds
- 1 yellow onion, chopped
- 4 garlic cloves, minced
- ¼ teaspoon turmeric powder

Directions:
1. Set your instant pot on Sauté mode, add the oil, heat it up, add the onion and garlic, stir and sauté for 3 minutes.
2. Add the cardamom, cloves, mustard seeds, chili flakes and turmeric, stir and cook for 2 minutes more.
3. Add the rest of the ingredients, put the lid on and cook on High for 25 minutes.
4. Release the pressure naturally for 10 minutes, divide the mix between plates and serve as a side dish.

Nutrition: calories 351, fat 7, fiber 6, carbs 9.2, protein 6

Cardamom Basmati
Preparation time: 10 minutes
Cooking time: 25 minutes
Servings: 4
Ingredients:
- 1 and ½ cups basmati rice
- 2 tablespoons vegetable oil
- 1 tablespoon cumin seeds
- Salt to the taste
- 2 and ½ cups water
- 2 green cardamom pods
- 1 yellow onion, chopped
- 2 cloves
- 1 tablespoon chili powder
- 1 teaspoon turmeric powder

Directions:
1. Set your instant pot on Sauté mode, add oil, heat it up, add the onion, cloves, cardamom, chili powder and the turmeric, stir and cook for 5 minutes.
2. Add the rest of the ingredients, toss, put the lid on and cook on High for 20 minutes.
3. Release the pressure naturally for 10 minutes, divide the mix between plates and serve as a side dish.
Nutrition: calories 271, fat 4.5, fiber 5, carbs 11..6, protein 6

Cumin Quinoa
Preparation time: 5 minutes
Cooking time: 20 minutes
Servings: 4
Ingredients:
- 1 cup red quinoa
- 2 tablespoons vegetable oil
- 1 yellow onion, chopped
- 2 cups cauliflower florets
- 2 tablespoons chili peppers, chopped
- Salt to the taste
- ½ teaspoon turmeric powder
- ½ teaspoon red chili powder
- 1 and ½ teaspoon cumin, ground
- ½ cup peas
- 2 tablespoons lemon juice
- ½ cup cilantro, chopped
- 1 tablespoon cashews, chopped

Directions:
1. Set your instant pot on Sauté mode, add the oil, heat it up, add the onion, chili peppers, turmeric, chili powder, cumin and salt, stir and cook for 5 minutes.
2. Add the quinoa and the rest of the ingredients, put the lid on and cook on High for 15 minutes.
3. Release the pressure fast for 5 minutes, divide the mix between plates and serve as a side dish.
Nutrition: calories 182, fat 6, fiber 3, carbs 5.6, protein 4.5

Coconut Curry
Preparation time: 5 minutes
Cooking time: 20 minutes
Servings: 4
Ingredients:
- 1 cup white quinoa
- 2 teaspoons tamari sauce
- 2 cups coconut milk
- 1 tablespoon curry powder
- 1 teaspoon cumin, ground

Directions:
1. In your instant pot, combine the quinoa with the tamari sauce and the other ingredients, put the lid on and cook on High for 20 minutes.
2. Release the pressure fast for 5 minutes, stir the mix, divide it between plates and serve as a side dish.
Nutrition: calories 262, fat 6, fiber 4, carbs 6, protein 3.5

Quinoa Pilaf
Preparation time: 5 minutes
Cooking time: 20 minutes
Servings: 4
Ingredients:
- 1 cup quinoa
- 1 and ½ cups water
- 1 tablespoon vegetable oil
- ½ teaspoon turmeric powder
- ½ cup corn
- ½ cup carrot, sliced
- 1 green chili, chopped
- ½ teaspoon cumin seeds
- 1 bay leaf
- ¼ teaspoon black mustard seeds
- 1 tablespoon lime juice
- 1 cup tomato, chopped

Directions:
1. Set your instant pot on Sauté mode, add the oil, heat it up, add the corn, carrot, chili, cumin and black mustard seeds, stir and cook for 5 minutes.
2. Add rest of the ingredients, put the lid on and cook on High for 15 minutes.
3. Release the pressure fast for 5 minutes, divide between plates and serve.
Nutrition: calories 200, fat 8, fiber 4, carbs 6, protein 7

Quinoa Curry Mix

Preparation time: 5 minutes
Cooking time: 20 minutes
Servings: 6
Ingredients:
- 2 tablespoons ghee, melted
- 1 teaspoon smoked paprika
- 2 teaspoons chili powder
- 2 teaspoons cumin, ground
- 2 teaspoons garam masala
- ¼ teaspoon red pepper flakes
- 2 teaspoons curry powder
- 1 yellow onion, chopped
- 1 red bell pepper, chopped
- 1 tablespoon ginger, grated
- 3 garlic cloves, minced
- 1 cup quinoa
- 1 and ½ cups water
- 1 green chili, chopped
- 28 ounces canned chickpeas, drained and rinsed
- 14 ounces canned tomatoes, chopped
- 4 cups spinach leaves, chopped
- Salt to the taste

Directions:
1. Set your instant pot on Sauté mode, add the ghee, heat it up, add the onion, garlic, ginger, paprika, chili powder, cumin, garam masala, curry powder and pepper flakes, stir and cook for 5 minutes.
2. Add the quinoa and the rest of the ingredients, toss, put the lid on and cook on High for 15 minutes.
3. Release the pressure fast for 5 minutes, divide the mix between plates and serve as a side dish.
Nutrition: calories 280, fat 7, fiber 4.4, carbs 11.7, protein 6

Beet Chili Sabzi

Preparation time: 10 minutes
Cooking time: 25 minutes
Servings: 4
Ingredients:
- 2 cups beets, peeled and cubed
- 2 tablespoons vegetable oil
- ¼ cup chicken stock
- ¼ teaspoon mustard seeds
- ½ teaspoon cumin seeds
- 2 red chilies, chopped
- 2 green chilies, chopped
- 10 curry leaves
- ¼ teaspoon turmeric powder
- 1 yellow onion, chopped
- ¼ cup coconut, grated
- Salt to the taste

Directions:
1. Set the instant pot on sauté mode, add the oil, heat it up, add the cumin, mustard, red and green chilies, curry leaves, onion and turmeric, stir and cook for 5 minutes.
2. Add the remaining ingredients, put the lid on and cook on High for 20 minutes.
3. Release the pressure naturally for 10 minutes, stir the mix, divide between plates and serve as a side dish.
Nutrition: calories 220, fat 8, fiber 4, carbs 6.6, protein 8

Curry Beet Rice

Preparation time: 10 minutes
Cooking time: 25 minutes
Servings: 4
Ingredients:
- 1 cup basmati rice
- 2 cups water
- 2 tablespoons vegetable oil
- 3 green cardamom
- 1-inch cinnamon, crushed
- 3 cloves
- ½ teaspoon mustard seeds
- ½ teaspoon cumin seeds
- 1 yellow onion, chopped
- 8 curry leaves
- 2 beets, peeled and chopped
- 1 teaspoon ginger-garlic paste
- ¼ cup coriander, chopped
- 1 green chili, chopped
- ¼ teaspoon turmeric powder
- ¼ teaspoon red chili powder
- ½ teaspoon coriander powder
- Salt to the taste

Directions:
1. Set the instant pot on Sauté mode, add the oil, heat it up, add the cardamom, cinnamon, cloves, mustard seeds, cumin, onion, curry, and green chili, stir and cook for 5 minutes.
2. Add the rest of the ingredients, toss, put the pressure lid on and cook on High for 20 minutes.
3. Release the pressure naturally for 10 minutes, divide the mix between plates and serve as a side dish.
Nutrition: calories 281, fat 11.7, fiber 3, carbs 8.6, protein 4.7

Beet Poriyal

Preparation time: 10 minutes
Cooking time: 20 minutes
Servings: 2
Ingredients:
- 2 tablespoons coconut oil
- 2 cups beets, peeled and grated
- 1 green chili, chopped
- 10 curry leaves, chopped
- 1 teaspoon black mustard seeds
- 1 teaspoon urad dal
- 1 teaspoon asafetida
- ½ cup water
- 4 tablespoons coconut, grated
- Salt to the taste

Directions:
1. Set your instant pot on Sauté mode, add the oil, heat it up, add the chili, curry leaves, mustard seeds and asafetida, stir and cook for 5 minutes.
2. Add the beets and the rest of the ingredients, stir, put the lid on and cook on High for 15 minutes.
3. Release the pressure naturally for 10 minutes, divide between plates and serve as a side dish.
Nutrition: calories 184, fat 6, fiber 3, carbs 6, protein 6

Coconut Thoran

Preparation time: 10 minutes
Cooking time: 20 minutes
Servings: 4
Ingredients:

- 3 beets, peeled and grated
- ¼ cup chicken stock
- 1 teaspoon mustard seeds
- ½ cup coconut, grated
- ½ teaspoon cumin seeds
- 4 shallots, chopped
- 10 curry leaves, chopped
- 2 red chilies, chopped
- 1 green chili, chopped
- 1 teaspoon ginger, grated
- 1 teaspoon turmeric powder
- 1 teaspoon red chili powder
- 2 tablespoons coconut oil
- 1 teaspoon coriander powder
- Salt to the taste

Directions:
1.   In your instant pot, combine beets with the mustard seeds, coconut, cumin and the other ingredients, toss, put the lid on and cook on High for 20 minutes.
2.   Release the pressure naturally for 10 minutes, divide between plates and serve as a side dish.
Nutrition: calories 200, fat 8, fiber 3, carbs 7, protein 8

Curry Carrot Poriyal

Preparation time: 10 minutes
Cooking time: 20 minutes
Servings: 4
Ingredients:

- 2 beets, peeled and cubed
- 1 green chili, minced
- 2 carrots, sliced
- 1 teaspoon mustard
- 1 teaspoon urad dal
- 10 curry leaves, chopped
- 1 teaspoon turmeric powder
- 1 tablespoon coconut oil
- 4 tablespoons coconut, grated
- Salt to the taste
- ¼ cup chicken stock

Directions:
1.   Set your instant pot on sauté mode, add the oil, heat it up, add the chilies, mustard, urad dal, curry, and turmeric, stir and sauté for 5 minutes.
2.   Add the beets and the rest of the ingredients except the spinach, put the lid on and cook on High for 15 minutes.
3.   Release the pressure naturally for 10 minutes, divide the mix between plates and serve as a side dish.
Nutrition: calories 200, fat 5.7, fiber 5.4, carbs 6.7, protein 5

Ginger Peas Pot

Preparation time: 10 minutes
Cooking time: 25 minutes
Servings: 4
Ingredients:

- 1 cup peas
- 1 teaspoon ginger, grated
- 2 tablespoons curd
- 2 tablespoon milk powder
- ½ teaspoon turmeric powder
- 1 teaspoon red chili powder
- 1 teaspoon coriander powder
- 1 teaspoon cumin powder
- ½ teaspoon garam masala
- ½ teaspoon fenugreek leaves, dried
- 1 cup water
- Salt to the taste
- 4 tablespoons ghee, melted

Directions:
1.   Set your instant pot on Sauté mode, add the ghee, heat up, add the ginger, turmeric, chili powder, coriander, cumin, garam masala and fenugreek leaves, stir and cook for 5 minutes.
2.   Add the rest of the ingredients, toss, put the lid on and cook on High for 20 minutes.
3.   Release the pressure naturally for 10 minutes, divide the mix between plates and serve as a side dish.
Nutrition: calories 185, fat 6, fiber 4, carbs 6, protein 5.8

Paneer Peas

Preparation time: 10 minutes
Cooking time: 25 minutes
Servings: 4
Ingredients:

- 1 cup paneer, cubed
- 1 cup peas
- 1 and ½ cups water
- ¼ teaspoon turmeric powder
- ½ teaspoon cumin seeds
- Salt to the taste
- ½ teaspoon red chili powder
- ½ teaspoon garam masala
- 1 tablespoon cream
- ½ teaspoon sugar
- 2 tablespoons ghee, melted
- Salt to the taste

Directions:
1.   Set your instant pot on Sauté mode, add the ghee, heat it up, add the cumin, turmeric, chili powder, garam masala, sugar and the salt, stir and cook for 5 minutes.
2.   Add the rest of the ingredients, put the lid on and cook on High for 20 minutes.
3.   Release the pressure naturally for 10 minutes, divide the mix between plates and serve as side dish.
Nutrition: calories 200, fat 7, fiber 2.3, carbs 5, protein 6

Peas Pulao

Preparation time: 10 minutes
Cooking time: 20 minutes
Servings: 4
Ingredients:

- 1 cup basmati rice
- 1 cup peas
- ½ cup onion, chopped
- 3 tablespoons ghee, melted
- 2 cups water
- Salt to the taste
- 1 teaspoon cumin seeds
- 1 black cardamom
- 2 green cardamom
- 3 cloves
- 1 bay leaf

Directions:

1. Set the instant pot on Sauté mode, add the ghee, heat it up, add the onion and sauté for 5 minutes.
2. Add the peas and the rest of the ingredients, put the lid on and cook on High for 15 minutes.
3. Release the pressure naturally for 10 minutes, divide between plates and serve as a side dish.

Nutrition: calories 226, fat 5.4, fiber 5, carbs 8, protein 5

White Peas & Mushrooms Mix

Preparation time: 10 minutes
Cooking time: 20 minutes
Servings: 4
Ingredients:

- ½ pound white mushrooms
- 1 cup peas
- 3 tomatoes, cubed
- 1 yellow onion, chopped
- 1 green chili, chopped
- ½ teaspoon chili powder
- ½ teaspoon turmeric powder
- ½ teaspoon garam masala
- 1 teaspoon coriander powder
- 1 teaspoon ginger-garlic paste
- 2 cups water
- Salt to the taste
- 2 tablespoons vegetable oil

Directions:

1. Set the instant pot on Sauté mode, add the oil, heat it up, add the onion and the chili, stir and sauté for 5 minutes.
2. Add the rest of the ingredients, toss, put the lid on and cook onHigh for 15 minutes.
3. Release the pressure naturally for 10 minutes, divide the mix between plates and serve as a side dish.

Nutrition: calories 175, fat 4, fiber 2, carbs 6, protein 8

Green Peas Matar

Preparation time: 10 minutes
Cooking time: 20 minutes

Servings: 4
Ingredients:

- 4 carrots, sliced
- 1 cup green peas
- 1 teaspoon cumin seeds
- 1-inch ginger, grated
- 2 green chilies, chopped
- ½ teaspoon red chili powder
- ¼ teaspoon garam masala
- 2 tablespoons vegetable oil
- ½ cup water
- 1 tablespoon coriander, chopped
- Salt to the taste

Directions:

1. Set the instant pot on Sauté mode, add the oil, heat it up, add the cumin, ginger, chilies, chili powder and garam masala, stir and cook for 5 minutes.
2. Add the rest of the ingredients, toss, put the lid on and cook on High for 15 minutes.
3. Release the pressure naturally for 10 minutes, divide the mix between plates and serve as a side dish.

Nutrition: calories 200, fat 5.5, fiber 3.3, carbs 6, protein 7

Spinach Potatoes Kabab

Preparation time: 10 minutes
Cooking time: 20 minutes
Servings: 4
Ingredients:

- 2 cups spinach, torn
- 1 cup water
- 2 potatoes, peeled and cubed
- ½ cup green peas
- 4 tablespoons gram flour
- 1 green chili, chopped
- 1 teaspoon ginger, grated
- 1 teaspoon chaat masala
- 1 teaspoon dry mango powder
- 8 cashews, chopped
- Salt to the taste
- 2 tablespoons coconut oil

Directions:

1. Set the pot on sauté mode, add the oil, heat it up, add the flour, chili, ginger, chaat masala, mango powder and salt, whisk well and cook for 3 minutes.
2. Add the rest of the ingredients, toss, put the lid on and cook on High for 17 minutes.
3. Release the pressure naturally for 10 minutes, divide the mix between plates and serve as a side dish.

Nutrition: calories 262, fat 8.6, fiber 2, carbs 7.6, protein 4

Soupy Peas Ka Nimona

Preparation time: 10 minutes
Cooking time: 20 minutes
Servings: 4
Ingredients:

- 1 yellow onion, chopped
- 1 teaspoon garlic, minced
- ½ teaspoon ginger, grated
- 2 green chilies, chopped
- 1 cup peas
- 2 tablespoons mustard oil
- 1 yellow potato, cubed
- 1 bay leaf
- 3 cloves
- ½ teaspoon cumin seeds
- 1 tomato, cubed
- ½ teaspoon turmeric powder
- ½ teaspoon red chili powder
- ½ teaspoon coriander powder
- 2 tablespoons coriander, chopped
- 1 cup water
- ½ teaspoon garam masala

Directions:
1.   Set your instant pot on Sauté mode, add the oil, heat it up, add the onion, garlic, ginger and the chilies and sauté for 5 minutes.
2.   Add the rest of the ingredients except the coriander, put the lid on and cook on High for 15 minutes.
3.   Release the pressure naturally for 10 minutes, divide the mix between plates and serve as a side dish with the coriander sprinkled on top.
Nutrition: calories 252, fat 6.4, fiber 2.5, carbs 6, protein 4.8

Eggplant Cumin Bhurtha

Preparation time: 10 minutes
Cooking time: 20 minutes
Servings: 4
Ingredients:

- 2 eggplants, roughly cubed
- ½ teaspoon turmeric powder
- ½ teaspoon cumin, ground
- 2 tablespoons vegetable oil
- ½ teaspoon cumin seeds
- 1 yellow onion, chopped
- ½ teaspoon coriander, ground
- 1 tomato, cubed
- 1 teaspoon ginger, grated
- ½ cup veggie stock

Directions:
1.   In your instant pot, combine the eggplant with the oil, turmeric and the other ingredients, put the lid on and cook on High for 20 minutes.
2.   Release the pressure naturally for 10 minutes, divide the mix between plates and serve.
Nutrition: calories 200, fat 11.8, fiber 4, carbs 7, protein 5.6

Eggplant Ka Bharta

Preparation time: 10 minutes
Cooking time: 20 minutes
Servings: 4
Ingredients:

- 2 eggplants, roughly cubed
- 1 yellow onion, chopped
- 2 tablespoons ghee, melted
- 1 teaspoon cumin seeds
- 1 teaspoon ginger, grated
- 5 garlic cloves, minced
- 1 chili pepper, chopped
- 2 teaspoons coriander powder
- ½ teaspoon garam masala
- ½ teaspoon turmeric powder
- ½ teaspoon sweet paprika
- 4 tomatoes, cubed
- 1 tablespoon cilantro, chopped

Directions:
1.   Set your instant pot on Sauté mode, add the ghee, heat it up, add the cumin, ginger, garlic, chili pepper, coriander and garam masala, stir and cook for 5 minutes.
2.   Add the rest of the ingredients, put the lid on and cook on High for 15 minutes.
3.   Release the pressure naturally for 10 minutes, divide the mix between plates and serve as a side dish.
Nutrition: calories 162, fat 4, fiber 4, carbs 6.9, protein 5.7

Parsnips and Carrots Mix

Preparation time: 10 minutes
Cooking time: 20 minutes
Servings: 4
Ingredients:

- 1 pound parsnips, peeled and cut into sticks
- ½ cup chicken stock
- Salt to the taste
- 2 tablespoons coconut oil
- 3 carrots, peeled and cut into sticks
- ½ teaspoon garam masala

Directions:
1.   In your instant pot, combine the parsnips with the carrots and the other ingredients, put the lid on and cook on High for 20 minutes.
2.   Release the pressure naturally for 10 minutes, divide the mix between plates and serve as a side dish.
Nutrition: calories 142, fat 2, fiber 4, carbs 9, protein 4

Cauliflower Mix

Preparation time: 10 minutes
Cooking time: 15 minutes
Servings: 4
Ingredients:
- 1 pound cauliflower florets
- 1 teaspoon cumin seeds
- ½ teaspoon mustard seeds
- 1 teaspoon garam masala
- 1 teaspoon sage, dried
- Salt and black pepper to the taste
- 1 tablespoon coriander, chopped
- ¼ cup coconut cream

Directions:
1. In your instant pot, mix the cauliflower with the cumin, mustard seeds and the other ingredients, toss, put the lid on and cook on High for 15 minutes.
2. Release the pressure naturally for 10 minutes, divide the mix between plates and serve as a side dish.
Nutrition: calories 242, fat 4, fiber 3, carbs 6, protein 4.5

Spiced Cauliflower Gobi

Preparation time: 5 minutes
Cooking time: 20 minutes
Servings: 4
Ingredients:
- 1 pound cauliflower florets
- 3 tablespoons ghee, melted
- 1 yellow onion, chopped
- 4 garlic cloves, minced
- 3 tablespoons curd
- ½ teaspoon red chili powder
- ¼ teaspoon turmeric powder
- ½ teaspoon garam masala powder
- ½ teaspoon cumin, ground
- 1 teaspoon coriander powder
- 1 bay leaf
- ½ teaspoon caraway seeds
- ½ teaspoon fenugreek leaves, dried
- 1 and ½ cups water
- 2 tablespoons cream
- Salt to the taste

Directions:
1. Set the instant pot on Sauté mode, add the ghee, heat it up, add the onion, garlic, chili powder, turmeric powder, garam masala, cumin and coriander, stir and sauté for 5 minutes.
2. Add the rest of the ingredients, toss, put the lid on and cook on High for 15 minutes.
3. Release the pressure fast for 5 minutes, divide between plates and serve as a side dish.
Nutrition: calories 232, fat 5.4, fiber 3, carbs 6, protein 4.5

Spicy Paprika Cauliflower

Preparation time: 5 minutes
Cooking time: 20 minutes
Servings: 4
Ingredients:
- 1 pound cauliflower florets
- ¼ teaspoon red chili powder
- ½ teaspoon smoked paprika
- 1 teaspoon soy sauce
- 1 cup chicken stock
- Salt and black pepper to the taste
- 3 tablespoons vegetable oil

Directions:
1. Set the instant pot on Sauté mode, add the oil, heat it up, add the cauliflower, chili powder and the paprika and brown for 5 minutes.
2. Add the rest of the ingredients, put the lid on and cook on High for 15 minutes.
3. Release the pressure fast for 5 minutes, divide the mix between plates and serve.
Nutrition: calories 142, fat 7, fiber 4, carbs 6, protein 3.4

Coconut Cauliflower Mix

Preparation time: 10 minutes
Cooking time: 20 minutes
Servings: 4
Ingredients:
- ½ pound cauliflower florets
- Salt to the taste
- ½ cup coconut, grated
- 2 green chilies, chopped
- 1 teaspoon ginger, grated
- 4 garlic cloves, minced
- 1 tablespoon chana dal
- 1 teaspoon poppy seeds
- ½ teaspoon fennel seeds
- 10 cashews, chopped
- ½ cup water
- 2 tablespoons coconut oil
- 2 cloves
- 1 yellow onion, chopped
- 1 teaspoon turmeric powder

Directions:
1. Set the instant pot on Sauté mode, add the oil, heat it up, add the coconut, chilies, ginger, garlic, chana dal, poppy seeds, fennel seeds and the onions, stir and sauté for 5 minutes.
2. Add the cauliflower and the other ingredients, put the lid on and cook on High for 15 minutes.
3. Release the pressure naturally for 10 minutes, divide the mix between plates and serve as a side dish.
Nutrition: calories 152, fat 7, fiber 2, carbs 7, protein 5

Brussels Sprouts Subzi

Preparation time: 10 minutes
Cooking time: 20 minutes
Servings: 2
Ingredients:

- 1 teaspoon coconut oil
- ½ teaspoon cumin seeds
- ½ teaspoon black mustard seeds
- 8 curry leaves, chopped
- 1 green chili, chopped
- 2 cups Brussels sprouts, halved
- 3 garlic cloves, minced
- 2 teaspoons sesame seeds
- ½ teaspoon coriander powder
- ½ teaspoon garam masala
- ½ teaspoon turmeric powder
- ¼ cup water
- Salt to the taste

Directions:
1. Set the instant pot on Sauté mode, add the oil, heat it up, add the cumin, mustard sees, curry leaves, chili, garlic, sesame seeds, coriander and garam masala, stir and cook for 5 minutes.
2. Add the other ingredients, toss, put the lid on and cook on High for 15 minutes.
3. Release the pressure naturally for 10 minutes, divide the mix between plates and serve.
Nutrition: calories 152, fat 4, fiber 3, carbs 4.4, protein 3

Chili Brussels Sprouts

Preparation time: 10 minutes
Cooking time: 20 minutes
Servings: 4
Ingredients:

- 2 tablespoons sunflower oil
- 2 garlic cloves, minced
- ½ teaspoon brown mustard seeds
- 2 red chilies, chopped
- 3 curry leaves
- 1 pound Brussels sprouts, halved
- ½ teaspoon garam masala
- ¼ teaspoon turmeric powder
- Salt to the taste
- 2 teaspoons lemon juice
- 1 tablespoon coriander, chopped

Directions:
1. Set the instant pot on Sauté mode, add the oil, heat it up, add the garlic, chilies, mustard seeds, curry leaves, garam masala and turmeric, stir and cook for 4 minutes.
2. Add the other ingredients, put the lid on and cook on High for 15 minutes.
3. Release the pressure naturally for 10 minutes, divide the mix between plates and serve as a side dish.
Nutrition: calories 187, fat 7, fiber 3, carbs 5, protein 5

Onion Brussels Sprouts

Preparation time: 10 minutes
Cooking time: 20 minutes
Servings: 4
Ingredients:

- ½ pound Brussels sprouts, halved
- 1 cup yellow onion, chopped
- 1 tomato, chopped
- 1 green chili, chopped
- 1 and ½ tablespoons coconut oil
- 2 garlic cloves, minced
- ½ teaspoon cumin, ground
- ½ teaspoon turmeric powder
- ½ teaspoon chili powder
- 1 teaspoon coriander powder
- 1 cup green peas
- 1 teaspoon fennel seeds, ground
- ½ cup veggie stock

Directions:
1. Set the instant pot on Sauté mode, add the oil, heat it up, add the onion, chili and the garlic, stir and cook for 2 minutes.
2. Add the cumin, turmeric, chili powder, coriander and fennel seeds, stir and cook for 3 minutes more.
3. Add the remaining ingredients, toss, put the lid on and cook on High for 15 minutes.
4. Release the pressure naturally for 10 minutes, divide everything between plates and serve.
Nutrition: calories 120, fat 4, fiber 3.4, carbs 8, protein 4

Kale and Dates Salad

Preparation time: 5 minutes
Cooking time: 15 minutes
Servings: 4
Ingredients:

- 2 bunches kale, torn
- 1 yellow onion, chopped
- 5 dates, chopped
- 2 tablespoons pistachios, chopped
- 2 tablespoons olive oil
- Juice of 1 lemon
- ¼ cup veggie stock
- Salt to the taste
- ½ teaspoon cumin, ground
- ½ teaspoon garam masala

Directions:
1. Set the instant pot on Sauté mode, add the oil, heat it up, add the onion, cumin and garam masala, toss and sauté for 5 minutes.
2. Add the rest of the ingredients, toss, put the lid on and cook on High for 10 minutes.
3. Release the pressure fast for 5 minutes, divide everything between plates and serve.
Nutrition: calories 165, fat 4, fiber 3, carbs 5.7, protein 6

Spiced Kale and Brussels Sprouts
Preparation time: 5 minutes
Cooking time: 15 minutes
Servings: 4
Ingredients:
- 1 tablespoon vegetable oil
- ½ teaspoon mustard seeds
- 1 teaspoon cumin seeds
- 4 green chilies, chopped
- 1 teaspoon ginger, grated
- ½ teaspoon turmeric powder
- 1 pound greens (kale, and Brussels sprouts), shredded
- Juice of 1 lemon
- ¼ cup veggie stock
- ½ teaspoon coriander, ground
- 1 tablespoon coriander, chopped

Directions:
1. In your instant pot, the greens with the oil, mustard sees, cumin and the other ingredients, put the lid on and cook on High for 15 minutes.
2. Release the pressure fast for 5 minutes, divide the mix between plates and serve.
Nutrition: calories 173, fat 4.5, fiber 2, carbs 5, protein 6

Mango and Kale Mix
Preparation time: 5 minutes
Cooking time: 15 minutes
Servings: 4
Ingredients:
- 1 bunch kale, torn
- Juice of 1 lemon
- 3 tablespoons vegetable oil
- 2 teaspoons honey
- Salt to the taste
- 1 mango, peeled and cubed
- 1 tablespoon pepitas
- ¼ cup chicken stock

Directions:
1. In your instant pot, combine the kale with the lemon juice and the other ingredients, toss, put the lid on and cook on High for 15 minutes.
2. Release the pressure fast for 5 minutes, divide between plates and serve as a side dish.
Nutrition: calories 173, fat 8, fiber 4.2, carbs 6, protein 6

Turmeric Broccoli Mix
Preparation time: 10 minutes
Cooking time: 15 minutes
Servings: 2
Ingredients:
- 1 broccoli head, florets separated
- ¼ cup chicken stock
- 1 teaspoon turmeric powder
- ½ teaspoon chili powder
- ½ teaspoon garam masala
- A pinch of salt and black pepper
- ¼ cup pine nuts, toasted
- 1 tablespoon olive oil

Directions:
1. In your instant pot, combine the broccoli with the stock and the other ingredients, put the lid on and cook on High for 15 minutes.
2. Release the pressure naturally for 10 minutes, divide the mix between plates and serve as a side dish.
Nutrition: calories 190, fat 5, fiber 3, carbs 4.5, protein 4.23

Citrus Cauliflower Mix
Preparation time: 10 minutes
Cooking time: 15 minutes
Servings: 4
Ingredients:
- 1 pound cauliflower florets
- ½ teaspoon garam masala
- ½ teaspoon cumin, ground
- ½ teaspoon coriander, ground
- Zest of 1 orange, grated
- Juice of 1 orange
- ¼ cup chicken stock
- 1 red chili pepper, chopped
- A pinch of salt and black pepper
- 2 tablespoons coconut oil

Directions:
1. In your instant pot, combine the cauliflower with the garam masala and the other ingredients, toss, put the lid on and cook on High for 15 minutes.
2. Release the pressure naturally for 10 minutes, divide everything between plates and serve as a side salad.
Nutrition: calories 242, fat 4, fiber 2.2, carbs 4, protein 5

Orange Pulao
Preparation time: 10 minutes
Cooking time: 20 minutes
Servings: 4
Ingredients:
- 1 cup basmati rice
- 4 carrots, chopped
- 1 cup orange juice
- 2 tablespoons vegetable oil
- Salt to the taste
- 1 yellow onion, chopped
- 1 teaspoon ginger garlic paste
- ½ teaspoon aniseed
- 2 curry leaves, chopped
- 1 cardamom

Directions:
1. Set the instant pot on Sauté mode, add the oil, heat it up, add the onion, ginger paste, aniseed, curry and cardamom, stir and cook for 5 minutes.
2. Add the rest of the ingredients, put the lid on and cook on High for 15 minutes.
3. Release the pressure naturally for 10 minutes, divide the mix between plates and serve.
Nutrition: calories 190, fat 6, fiber 2, carbs 6, protein 3.4

Narangi Rice Pulao

Preparation time: 10 minutes
Cooking time: 20 minutes
Servings: 4
Ingredients:
- 1 cup basmati rice
- 1 tablespoon ghee, melted
- 1-inch cinnamon stick
- 1 star anise
- 2 cloves
- 1 cardamom
- 2 cups orange juice
- 1 tablespoon milk
- ½ teaspoon saffron powder
- 2 tablespoons sugar
- Salt to the taste

Directions:
1.   Set the instant pot on Sauté mode, add the ghee, heat it up, add the cinnamon, star anise, cloves, cardamom and the saffron mixed with the milk, whisk and cook for 3 minutes.
2.   Add the rest of the ingredients, put the lid on and cook on High for 17 minutes.
3.   Release the pressure naturally for 10 minutes, divide the mix between plates and serve.
Nutrition: calories 181, fat 6, fiber 5, carbs 3.7, protein 7

Rice and Kale

Preparation time: 5 minutes
Cooking time: 20 minutes
Servings: 4
Ingredients:
- 2 cups basmati rice
- 3 cups chicken stock
- 2 cups kale, torn
- ½ teaspoon turmeric powder
- 1 teaspoon cumin seeds
- 2 tablespoons ghee, melted
- 3 garlic cloves, minced

Directions:
1.   Set the instant pot on Sauté mode, add the ghee, heat it up, add the garlic, cumin and the turmeric, stir and cook for 3 minutes.
2.   Add the rest of the ingredients, put the lid on and cook on High for 17 minutes.
3.   Release the pressure fast for 5 minutes, divide the mix between plates and serve.
Nutrition: calories 181, fat 5, fiber 4, carbs 6, protein 3.6

Garlic Rice Mix

Preparation time: 10 minutes
Cooking time: 20 minutes
Servings: 6
Ingredients:
- 2 tablespoons butter
- 4 garlic cloves, minced
- Salt to the taste
- 1 and ½ cups rice
- 2 and ½ cups chicken stock
- 1/3 cup almonds, chopped

- 1 tablespoon cilantro, chopped

Directions:
1.   Set your instant pot on Sauté mode, add the butter, heat it up, add the garlic and sauté for 2 minutes.
2.   Add the rest of the ingredients, put the lid on and cook on High for 18 minutes
3.   Release the pressure fast for 10 minutes, divide between plates and serve.
Nutrition: calories 182, fat 4, fiber 3, carbs 3.4, protein 4

Asparagus Rice Mix

Preparation time: 5 minutes
Cooking time: 20 minutes
Servings: 4
Ingredients:
- 1 cup basmati rice
- 1 cup chicken stock
- 1 cup water
- Salt to the taste
- 2 garlic cloves, minced
- ½ teaspoon sweet paprika
- ½ teaspoon turmeric powder
- ½ teaspoon orange zest, grated
- 1 pound asparagus, trimmed and chopped

Directions:
1.   In the instant pot, combine the rice with the stock, water and the other ingredients, toss, put the lid on and cook on High for 20 minutes.
2.   Release the pressure fast for 5 minutes, divide the mix between plates and serve as a side dish.
Nutrition: calories 218, fat 20, fiber 3.4, carbs 41.6, protein 7.3

Spicy Eggplant Mix

Preparation time: 10 minutes
Cooking time: 15 minutes
Servings: 4
Ingredients:
- 2 eggplants, roughly cubed
- ½ cup chicken stock
- ½ teaspoon cumin, ground
- ½ teaspoon coriander powder
- ½ teaspoon ginger, grated
- 2 teaspoons turmeric powder
- A pinch of salt and black pepper
- 2 tablespoons coconut oil, melted
- 2 garlic cloves, minced
- 1 teaspoon hot pepper flakes

Directions:
1.   Set your instant pot on Sauté mode, add the oil, heat it up, add the garlic, cumin, coriander, ginger, and turmeric, stir and cook for 2 minutes.
2.   Add the rest of the ingredients, put the lid on and cook on High for 13 minutes.
3.   Release the pressure naturally for 10 minutes, divide between plates and serve.
Nutrition: calories 233, fat 4, fiber 4, carbs 4.7, protein 2.4

Ginger Broccoli and Orange Mix

Preparation time: 5 minutes
Cooking time: 20 minutes
Servings: 4
Ingredients:
- 1 pound broccoli florets
- 1 orange, peeled and cut into segments
- ½ teaspoon turmeric powder
- ½ teaspoon garam masala
- ½ teaspoon ginger powder
- ½ teaspoon dry mango powder
- ¼ cup veggie stock
- 2 teaspoons ginger, grated
- 2 garlic cloves, minced
- Salt and white pepper to the taste

Directions:
1. In your instant pot, combine the broccoli with the orange and the other ingredients, put the lid on and cook on High for 20 minutes.
2. Release the pressure fast for 5 minutes, divide the mix between plates and serve.

Nutrition: calories 230, fat 4.4, fiber 3, carbs 7, protein 4

Saffron Red Cabbage

Preparation time: 10 minutes
Cooking time: 15 minutes
Servings: 4
Ingredients:
- 1 pound red cabbage, shredded
- 2 tablespoons coconut oil
- ½ teaspoon saffron powder mixed with 1 tablespoon milk
- ½ cup yellow onion, chopped
- 1 teaspoon hot paprika
- ½ teaspoon chili powder
- 2 green chilies, chopped
- Salt and black pepper to the taste
- 1 tablespoon apple cider vinegar

Directions:
1. Set your instant pot on Sauté mode, add the oil, heat it up, add the onion, paprika, chilies and green chilies, stir and cook for 2 minutes.
2. Add the saffron, stir and cook for 3 minutes more.
3. Add the rest of the ingredients, toss, put the lid on and cook on High for 10 minutes.
4. Release the pressure naturally for 10 minutes, divide the mix between plates and serve as a side dish.

Nutrition: calories 232, fat 3.7, fiber 3, carbs 6, protein 2.4

Cabbage Rice

Preparation time: 10 minutes
Cooking time: 20 minutes
Servings: 8
Ingredients:
- 2 cups basmati rice
- 3 and ½ cups water
- Salt to the taste
- ¼ teaspoon asafetida powder
- 2 tablespoons coconut oil
- ½ cup peanuts
- 1 teaspoon mustard seeds
- ½ teaspoon turmeric powder
- 15 curry leaves
- 2 tablespoons ginger, grated
- 4 green chilies, chopped
- 8 cups green cabbage, shredded
- 2 tablespoons lemon juice
- 2 tablespoons cilantro, chopped

Directions:
1. Set the instant pot on Sauté mode, add the oil, heat it up, add the mustard seeds, turmeric, curry leaves, ginger and the chilies, stir and cook for 3 minutes.
2. Add the rice, water and the rest of the ingredients, put the lid on and cook on High for 17 minutes.
3. Release the pressure naturally for 10 minutes, divide the mix between plates and serve.

Nutrition: calories 263, fat 4.6, fiber 4, carbs 8, protein 6

Creamy Beans and Rice

Preparation time: 10 minutes
Cooking time: 20 minutes
Servings: 4
Ingredients:
- 1 pound green beans, trimmed
- 1 cup basmati rice
- 1 and ½ cups coconut cream
- 5 garlic cloves, minced
- ½ teaspoon chili powder
- ½ teaspoon garam masala
- ½ teaspoon coriander powder
- A pinch of salt and black pepper
- 1 teaspoon sweet paprika

Directions:
1. In your instant pot, mix the beans with the rice, cream and the other ingredients, put the lid on and cook on High for 20 minutes.
2. Release the pressure naturally for 10 minutes, divide the mix between plates and serve as a side dish.

Nutrition: calories 251, fat 11.7, fiber 4, carbs 6.9, protein 11

Tomato Salad

Preparation time: 10 minutes
Cooking time: 15 minutes
Servings: 4
Ingredients:

- 3 tomatoes, cut into wedges
- ½ teaspoon garam masala
- ½ red onion, chopped
- 1 cup curd
- 1 tablespoon lemon juice
- 1 cup mint leaves
- Salt to the taste
- 1 tablespoon water

Directions:
1.   In a blender, combine the curd with the other ingredients except the tomatoes, garam masala and the onion and pulse well.
2.   In your instant pot, combine the tomatoes with the onion, garam masala and the mint mix, toss, put the lid on and cook on High for 15 minutes.
3.   Release the pressure naturally for 10 minutes, divide the mix between plates and serve.
Nutrition: calories 182, fat 4, fiber 4, carbs 4.5, protein 8

Beets and Almonds

Preparation time: 10 minutes
Cooking time: 20 minutes
Servings: 4
Ingredients:

- ½ cup chicken stock
- ½ cup almonds, chopped
- ½ teaspoon red chili powder
- ½ teaspoon cumin, ground
- ½ teaspoon mustard seeds
- ½ teaspoon turmeric powder
- 1 red onion, sliced
- 4 beets, peeled and cut into cubes
- 2 tablespoons coconut oil
- A pinch of salt and black pepper
- 2 tablespoons coriander, chopped

Directions:
1.   In your instant pot, combine the beets with the stock, almonds and the other ingredients, toss, put the lid on and cook on High for 20 minutes.
2.   Release the pressure naturally for 10 minutes, divide the mix between plates and serve as a side dish.
Nutrition: calories 142, fat 5, fiber 3, carbs 8, protein 6

Spicy Artichokes and Rice

Preparation time: 10 minutes
Cooking time: 20 minutes
Servings: 4
Ingredients:

- 1 cup canned artichoke hearts, drained and roughly chopped
- 1 cup basmati rice
- 2 cups chicken stock
- 1 tablespoon coconut oil
- ½ teaspoon cumin, ground
- ½ teaspoon turmeric powder

- ½ teaspoon garam masala
- 2 tablespoons lemon juice
- A pinch of cayenne pepper
- ½ teaspoon red pepper flakes

Directions:
1.   Set the instant pot on Sauté mode, add the oil, heat it up, add the cumin, turmeric, garam masala, cayenne and pepper flakes, stir and cook for 5 minutes.
2.   Add the rest of the ingredients, put the lid on and cook on High for 15 minutes.
3.   Release the pressure naturally for 10 minutes, divide the mix between plates and serve.
Nutrition: calories 152, fat 4, fiber 4, carbs 8, protein 6

Spicy Cumin Tomatoes

Preparation time: 5 minutes
Cooking time: 12 minutes
Servings: 4
Ingredients:

- 2 tomatoes, cut into wedges
- ½ tablespoon coconut oil
- 1 yellow onion, chopped
- 2 tablespoons lemon juice
- Salt to the taste
- ½ teaspoon cayenne pepper
- ½ teaspoon cumin, ground
- ½ teaspoon dry mango powder

Directions:
1.   In your instant pot, combine the tomatoes with the oil and the other ingredients, put the lid on and cook on High for 12 minutes.
2.   Release the pressure fast for 5 minutes, divide the mix between plates and serve.
Nutrition: calories 140, fat 4, fiber 4, carbs 8, protein 4

Parsley Endives and Tomatoes

Preparation time: 5 minutes
Cooking time: 15 minutes
Servings: 4
Ingredients:

- 2 endives, trimmed and shredded
- 1 pound tomatoes, cut into wedges
- 2 tablespoons coconut oil
- ½ teaspoon cumin, ground
- ½ teaspoon sweet paprika
- ½ teaspoon chili powder
- Salt and black pepper to the taste
- Juice of 1 lime
- ¼ cup veggie stock
- 2 tablespoons parsley, chopped

Directions:
1.   In your instant pot, combine the endives with the tomatoes and the other ingredients except the parsley, put the lid on and cook on High for 15 minutes.
2.   Release the pressure fast for 5 minutes, divide the mix between plates and serve with the parsley sprinkled on top.
Nutrition: calories 140, fat 4, fiber 4, carbs 8, protein 5

Endives and Cumin Walnuts Pot
Preparation time: 10 minutes
Cooking time: 15 minutes
Servings: 2
Ingredients:
- 4 endives, trimmed and shredded
- 1 cup walnuts, chopped
- 2 tablespoons coconut oil, melted
- 2 shallots, chopped
- ½ teaspoon turmeric powder
- ½ teaspoon chili powder
- ½ teaspoon cumin, ground
- ½ teaspoon dry mango powder
- ½ cup chicken stock

Directions:
1. Set your instant pot on Sauté mode, add the oil, heat it up, add the shallots, walnuts, turmeric, chili powder, cumin and mango powder, stir and cook for 3 minutes.
2. Add the rest of the ingredients, put the lid on and cook on High for 12 minutes.
3. Release the pressure naturally for 10 minutes, divide the mix between plates and serve as a side dish.
Nutrition: calories 180, fat 4, fiber 5, carbs 9, protein 6

Endives with Orange Mix
Preparation time: 10 minutes
Cooking time: 15 minutes
Servings: 4
Ingredients:
- 2 endives, trimmed and shredded
- 2 oranges, peeled and cut into wedges
- 1 tablespoon coconut oil
- 1 yellow onion, chopped
- ½ cup chicken stock
- 6 garlic cloves, chopped
- Salt and black pepper to the taste
- 2 tablespoons coriander, chopped
- 1 teaspoon turmeric powder
- ½ teaspoon garam masala

Directions:
1. Set your instant pot on Sauté mode, add the oil, heat up, add the onion and garlic cloves, stir and cook for 3 minutes.
2. Add the rest of the ingredients, put the lid on and cook on High for 12 minutes.
3. Release the pressure naturally for 10 minutes, divide the mix between plates and serve.
Nutrition: calories 183, fat 4, fiber 4, carbs 8, protein 6

Indian Spicy Asparagus
Preparation time: 5 minutes
Cooking time: 12 minutes
Servings: 4
Ingredients:
- 1 pound fresh asparagus, trimmed and halved
- 1-inch ginger, grated
- 1 teaspoon cumin seeds
- 2 tablespoons lemon juice
- 1 tablespoon vegetable oil
- Salt to the taste
- ½ cup chicken stock
- ½ teaspoon turmeric powder
- ½ teaspoon chili powder
- ½ teaspoon garam masala

Directions:
1. Set your instant pot on Sauté mode, add the oil, heat it up, add the ginger, cumin, turmeric, chili powder and garam masala, stir and cook for 2 minutes.
2. Add the rest of the ingredients, toss, put the lid on and cook on High for 10 minutes.
3. Release the pressure fast for 5 minutes, divide the mix between plates and serve.
Nutrition: calories 169, fat 5.4, fiber 4, carbs 6.8, protein 6

Turmeric Fennel Basmati
Preparation time: 5 minutes
Cooking time: 20 minutes
Servings: 4
Ingredients:
- 1 fennel bulb, sliced
- 2 teaspoons turmeric powder
- 1 cup basmati rice
- ½ cup chicken stock
- ½ teaspoon chili powder
- ½ teaspoon garam masala
- 1 cup coconut cream
- A pinch of salt and black pepper

Directions:
1. In your instant pot, combine the rice with the stock, the fennel and the other ingredients, put the lid on and cook on High for 20 minutes.
2. Release the pressure fast for 5 minutes, divide the mix between plates and serve as a side dish.
Nutrition: calories 152, fat 5, fiber 4, carbs 8, protein 7

Peas and Fennel Mix
Preparation time: 10 minutes
Cooking time: 15 minutes
Servings: 4
Ingredients:
- 1 pound fresh peas
- 1 fennel bulb, shredded
- Salt to the taste
- 1 yellow onion, chopped
- 1 tablespoon mint, chopped
- ½ cup coconut cream
- ½ teaspoon chili powder
- ½ teaspoon smoked paprika

Directions:
1. In your instant pot, combine the peas with the fennel and the other ingredients, put the lid on and cook on High for 15 minutes.
2. Release the pressure naturally for 10 minutes, divide the mix between plates and serve.
Nutrition: calories 182, fat 5, fiber 5, carbs 4.9, protein 7

Indian Instant Pot Snack and Appetizer Recipes

Chili Paneer
Preparation time: 10 minutes
Cooking time: 20 minutes
Servings: 3
Ingredients:
- ½ green bell pepper, cubed
- ½ red bell pepper, cubed
- ½ yellow bell pepper, cubed
- 1 cup paneer, cubed
- ½ teaspoon cayenne pepper
- 2 teaspoons soy sauce
- ¼ teaspoon sugar
- ¼ cup spring onions, chopped
- 2 tablespoons vegetable oil
- Salt to the taste

Directions:
1. In your instant pot, combine the bell peppers with the other ingredients, put the lid on and cook on High for 15 minutes.
2. Divide the mix into bowls and serve as an appetizer.
Nutrition: calories 207, fat 13.2, fiber 1.8, carbs 17.4, protein 5.8

Turmeric Okra Pot
Preparation time: 5 minutes
Cooking time: 15 minutes
Servings: 3
Ingredients:
- 20 okra
- 2 tablespoons gram flour
- ½ teaspoon turmeric powder
- ½ teaspoon turmeric powder
- 2 tablespoons vegetable oil
- 1 cup water

Directions:
1. In a bowl, combine the okra with the flour and the other ingredients except the water and toss.
2. Put the water into the instant pot, add the trivet inside, put the bowls into the pot and cook on High for 15 minutes.
3. Release the pressure fast for 5 minutes, divide everything into smaller bowls and serve as a snack.
Nutrition: calories 124, fat 9.5, fiber 2.7, carbs 7.7, protein 2.2

Khara Wheat and Curry Biscuits
Preparation time: 10 minutes
Cooking time: 15 minutes
Servings: 10
Ingredients:
- 1 and ½ cups whole wheat flour
- ½ cup butter
- 1 tablespoon milk powder
- 3 tablespoons curd
- 2 tablespoons sugar
- ½ cup cilantro, chopped
- 20 curry leaves, chopped
- 7 green chilies, chopped
- Salt to the taste
- 1 cup water

Directions:
1. In a bowl, combine the flour with the milk powder, butter and the other ingredients except the water and stir well until you obtain a dough.
2. Transfer the dough to a baking sheet that fits the instant pot and press well on the bottom.
3. Add the water to the instant pot, add the trivet and the baking sheet inside, and cook on High for 15 minutes.
4. Release the pressure naturally for 10 minutes, cool the mix down, cut into biscuits and serve.
Nutrition: calories 194, fat 9.8, fiber 1.2, carbs 23, protein 3.7

Pyaaz Onion Chutney
Preparation time: 10 minutes
Cooking time: 10 minutes
Servings: 10
Ingredients:
- 3 yellow onions, chopped
- 2 green chilies, chopped
- 1 tablespoon ginger, grated
- 2 tablespoons sunflower oil
- Salt to the taste
- 3 red chilies, chopped
- 1 teaspoon cumin seeds

Directions:
1. Set the instant pot on Sauté mode, add the oil, heat it up, add the onions and sauté for 4 minutes.
2. Add the rest of the ingredients, put the lid on and cook on High for 6 minutes.
3. Release the pressure naturally for 10 minutes, transfer the mix to a blender, pulse well, divide into bowls and serve.
Nutrition: calories 70, fat 2.9, fiber 0.8, carbs 3.6, protein 0.5

Tomato Chili Chutney
Preparation time: 10 minutes
Cooking time: 20 minutes
Servings: 6
Ingredients:
- 1 pound red onions, chopped
- 2 pounds tomatoes, chopped
- 1 red chili, minced
- 2 garlic cloves, minced
- 1 tablespoon ginger, grated
- 1 tablespoon sugar
- 2 tablespoons red wine vinegar
- Salt to the taste
- 4 cardamom pods
- ½ teaspoon paprika

Directions:
1. In your instant pot, combine the onions with the tomatoes and the other ingredients, put the lid on and cook on High for 20 minutes.
2. Release the pressure naturally for 10 minutes, whisk the mix, divide into jars and serve as a party dip.
Nutrition: calories 221, fat 2.4, fiber 4.5, carbs 9.4, protein 3.4

Garlic Chili Dip

Preparation time: 10 minutes
Cooking time: 10 minutes
Servings: 4
Ingredients:

- 4 tablespoons chana daal
- 3 tablespoons urad daal
- 5 red chilies, minced
- 1 tablespoon cumin seeds
- 3 tablespoons garlic, minced
- 1 tablespoon vegetable oil
- 1 teaspoon sugar
- Salt to the taste

Directions:

1. In your instant pot, combine the urad dal with the chilies and the other ingredients, put the lid on and cook on High for 10 minutes.
2. Release the pressure naturally for 10 minutes, transfer this to a blender, pulse, divide into bowls and serve.

Nutrition: calories 200, fat 3.4, fiber 3.4, carbs 9.7, protein 5.6

Minty Yogurt Dip

Preparation time: 5 minutes
Cooking time: 5 minutes
Servings: 4
Ingredients:

- 2 cup yogurt
- ½ cup mint leaves, chopped
- 1 cucumber, grated
- 1 teaspoon cumin powder
- ½ teaspoon red chili powder
- ½ teaspoon sugar
- Salt to the taste

Directions:

1. In your instant pot, combine the yogurt with the mint and the other ingredients, put the lid on and cook on High for 5 minutes.
2. Release the pressure fast for 5 minutes, divide the mix into bowls and serve.

Nutrition: calories 200, fat 6.7, fiber 3.5, carbs 5.6, protein 6.7

Masala Chickpeas Hummus

Preparation time: 5 minutes
Cooking time: 15 minutes
Servings: 6
Ingredients:

- 15 ounces canned chickpeas, drained and rinsed
- ¼ cup lemon juice
- 3 garlic cloves, minced
- ½ cup tahini paste
- Salt to the taste
- ½ teaspoon sweet paprika
- 3 tablespoons olive oil
- 1 teaspoon garam masala

Directions:

1. In your instant pot, combine the chickpeas with the lemon juice and the other ingredients, toss, put the lid on and cook on High for 15 minutes.
2. Release the pressure fast for 5 minutes, blend the mix using an immersion blender, divide into bowls and serve as an appetizer.

Nutrition: calories 300, fat 3.4, fiber 6.5, carbs 11, protein 4.5

Avocado Yogurt Raita

Preparation time: 5 minutes
Cooking time: 5 minutes
Servings: 4
Ingredients:

- 1 yellow onion, chopped
- 2 avocados, peeled, pitted and chopped
- 2 tomatoes, chopped
- ½ teaspoon red chili powder
- 1 green chili, chopped
- 1 teaspoon cumin powder
- ½ cup coriander, chopped
- 1 tablespoon lemon juice
- 1 cup yogurt
- Salt to the taste

Directions:

1. In your instant pot, combine the avocado with the chili powder and the other ingredients, toss, put the lid on and cook on High for 5 minutes.
2. Release the pressure fast for 5 minutes, transfer the mix to a blender, pulse well, divide into bowls and serve.

Nutrition: calories 299, fat 4.5, fiber 5.4, carbs 11.3, protein 5.6

Tamarind Yogurt Dip

Preparation time: 10 minutes
Cooking time: 20 minutes
Servings: 4
Ingredients:

- 2 cups yogurt
- 2 red onions, chopped
- 2 tablespoons coconut oil, melted
- 1 cup tamarind chutney
- 1 cup mint, chopped
- 2 tomatoes, chopped
- 2 teaspoons red chili powder
- 2 tablespoons cumin seeds

Directions:

1. In your instant pot, combine the yogurt with the onions and other ingredients, put the lid on and cook on High for 20 minutes.
2. Release the pressure naturally for 10 minutes, whisk the mix, divide into bowls and serve as a party dip.

Nutrition: calories 244, fat 4.4, fiber 3.4, carbs 11, protein 2.5

Cashew Paneer Dip

Preparation time: 5 minutes
Cooking time: 10 minutes
Servings: 4
Ingredients:
- 8 ounces paneer, cubed
- 1 cup cashews, chopped
- 8 tablespoons water
- 2 tablespoons vinegar
- ½ teaspoon turmeric powder
- A pinch of salt and black pepper
- 1 and ½ teaspoons sweet paprika
- 1 tablespoon lime juice
- 1 cup water

Directions:
1. In a bowl, combine all the ingredients except the water, whisk well and transfer to a ramekin.
2. Put the water in the instant pot, add the trivet inside, put the ramekin inside, put the lid on and cook on High for 10 minutes.
3. Release the pressure fast for 5 minutes and serve as a dip.

Nutrition: calories 232, fat 11.1, fiber 2, carbs 6.6, protein 5

Capsicum Bell Masala

Preparation time: 10 minutes
Cooking time: 15 minutes
Servings: 4
Ingredients:
- 1 pound green bell peppers, deseeded and roughly cubed
- 2 tablespoons vegetable oil
- ½ teaspoon cumin seeds
- 1 tablespoon coconut powder
- 1 and ½ tablespoon sesame seed powder
- 2 teaspoons coriander powder
- 2 teaspoons fennel seed powder
- ½ teaspoon chili powder
- ¼ teaspoon turmeric powder
- 1 teaspoon lemon juice
- ¼ cup veggie stock

Directions:
1. In your instant pot, combine the bell peppers with the oil, cumin seeds and the rest of the ingredients, put the lid on and cook on High for 15 minutes.
2. Release the pressure naturally for 10 minutes, transfer the mix to small bowls and serve cold as an appetizer.

Nutrition: calories 240, fat 4.6, fiber 3, carbs 7.6, protein 6

Bell Almonds Dip

Preparation time: 5 minutes
Cooking time: 20 minutes
Servings: 4
Ingredients:
- 2 red bell peppers, chopped
- 4 tomatoes, chopped
- 12 garlic cloves, minced
- 20 almonds, chopped
- 1 tablespoon white wine vinegar
- 2 tablespoons vegetable oil
- Salt and black pepper to the taste

Directions:
1. Set the instant pot on Sauté mode, add the oil ,heat it up, add the garlic and the almonds and sauté for 5 minutes.
2. Add the bell peppers and the other ingredients, put the lid on and cook on High for 15 minutes.
3. Release the pressure fast for 5 minutes, blend the mix using an immersion blender, divide into bowls and serve.

Nutrition: calories 160, fat 9, fiber 4, carbs 7.6, protein 7

Shrimp Bowls

Preparation time: 30 minutes
Cooking time: 6 minutes
Servings: 4
Ingredients:
- 1 pound shrimp, peeled and deveined
- 1 tablespoon vegetable oil
- Juice of 1 lime
- ½ tablespoon cilantro, chopped
- ¼ cup curd
- 1 teaspoon garlic, minced
- ½ teaspoon garam masala
- ¼ teaspoon chili powder
- Salt to the taste
- ¼ teaspoon turmeric powder

Directions:
1. In a bowl, combine the shrimp with the oil, lime juice and the other ingredients, toss and keep in the fridge for 25 minutes.
2. Transfer everything to your instant pot, put the lid on and cook on High for 6 minutes.
3. Release the pressure fast for 5 minutes, transfer the shrimp mixture to small bowls and serve as an appetizer.

Nutrition: calories 170, fat 11.9, fiber 4, carbs 9.5, protein 6

Pepper Shrimp Mix

Preparation time: 10 minutes
Cooking time: 6 minutes
Servings: 4
Ingredients:
- 1 pound shrimp, peeled and deveined
- 2 teaspoons red pepper flakes
- ½ teaspoon cumin, ground
- ½ teaspoon turmeric powder
- Salt to the taste
- ½ teaspoon turmeric powder
- 1 tablespoon vegetable oil

Directions:
1. In your instant pot, combine the shrimp with the pepper flakes and the other ingredients, put the lid on and cook on High for 6 minutes.
2. Release the pressure naturally for 10 minutes, divide the shrimp into bowls and serve as an appetizer.

Nutrition: calories 280, fat 13.4, fiber 3, carbs 7, protein 9

Cumin Eggplant and Tomato Bowls
Preparation time: 5 minutes
Cooking time: 15 minutes
Servings: 4
Ingredients:
- 2 eggplants, roughly cubed
- 2 tomatoes, cubed
- Juice of 1 lime
- ½ teaspoon turmeric powder
- ½ teaspoon garam masala
- 2 teaspoons cumin, ground
- 2 tablespoons sunflower oil
- 2 tablespoons garlic, minced
- 1 chili pepper, chopped
- ¼ cup cilantro, chopped

Directions:
1. Set the instant pot on Sauté mode, add the oil, heat it up, add the turmeric, garam masala, cumin, garlic and the chili pepper, stir and cook for 5 minutes.
2. Add the rest of the ingredients, put the lid on and cook on High for 10 minutes.
3. Release the pressure fast for 5 minutes, divide the salad into cups and serve.
Nutrition: calories 250, fat 9, fiber 2.5, carbs 6, protein 6

Hot Shrimp and Peppers Salad
Preparation time: 5 minutes
Cooking time: 6 minutes
Servings: 4
Ingredients:
- 2 tablespoons lemon juice
- 1 yellow onion, chopped
- 1 tablespoon coconut oil
- ½ teaspoon hot paprika
- 2 red bell peppers, cut into strips
- 1 teaspoon turmeric powder
- ½ teaspoon coriander powder
- ½ teaspoon dry mango powder
- 2 pounds shrimp, peeled and deveined
- 2 tablespoons basil, chopped

Directions:
1. Set the instant pot on Sauté mode, add the oil, heat it up, add the onion , paprika, turmeric, coriander powder and mango powder and cook for 2 minutes.
2. Add the rest of the ingredients, put the lid on and cook on High for 4 minutes.
3. Release the pressure fast for 5 minutes, divide the shrimp mix into small bowls and serve.
Nutrition: calories 273, fat 9, fiber 3, carbs 5.5, protein 8

Spinach and Coconut Avocado Dip
Preparation time: 5 minutes
Cooking time: 5 minutes
Servings: 4
Ingredients:
- 4 cups spinach
- 1 avocado, peeled, pitted and chopped
- ¼ cup coconut cream
- 1 tablespoon lemon juice
- Salt to the taste
- ¼ teaspoon curry powder
- 1 garlic clove, minced
- 1 teaspoon ginger, grated

Directions:
1. In your instant pot, combine the spinach with the avocado and the other ingredients, put the lid on and cook on High for 5 minutes.
2. Release the pressure fast for 5 minutes, blend the mix using an immersion blender, divide into bowls and serve.
Nutrition: calories 242, fat 8.4, fiber 5, carbs 11.8, protein 2.5

Milky Spinach Spread
Preparation time: 5 minutes
Cooking time: 20 minutes
Servings: 4
Ingredients:
- 2 tablespoons ghee, melted
- 2 garlic cloves, minced
- 1 yellow onion, chopped
- 10 ounces spinach, chopped
- 1 tablespoon ginger, grated
- 2 teaspoons garam masala
- 2 teaspoons cumin
- 1 cup evaporated milk

Directions:
1. Set the instant pot on Sauté mode, add the ghee, heat it up, add the onion and the garlic and sauté for 5 minutes
2. Add the rest of the ingredients, put the lid on and cook on High for 15 minutes
3. Release the pressure fast for 5 minutes, blend the mix with an immersion blender, divide into bowls and serve as a spread.
Nutrition: calories 280, fat 9, fiber 2.5, carbs 7.6, protein 9

Beans Pepper Dip
Preparation time: 10 minutes
Cooking time: 20 minutes
Servings: 8
Ingredients:
- ¼ teaspoon cumin, ground
- ½ teaspoon allspice, ground
- 16 ounces canned navy beans, drained and rinsed
- ¼ teaspoon ginger, grated
- 1 teaspoon curry powder
- 1 cup yellow bell pepper, chopped
- 1 zucchini, chopped
- 1 red onion , chopped
- 2 garlic cloves, minced
- ¼ cup mango chutney
- Salt to the taste
- 2 tablespoons yogurt

Directions:
1. In your instant pot, combine the beans with the cumin, allspice, ginger and the other ingredients, stir, put the lid on and cook on High for 20 minutes.
2. Release the pressure naturally for 10 minutes, divide everything into bowls and serve as an appetizer.
Nutrition: calories 25, fat 0.1, fiber 0.8, carbs 5.1, protein 1.1

Masala Beans Spread

Preparation time: 10 minutes
Cooking time: 20 minutes
Servings: 4
Ingredients:
- 10 ounces canned white beans, drained and rinsed
- ½ teaspoon garam masala
- ¼ teaspoon turmeric powder
- 2 garlic cloves, minced
- Salt to the taste
- 1 tablespoon lemon juice
- ¼ cup olive oil

Directions:
1. Set the instant pot on Sauté mode, add the oil, heat it up, add the garlic and cook for 2 minutes.
2. Add the rest of the ingredients, put the lid on and cook on High for 18 minutes.
3. Release the pressure naturally for 10 minutes, blend the mix using an immersion blender, divide into bowls and serve.
Nutrition: calories 180, fat 9, fiber 4, carbs 11.2, protein 8

Paprika Shrimp Salad

Preparation time: 5 minutes
Cooking time: 8 minutes
Servings: 4
Ingredients:
- 2 pounds shrimp, peeled and deveined
- 2 tablespoons turmeric powder
- 1 teaspoon smoked paprika
- 2 tablespoons curd
- 2 teaspoons lime juice
- 1 tablespoon coconut oil
- A pinch of salt and black pepper

Directions:
1. In your instant pot, combine the shrimp with the turmeric and the other ingredients, toss, put the lid on and cook on High for 8 minutes.
2. Release the pressure fast for 5 minutes, transfer the mix to small bowls and serve as an appetizer.
Nutrition: calories 177, fat 8, fiber 2, carbs 6.5, protein 7

Curd & Spinach Chicken Salad

Preparation time: 10 minutes
Cooking time: 20 minutes
Servings: 4
Ingredients:
- 1 pound chicken breast, skinless, boneless and cubed
- 1 cup curd
- 1 cup spinach, torn
- 1 teaspoon turmeric powder
- ½ teaspoon chili powder
- ½ teaspoon garam masala
- 2 tablespoons ghee, melted
- 1 red onion, chopped
- 2 tablespoons garlic, chopped
- 1 cup tomatoes, cubed
- 1 tablespoon coriander, chopped

Directions:

1. Set your instant pot on Sauté mode, add the ghee, heat it up, add the chicken, turmeric, chili powder and the garam masala, stir and brown for 5 minutes.
2. Add the rest of the ingredients except the coriander, put the lid on and cook on High for 15 minutes.
3. Release the pressure naturally for 10 minutes, divide the mix into bowls, sprinkle the coriander on top and serve as an appetizer.
Nutrition: calories 221, fat 12, fiber 4, carbs 7, protein 11

Chicken Chutney Salad

Preparation time: 10 minutes
Cooking time: 20 minutes
Servings: 4
Ingredients:
- 2 tablespoons mango chutney
- 1 tablespoon ghee, melted
- 1 teaspoon nigella seeds
- 1 red bell pepper, cut into strips
- 1 cup baby arugula
- 1 cup basmati rice
- 2 cup chicken stock
- 1 teaspoon turmeric powder
- 1 carrot, sliced
- 1 tablespoon curry powder
- Juice of 1 lime
- 1 tablespoon coriander, chopped
- 1 chicken breast, skinless, boneless and cubed
- Salt to the taste

Directions:
1. Set instant pot on Sauté mode, add the ghee, heat it up, add the chicken and brown for 5 minutes.
2. Add the rest of the ingredients, put the lid on and cook on High for 15 minutes.
3. Release the pressure naturally for 10 minutes, divide the mix into small bowls and serve as an appetizer.
Nutrition: calories 180, fat 9, fiber 3, carbs 5, protein 7

Creamy Mango Salad

Preparation time: 5 minutes
Cooking time: 7 minutes
Servings: 4
Ingredients:
- 1 cup mango, peeled and cubed
- ½ cup coconut cream
- ¼ cup yellow onion, chopped
- ½ teaspoon chili powder
- 2 teaspoons jaggery powder
- Salt to the taste
- ½ teaspoon cumin seeds, roasted and crushed
- 1 tablespoon coriander, chopped

Directions:
1. In your instant pot, combine the mangoes with the cream and the other ingredients, put the lid on and cook on High for 7 minutes.
2. Release the pressure fast for 5 minutes, divide into cups and serve.
Nutrition: calories 140, fat 4.4, fiber 3, carbs 5, protein 4

Cucumber and Mango Salad

Preparation time: 6 minutes
Cooking time: 6 minutes
Servings: 4
Ingredients:

- 2 tablespoons sesame oil
- Juice of 2 limes
- 1-inch ginger, grated
- 2 garlic cloves, minced
- 2 green chilies, chopped
- 2 mangoes, peeled and cubed
- 2 cucumbers, cubed
- 1 tomato, cubed
- 20 peanuts, chopped
- 1 tablespoon mint, chopped
- 1 tablespoon coriander, chopped
- Salt to the taste

Directions:

1. In your instant pot, combine the mangoes with the cucumbers and the other ingredients, put the lid on and cook on High for 6 minutes.
2. Release the pressure fast for 6 minutes, divide the mix into small bowls and serve as an appetizer.

Nutrition: calories 176, fat 4, fiber 3.3, carbs 6, protein 7

Spinach Turkey Bowls

Preparation time: 10 minutes
Cooking time: 20 minutes
Servings: 4
Ingredients:

- 1 pound turkey breast, skinless, boneless and cubed
- 2 tomatoes, cubed
- 1 tablespoon coconut oil, melted
- 1 yellow onion, chopped
- ½ teaspoon sweet paprika
- ½ teaspoon chili powder
- ½ teaspoon turmeric powder
- ½ teaspoon garam masala
- ½ cup parsley, chopped
- ½ cup chicken stock
- Salt to the taste
- ½ cup spinach, torn

Directions:

1. Set your instant pot on Sauté mode, add the oil, heat it up, add the onion, paprika, chili powder, turmeric and the garam masala, stir and cook for 5 minutes.
2. Add the meat and brown for 5 minutes more.
3. Add the rest of the ingredients, put the lid on and cook on High for 10 minutes.
4. Release the pressure naturally for 10 minutes, transfer the mix bowls and serve as an appetizer.

Nutrition: calories 281, fat 4.4, fiber 3, carbs 7, protein 15

Potato Coconut Dip

Preparation time: 10 minutes
Cooking time: 20 minutes
Servings: 4
Ingredients:

- 1 pound sweet potatoes, peeled and chopped
- ¼ cup coconut cream
- 2 tablespoons raisins
- ½ teaspoon turmeric powder
- 2 garlic cloves, minced
- ½ teaspoon chili powder
- 1 teaspoon ginger, grated
- 1 teaspoon cumin, ground
- ½ teaspoon sugar
- 2 tablespoons red vinegar
- ¼ cup sunflower oil

Directions:

1. Set your instant pot on Sauté mode, add the oil, heat it up, add the garlic, turmeric, chili powder, cumin and the ginger and sauté for 5 minutes.
2. Add the potatoes and the rest of the ingredients, put the lid on and cook on High for 15 minutes.
3. Release the pressure naturally for 10 minutes, blend the mix in your blender, divide into bowls and serve.

Nutrition: calories 201, fat 9, fiber 4, carbs 7, protein 7.6

Cream Cheese Dip

Preparation time: 10 minutes
Cooking time: 10 minutes
Servings: 6
Ingredients:

- 8 ounces cream cheese, soft
- ½ cup milk
- 1 tablespoon almond milk
- 2 tablespoons red bell pepper, chopped
- 2 teaspoons corn flour
- ¼ teaspoon mustard powder

Directions:

1. In your instant pot, combine the cream cheese with the corn flour and the other ingredients, toss, put the lid on and cook on High for 10 minutes.
2. Release the pressure naturally for 10 minutes, whisk the mix, divide into bowls and serve as a party dip.

Nutrition: calories 200, fat 8, fiber 2.5, carbs 6, protein 8

Coconut Creamy Endives Dip

Preparation time: 5 minutes
Cooking time: 12 minutes
Servings: 4
Ingredients:

- 4 endives, roughly shredded
- ¼ cup coconut cream
- 1 teaspoon turmeric powder
- ½ teaspoon chili powder
- ½ teaspoon garam masala
- A pinch of salt and black pepper
- 2 garlic cloves, chopped
- 2 tablespoons coconut oil, melted
- 2 tablespoons lemon juice

Directions:

3. Set the instant pot on Sauté mode, add the oil, heat it up, add the turmeric, chili powder, garam masala and the garlic, stir and sauté for 2 minutes.
4. Add the rest of the ingredients, put the lid on and cook on High for 10 minutes.
5. Release the pressure fast for 5 minutes, divide into bowls and serve as a party dip.

Nutrition: calories 171, fat 3.4, fiber 4, carbs 7, protein 5

Saffron Cumin Shrimp

Preparation time: 5 minutes
Cooking time: 5 minutes
Servings: 4
Ingredients:
- 1 pound shrimp, peeled and deveined
- ¼ cup coconut cream
- 1 teaspoon saffron powder mixed with 1 tablespoon milk
- 1 tablespoon ghee, melted
- 1 teaspoon cumin, ground
- 1 teaspoon mustard seeds
- 1 teaspoon chili powder
- A pinch of salt and black pepper

Directions:
1. Set the instant pot on Sauté mode, add the shrimp, the cream and the other ingredients, toss, put the lid on and cook on High for 5 minutes.
2. Release the pressure fast for 5 minutes, arrange the shrimp into bowls and serve.
Nutrition: calories 242, fat 5.6, fiber 4, carbs 7, protein 6

Chili Lentils Dip

Preparation time: 10 minutes
Cooking time: 20 minutes
Servings: 8
Ingredients:
- 1 and ½ cups red lentils, canned, drained and rinsed
- 2 teaspoons ginger, grated
- 2 tablespoons coconut oil
- 1 teaspoon coriander seeds
- 2 garlic cloves, minced
- 1 chili pepper, chopped
- 1 teaspoon garam masala
- 1 teaspoon turmeric powder
- Salt to the taste
- 2 and ½ cups tomatoes, chopped
- 2 tablespoons lemon juice
- ¼ cup scallions, chopped

Directions:
1. In your instant pot, mix the lentils with the oil, ginger and the other ingredients, toss, put the lid on and cook on High for 20 minutes.
2. Release the pressure naturally for 10 minutes, transfer the mix to a food processor, pulse well, divide into small bowls, and serve.
Nutrition: calories 217, fat 5.4, fiber 3, carbs 8, protein 6

Turmeric Chickpeas Dip

Preparation time: 10 minutes
Cooking time: 20 minutes
Servings: 4
Ingredients:
- 2 teaspoons cumin seeds
- ½ teaspoon coriander seeds
- ¼ teaspoon mustard seeds
- ¼ teaspoon red pepper flakes
- ¼ teaspoon turmeric powder
- 16 ounces canned chickpeas, drained and rinsed
- ½ cup cilantro, chopped
- Salt to the taste
- 4 tablespoons lemon juice
- 2 garlic cloves, minced
- 3 tablespoons tahini paste

Directions:
1. In your instant pot, combine the cumin seeds with the coriander seeds and the other ingredients, put the lid on and cook on High for 20 minutes.
2. Release the pressure naturally for 10 minutes, blend the mix using an immersion blender, divide into bowls and serve as a dip.
Nutrition: calories 241, fat 7.2, fiber 4, carbs 5, protein 4

Coconut Onion Dip

Preparation time: 5 minutes
Cooking time: 10 minutes.
Servings: 4
Ingredients:
- 1 cup coconut cream
- ½ teaspoon turmeric powder
- ½ teaspoon chili powder
- A pinch of salt and black pepper
- 1 tablespoon coconut oil
- 2 yellow onion, chopped
- Juice of 1 orange

Directions:
1. In your instant pot, combine the cream with the turmeric, onion and the other ingredients, whisk, put the lid on and cook on High for 10 minutes.
2. Release the pressure fast for 5 minutes, divide the mix into bowls and serve as a party dip.
Nutrition: calories 220, fat 6.2, fiber 3.6, carbs 5, protein 4

Zucchini Bell Salad

Preparation time: 10 minutes
Cooking time: 15 minutes
Servings: 4
Ingredients:
- 1 teaspoon vegetable oil
- 1 teaspoon mustard seeds
- 1 yellow onion, chopped
- 2 tablespoons peanuts, chopped
- 1 teaspoon ginger, grated
- 2 garlic cloves, minced
- 3 zucchinis, cut into medium cubes
- 1 red bell pepper, cut into strips
- 1 green chili, chopped
- Juice of 1 lime
- ¼ cup cilantro, chopped

Directions:
1. Set your instant pot on Sauté mode, add the oil, heat it up, add the onion, ginger, garlic and the chili, stir and sauté for 2 minutes.
2. Add the rest of the ingredients, toss gently, put the lid on and cook on High for 13 minutes.
3. Release the pressure naturally for 10 minutes, divide into bowls and serve as an appetizer.
Nutrition: calories 200, fat 5, fiber 3, carbs 7.5, protein 6

Mango Broccoli Spread

Preparation time: 10 minutes
Cooking time: 15 minutes
Servings: 4
Ingredients:
- 1 yellow onion, chopped
- 1 tablespoon coconut oil
- 1 pound broccoli florets
- 1 teaspoon chili powder
- ½ teaspoon coriander powder
- ½ teaspoon dry mango powder
- A pinch of salt and black pepper
- 3 garlic cloves, minced
- 1 cup coconut cream
- 1 tablespoons coriander, chopped

Directions:
1. Set your instant pot on Sauté mode, add the oil, heat it up, add the onion, chili powder, coriander and mango powder, stir and cook for 2 minutes.
2. Add the rest of the ingredients, put the lid on and cook on High for 13 minutes.
3. Release the pressure naturally for 10 minutes, blend the mix using an immersion blender, divide into bowls, and serve.

Nutrition: calories 270, fat 12.2, fiber 2, carbs 6, protein 7

Coconut Cauliflower Dip

Preparation time: 10 minutes
Cooking time: 15 minutes
Servings: 4
Ingredients:
- 2 tablespoons ghee, melted
- 1 pound cauliflower florets
- 8 garlic cloves, minced
- ½ teaspoon garam masala
- 1 teaspoon red chili powder
- ½ teaspoon smoked paprika
- 1 red chili pepper, chopped
- ½ cup coconut cream

Directions:
1. Set your instant pot on Sauté mode, add the ghee, heat it up, add the garlic, chili powder, paprika, garam masala and the chili pepper, stir and cook for 2 minutes.
2. Add the rest of the ingredients, put the lid on and cook on High for 13 minutes.
3. Release the pressure naturally for 10 minutes, transfer the mix to a blender, pulse, divide into bowls and serve as a party dip.

Nutrition: calories 178, fat 3, fiber 3, carbs 5, protein 8

Zucchini Dip

Preparation time: 5 minutes
Cooking time: 15 minutes
Servings: 4
Ingredients:
- 2 tablespoons coconut oil
- 2 tablespoons lemon juice
- 2 tablespoons mint, chopped
- Salt to the taste
- 2 zucchinis, chopped
- 2 garlic cloves, minced

- ½ cup curd
- ½ teaspoon chili powder
- ½ teaspoon cumin, ground

Directions:
1. Set the instant pot on Sauté mode, add the oil, heat it up, add the garlic, chili powder and the cumin, stir and cook for 2 minutes.
2. Add the rest of the ingredients, put the lid on, and cook on High for 13 minutes.
3. Release the pressure fast for 5 minutes, blend the mix using an immersion blender and serve the dip

Nutrition: calories 170, fat 2, fiber 3, carbs 6, protein 8

Basil Corn Bowls

Preparation time: 10 minutes
Cooking time: 15 minutes
Servings: 4
Ingredients:
- 1 tablespoon ghee, melted
- ½ teaspoon cumin seeds
- 1 leek, sliced
- 4 cups corn
- Salt and black pepper to the taste
- 1 tablespoon lemon juice
- ½ cup corn
- 2 tablespoons basil, chopped

Directions:
1. In your instant pot, combine the corn with the cumin, leek and the other ingredients, toss, put the lid on and cook on High for 15 minutes.
2. Release the pressure naturally for 10 minutes, divide the mix into small bowls and serve as an appetizer.

Nutrition: calories 180, fat 4, fiber 3, carbs 7, protein 9

Tomato Cucumber Salad

Preparation time: 5 minutes
Cooking time: 5 minutes
Servings: 4
Ingredients:
- 2 cucumbers, sliced
- 1 carrot, grated
- 1 red onion, chopped
- 2 cups cherry tomatoes, halved
- 4 radishes, chopped
- 1 red chili pepper, minced
- ¼ cup cilantro, chopped
- 2 tablespoons lemon juice
- Salt and black pepper to the taste
- ¼ teaspoon cumin, ground
- ¼ cup veggie stock

Directions:
1. In your instant pot, combine the cucumbers with the carrot and the other ingredients, toss gently, put the lid on and cook on High for 5 minutes.
2. Release the pressure fast for 5 minutes, divide into small bowls and serve as an appetizer.

Nutrition: calories 224, fat 12, fiber 4, carbs 7, protein 12

Barley and Chickpeas Salad
Preparation time: 10 minutes
Cooking time: 20 minutes
Servings: 4
Ingredients:
- 1 cup barley, cooked
- 1 cup chickpeas, canned, drained and rinsed
- ¼ cup cherry tomatoes, halved
- ½ cup red cabbage, shredded
- ½ cup carrots, grated
- ¼ cup red onion, sliced
- 1 cup baby spinach
- 4 tablespoons peanuts, toasted
- 1 cup curd
- 1 teaspoon turmeric powder
- ½ teaspoon cumin powder
- 2 garlic cloves, minced
- Salt to the taste

Directions:
1. In your instant pot, combine the barley with the chickpeas, tomatoes and the other ingredients, toss, put the lid on and cook on High for 20 minutes.
2. Release the pressure naturally for 10 minutes, divide into bowls and serve as an appetizer.
Nutrition: calories 372, fat 11.4, fiber 4, carbs 7, protein 9.4

Barley and Tomatoes Salad
Preparation time: 5 minutes
Cooking time: 15 minutes
Servings: 4
Ingredients:
- 1 cup barley, cooked
- ½ cup curd
- 1 tablespoon ghee, melted
- 1 cup black olives, pitted and halved
- 1 cup cherry tomatoes, halved
- ½ teaspoon turmeric powder
- ½ teaspoon garam masala
- 1 handful coriander leaves, chopped

Directions:
1. Set your instant pot on Sauté mode, add the ghee, heat it up, add the barley, turmeric and garam masala, stir and cook for 5 minutes.
2. Add the rest of the ingredients, toss, put the lid on and cook on High for 10 minutes.
3. Release the pressure fast for 5 minutes, divide the salad bowls and serve cold as an appetizer.
Nutrition: calories 252, fat 12.2, fiber 3, carbs 6.6, protein 7

Broccoli Chana Dal Bites
Preparation time: 10 minutes
Cooking time: 15 minutes
Servings: 4
Ingredients:
- 1 cup chicken stock
- 1 pound broccoli florets
- A pinch of salt and black pepper
- ¼ teaspoon mustard seeds
- ¼ teaspoon cumin, ground
- 1 teaspoon ginger, grated
- 1 tablespoon chana dal
- 2 garlic cloves, minced
- 2 teaspoons sunflower oil

- ¼ teaspoon garam masala
- ¼ teaspoon turmeric powder

Directions:
1. Set your instant pot on Sauté mode, add the oil, heat it up, add mustard seeds, cumin, ginger, garlic, turmeric and garam masala, toss and cook for 5 minutes.
2. Add the broccoli and the other ingredients, put the lid on and cook on High for 10 minutes.
3. Release the pressure naturally for 10 minutes, divide the broccoli into bowls and serve as a snack.
Nutrition: calories 154, fat 2.89, fiber 3, carbs 4, protein 4

Quinoa, Mango and Avocado Salad
Preparation time: 5 minutes
Cooking time: 15 minutes
Servings: 4
Ingredients:
- 1 cup red quinoa, cooked
- ½ cup almonds, toasted and chopped
- ½ cup coconut cream
- 1 avocado, peeled, pitted and cubed
- 1 tablespoon cilantro, chopped
- ½ teaspoon chana masala
- ½ teaspoon sweet paprika
- ½ teaspoon turmeric powder
- 1 cup mango, peeled and cubed
- A pinch of salt and black pepper

Directions:
1. In your instant pot, combine the quinoa with the almonds, the cream and the other ingredients, toss, put the lid on and cook on High for 15 minutes.
2. Release the pressure fast for 5 minutes, divide the mix into small bowls and serve as an appetizer.
Nutrition: calories 242, fat 8.2, fiber 3, carbs 5, protein 7

Barley and Chickpeas Pot
Preparation time: 10 minutes
Cooking time: 15 minutes
Servings: 4
Ingredients:
- 1 cup barley, cooked
- 1 cup canned chickpeas, drained and rinsed
- 2 tablespoons ghee, melted
- Juice of 1 orange
- 2 garlic cloves, minced
- 2 tablespoons ginger, grated
- 1 yellow onion, chopped
- ½ teaspoon garam masala
- A pinch of salt and black pepper
- ½ cup coconut cream

Directions:
1. Set your instant pot on Sauté mode, add the ghee, heat it up, add the ginger, garlic, onion and the garam masala, stir and cook for 5 minutes.
2. Add the barley and the rest of the ingredients, put the lid on and cook on High for 10 minutes.
3. Release the pressure naturally for 10 minutes, divide everything into bowls and serve.
Nutrition: calories 342, fat 15.2, fiber 3, carbs 11.5, protein 8

Thyme Lentils and Tomatoes Bowls

Preparation time: 10 minutes
Cooking time: 15 minutes
Servings: 4
Ingredients:
- ½ cup coconut cream
- 1 cup canned lentils, drained and rinsed
- ½ teaspoon thyme, dried
- 1 yellow onion, chopped
- 2 tablespoons ghee, melted
- ½ teaspoon turmeric powder
- ¼ teaspoon chili powder
- 1 cup cherry tomatoes, cubed
- 1 tablespoon garlic, minced
- Juice of 1 lime
- 2 tablespoons parsley, chopped
- Salt and black pepper to the taste

Directions:
1. Set the instant pot on Sauté mode, add the ghee, heat it up, add the onion, turmeric, chili powder and the garlic, stir and cook for 5 minutes.
2. Add the rest of the ingredients, toss gently, put the lid on and cook on High for 10 minutes.
3. Release the pressure naturally for 10 minutes, divide the mix into bowls and serve as an appetizer.
Nutrition: calories 312, fat 4.5, fiber 3, carbs 5.9, protein 7

Mushroom Curd Dip

Preparation time: 10 minutes
Cooking time: 25 minutes
Servings: 4
Ingredients:
- 1 pound mushrooms, sliced
- 2 garlic cloves, minced
- 1 tablespoon ghee, melted
- Salt to the taste
- 1 tablespoon parsley, chopped
- 1 cup curd
- 1 tablespoon lemon juice
- 1 teaspoon coriander powder
- ½ teaspoon turmeric powder
- 1 teaspoon cayenne pepper

Directions:
1. Set the instant pot on Sauté mode, add the ghee, heat it up, add the mushrooms and the garlic and sauté for 5 minutes.
2. Add the rest of the ingredients, toss, put the lid on and cook on High for 20 minutes.
3. Release the pressure naturally for 10 minutes, whisk the dip, divide it into bowls and serve.
Nutrition: calories 152, fat 3, fiber 4, carbs 5, protein 9

Mushroom and Paneer Dip

Preparation time: 5 minutes
Cooking time: 20 minutes
Servings: 4
Ingredients:
- ½ cup broccoli florets, chopped
- 2 tablespoons butter
- ½ cup mushrooms, chopped
- ¼ cup yellow onion, chopped
- ½ teaspoon garlic paste
- ¼ teaspoon green chili paste
- 1 and ¼ cups milk
- 1 cup paneer, cubed
- Salt to the taste
- 1 tablespoon lime juice
- Zest of 1 lime, grated

Directions:
1. Set your instant pot on Sauté mode, add the butter, heat it up, add the onion, garlic paste, chili paste and the mushrooms, stir and cook for 5 minutes.
2. Add the rest of the ingredients, put the lid on and cook on High for 15 minutes.
3. Release the pressure fast for 5 minutes, blend the mix using an immersion blender, divide into bowls and serve.
Nutrition: calories 210, fat 12.2, fiber 3, carbs 5.9, protein 4

Creamy Mushrooms

Preparation time: 10 minutes
Cooking time: 20 minutes
Servings: 4
Ingredients:
- 1 cup mushrooms, sliced
- 1 tablespoon butter
- ½ cup yellow onion, chopped
- ½ teaspoon green chilies, minced
- Salt to the taste
- 1 cup coconut cream
- ½ teaspoon smoked paprika
- ½ teaspoon cumin, ground
- ½ teaspoon mustard seeds, toasted and crushed

Directions:
1. Set your instant pot on Sauté mode, add the butter, heat it up, add the onion, chilies and the mushrooms, stir and cook for 5 minutes.
2. Add the rest of the ingredients, put the lid on and cook on High for 15 minutes.
3. Release the pressure naturally for 10 minutes, blend the mix using an immersion blender, divide into bowls and serve as a party spread.
Nutrition: calories 232, fat 7.2, fiber 3, carbs 4, protein 4

Shrimp and Creamy Beans Appetizer

Preparation time: 5 minutes
Cooking time: 8 minutes
Servings: 4
Ingredients:
- 1 pound shrimp, peeled and deveined
- 1 tablespoon coconut oil
- 1 cup green beans, trimmed and halved
- 2 red onions, chopped
- ½ cup coconut cream
- 2 teaspoons turmeric powder
- ½ teaspoon coriander, ground
- ½ teaspoon cumin, ground
- ½ teaspoon sweet paprika
- 2 tablespoons cilantro, chopped

Directions:
1. Set your instant pot on Sauté mode, add the oil, heat it up, add the onions, turmeric, coriander, cumin and the paprika, stir and cook for 2 minutes.
2. Add the shrimp and the rest of the ingredients, put the lid on and cook on High for 6 minutes.
3. Release the pressure fast for 5 minutes, divide the mix into small bowls and serve as an appetizer.
Nutrition: calories 200, fat 5, fiber 2, carbs 5, protein 7

Indian Instant Pot Fish and Seafood Recipes

Creamy Cod Tikka
Preparation time: 10 minutes
Cooking time: 15 minutes
Servings: 3
Ingredients:
- 1 pound cod fillets, boneless, skinless and cubed
- 1 and ½ teaspoon ginger garlic paste
- A pinch of salt and black pepper
- 2 teaspoons red chili powder
- 1 cup yogurt
- ½ teaspoon turmeric powder
- ½ teaspoon fenugreek leaves, dried
- 2 tablespoons lemon juice
- ¼ teaspoon garam masala
- ½ teaspoon coriander powder
- 1 tablespoon vegetable oil

Directions:
1. Set the instant pot on Sauté mode, add the oil, heat it up, add the ginger paste chili powder, turmeric, fenugreek, coriander and garam masala, stir and cook for 4 minutes.
2. Add the fish and the rest of the ingredients, toss, put the lid on and cook on High for 11 minutes.
3. Release the pressure naturally for 10 minutes, divide the mix into bowls and serve.

Nutrition: calories 173, fat 5.5, fiber 0.7, carbs 5.7, protein 24.1

White Fish Pulusu
Preparation time: 10 minutes
Cooking time: 20 minutes
Servings: 4
Ingredients:
- 2 pounds white fish, skinless, boneless and cubed
- 3 green chilies, chopped
- 1 cup yellow onion, chopped
- 1 tablespoon ginger garlic paste
- 3 tablespoons sunflower oil
- 2 tablespoons poppy seeds
- 2 teaspoons garam masala
- 1 teaspoon red chili powder
- 1 tablespoon coriander, chopped
- 2 tablespoons tamarind paste
- 1 bay leaf
- 1 teaspoon cumin, ground

Directions:
1. Set the instant pot on Sauté mode, add the oil, heat it up, add the onion, ginger and the chilies, stir and cook for 4 minutes.
2. Add the fish and the rest of the ingredients, toss, put the lid on and cook on High for 16 minutes.
3. Release the pressure naturally for 10 minutes, divide the mix into bowls and serve.

Nutrition: calories 331, fat 13.4, fiber 1.5, carbs 6.7, protein 47.7

Creamy White Fish Mix
Preparation time: 10 minutes
Cooking time: 20 minutes
Servings: 2
Ingredients:
- 4 garlic cloves, minced
- 2 tablespoons spring onions, chopped
- ¼ cup green bell pepper, cubed
- ¼ cup red bell pepper, cubed
- 1 teaspoon soy sauce
- 1 teaspoon white vinegar
- 2 teaspoons red chili sauce
- ½ teaspoon sugar
- Salt to the taste
- ¼ cup coconut cream
- 1 pound white fish fillets, boneless, skinless and cubed

Directions:
1. In your instant pot, combine the fish with the garlic, onions and the other ingredients, toss gently, put the lid on and cook on High for 20 minutes.
2. Release the pressure naturally for 10 minutes, divide everything into bowls and serve.

Nutrition: calories 486, fat 24.3, fiber 1.4, carbs 7.6, protein 57.2

Shallot Salmon Curry
Preparation time: 5 minutes
Cooking time: 20 minutes
Servings: 4
Ingredients:
- 4 salmon fillets, boneless and cubed
- ¼ teaspoon mustard seeds
- ¼ teaspoon fenugreek leaves, dried
- 4 shallots, chopped
- 2 curry leaves, chopped
- 2 teaspoons ginger, grated
- 1 tablespoon chili powder
- 3 garlic cloves, minced
- ½ teaspoon turmeric powder
- ½ tablespoon coriander powder
- 1 cup water
- 2 tablespoons vegetable oil
- Salt to the taste

Directions:
1. Set the instant pot on sauté mode, add the oil, heat it up, add the mustard seeds, fenugreek leaves, shallots, curry leaves, ginger and the garlic, stir and cook for 5 minutes.
2. Add the salmon fillets and the rest of the ingredients, put the lid on and cook on High for 15 minutes.
3. Release the pressure fast for 5 minutes, divide the mix into bowls and serve.

Nutrition: calories 318, fat 18.3, fiber 1, carbs 4.5, protein 35.4

Cod and Tomato Bowls

Preparation time: 5 minutes
Cooking time: 15 minutes
Servings: 4
Ingredients:

- 1 pound cod fillets, boneless, skinless and cubed
- ½ teaspoon chili powder
- ½ teaspoon smoked paprika
- ½ teaspoon turmeric powder
- 1 pound cherry tomatoes, halved
- 2 garlic cloves, minced
- 1 tablespoon coconut oil, melted
- Salt and black pepper to the taste
- 1 tablespoon coriander, chopped
- ½ teaspoon cumin, ground

Directions:
1. Set the instant pot on Sauté mode, add the oil, heat it up, add the chili powder, paprika, turmeric, cumin and the garlic and sauté for 2 minutes.
2. Add the rest of the ingredients, put the lid on and cook on High for 13 minutes.
3. Release the pressure fast for 5 minutes, divide everything into bowls and serve.
Nutrition: calories 332, fat 9, fiber 2, carbs 7.5, protein 11

Coconut Cod Curry

Preparation time: 10 minutes
Cooking time: 15 minutes
Servings: 4
Ingredients:

- 1 pound cod fillets, boneless, skinless and cubed
- 1 cup coconut milk
- 2 red onions, sliced
- 2 garlic cloves, minced
- 1 tablespoons cumin, ground
- 1 tablespoon ginger, grated
- ½ teaspoon turmeric powder
- A pinch of salt and black pepper
- 2 tablespoons lime juice

Directions:
1. Set your instant pot on Sauté mode, add the oil, heat it up, add the onions, garlic and the ginger and sauté for 2 minutes.
2. Add the fish and the rest of the ingredients, put the lid on and cook on High for 13 minutes.
3. Release the pressure naturally for 10 minutes, divide the curry into bowls and serve.
Nutrition: calories 310, fat 12, fiber 2.6, carbs 6, protein 11

Herbed Salmon and Broccoli

Preparation time: 10 minutes
Cooking time: 12 minutes
Servings: 4
Ingredients:

- 4 salmon fillets, boneless and cubed
- 1 cup broccoli florets
- 2 tablespoons ghee
- ½ teaspoon turmeric powder
- ½ teaspoon garam masala
- 2 garlic cloves, minced
- Salt and black pepper to the taste
- ½ cup veggie stock

Directions:
1. Set the instant pot on Sauté mode, add the ghee, heat it up, add the garlic, turmeric and garam masala, toss and cook for 2 minutes.
2. Add the rest of the ingredients, put the lid on and cook on High for 10 minutes.
3. Release the pressure naturally for 10 minutes, divide the mix between plates and serve.
Nutrition: calories 356, fat 12, fiber 2, carbs 15.,6, protein 9

Charred Yogurt Salmon

Preparation time: 10 minutes
Cooking time: 15 minutes
Servings: 4
Ingredients:

- 4 salmon fillets, boneless
- 1 tablespoon ginger, grated
- 1 cup yogurt
- 1 red chili pepper, chopped
- 2 garlic cloves, minced
- 2 teaspoons garam masala
- 1 tablespoon vegetable oil
- 1 bunch asparagus, trimmed and chopped
- 1 tablespoon cilantro, chopped

Directions:
1. In your instant pot, combine the salmon with the yogurt, oil, chili pepper and the other ingredients, toss gently, put the lid on and cook on High for 15 minutes.
2. Release the pressure naturally for 10 minutes, divide the salmon mix between plates and serve.
Nutrition: calories 311, fat 13, fiber 2, carbs 7.7, protein 11

Cumin Cod and Rice

Preparation time: 10 minutes
Cooking time: 20 minutes
Servings: 4
Ingredients:

- 4 cod fillets, boneless, skinless and cubed
- 1 cup basmati rice
- 2 cups chicken stock
- ½ teaspoon cumin, ground
- ½ teaspoon fenugreek leaves, dried
- Salt to the taste
- Zest of 1 lemon, grated
- Juice of ½ lemon
- 1 yellow onion, chopped
- 1 tablespoon ghee, melted
- ¼ cup parsley, chopped

Directions:
1. Set the instant pot on Sauté mode, add the ghee, heat it up, add the cumin, fenugreek, and the onion, stir and cook for 5 minutes.
2. Add the fish and the other ingredients, toss, put the lid on and cook on High for 15 minutes.
3. Release the pressure naturally for 10 minutes, divide the mix between plates and serve.
Nutrition: calories 320, fat 12, fiber 4, carbs 11.6, protein 8

Shrimp and White Rice

Preparation time: 5 minutes
Cooking time: 15 minutes
Servings: 4
Ingredients:

- 1 pound shrimp, peeled and deveined
- 1 tablespoon lime juice
- 1 tablespoon lime zest, grated
- 1 cup white rice
- 2 cups chicken stock
- ½ teaspoon turmeric powder
- ½ teaspoon dried mango powder
- 1 yellow onion, chopped
- 2 tomatoes, cubed
- A pinch of salt and black pepper
- 1 tablespoon parsley, chopped
- ½ tablespoon sweet paprika, chopped
- 2 garlic cloves, minced

Directions:
1. In your instant pot, combine the shrimp with the lime juice, lime zest, rice and the rest of the ingredients, put the lid on and cook on High for 15 minutes.
2. Release the pressure fast for 5 minutes, divide the mix into bowls and serve.

Nutrition: calories 232, fat 7, fiber 3, carbs 11.7, protein 9

Coriander Cod

Preparation time: 5 minutes
Cooking time: 15 minutes
Servings: 4
Ingredients:

- 4 cod fillets, boneless
- A pinch of salt and black pepper
- 2 teaspoons cumin, ground
- 1 teaspoon coriander, ground
- ½ teaspoon ginger, grated
- 4 tablespoons lemon juice
- ½ cup chicken stock
- ½ teaspoon garam masala
- ½ teaspoon chili powder

Directions:
1. In your instant pot, combine the fish with the cumin, coriander and the other ingredients, put the lid on and cook on High for 15 minutes.
2. Release the pressure fast for 5 minutes, divide the fish mix between plates and serve.

Nutrition: calories 332, fat 9.6, fiber 2, carbs 13.6, protein 8

Crab and Shrimp Salad

Preparation time: 10 minutes
Cooking time: 15 minutes
Servings: 4
Ingredients:

- ¼ pound shrimp, peeled and deveined
- 2 shallots, chopped
- ¼ pound squid rings
- 1 cup crab meat, drained
- 3 tablespoons yogurt
- ½ cup chicken stock
- 1 teaspoon fennel seeds
- 1 teaspoon black mustard seeds

- 1 tablespoon lime juice
- 1 tablespoon coriander, chopped

Directions:
1. In your instant pot, combine the shrimp with the shallots and the other ingredients, toss, put the lid on and cook on High for 15 minutes.
2. Release the pressure naturally for 10 minutes, divide the mix into bowls and serve.

Nutrition: calories 356, fat 13, fiber 3, carbs 11.6, protein 11

Trout and Cardamom Tomatoes

Preparation time: 5 minutes
Cooking time: 20 minutes
Servings: 4
Ingredients:

- 2 trout, cut into chunks
- Salt and black pepper to the taste
- 1 teaspoon turmeric powder
- 2 yellow onions, chopped
- 10 ounces canned tomatoes, chopped
- 2 bay leaves
- 2 green cardamom pods
- 1 teaspoon chili powder
- ½ teaspoon garam masala
- 1 teaspoon cinnamon powder
- 2 teaspoon coriander, ground

Directions:
1. In your instant pot, mix the trout chunks with the turmeric, salt, pepper and the other ingredients, toss gently, put the lid on and cook on High for 20 minutes.
2. Release the pressure fast for 5 minutes, divide everything into bowls and serve.

Nutrition: calories 290, fat 14.3, fiber 2, carbs 11.6, protein 9

Coconut Cod Mix

Preparation time: 10 minutes
Cooking time: 20 minutes
Servings: 4
Ingredients:

- 4 cod fillets, boneless
- 1 tablespoon sunflower oil
- 1 cup cauliflower florets
- 1 red onion, chopped
- 1 teaspoon turmeric powder
- ½ teaspoon chana masala
- ½ teaspoon dry mango powder
- 2 tablespoons coriander, chopped
- 3 tablespoons coconut oil, melted
- A pinch of salt and black pepper
- ½ cup coconut cream

Directions:
1. Set the instant pot on Sauté mode, add the oil, heat it up, add the onion, turmeric and chana masala, stir and cook for 5 minutes.
2. Add the cod and the rest of the ingredients, put the lid on and cook on High for 15 minutes.
3. Release the pressure naturally for 10 minutes, divide the whole mix into bowls and serve.

Nutrition: calories 280, fat 12, fiber 2, carbs 5.5, protein 6

Salmon and Chili Sauce

Preparation time: 10 minutes
Cooking time: 15 minutes
Servings: 4
Ingredients:

- 1 tablespoon sunflower oil
- 1 pound salmon meat, skinless, boneless and cubed
- 1 teaspoon red chili powder
- ½ teaspoon fenugreek leaves, dried
- ½ teaspoon turmeric powder
- ½ cup spring onions, chopped
- 1 cup coconut cream
- 2 tablespoons lemon zest, grated
- 1 teaspoon lemon juice
- A pinch of salt and black pepper

Directions:
1. Set the instant pot on Sauté mode, add the oil, heat it up, add the chili powder, fenugreek, turmeric and the onions, stir and cook for 3 minutes.
2. Add the salmon and the other ingredients, put the lid on and cook on High for 12 minutes.
3. Release the pressure naturally for 10 minutes, divide the mix into bowls and serve.
Nutrition: calories 392, fat 14.5, fiber 2, carbs 22.4, protein 7

Creamy Salmon and Saffron Asparagus

Preparation time: 10 minutes
Cooking time: 20 minutes
Servings: 4
Ingredients:

- 1 pound salmon fillets, skinless, boneless and cubed
- 1 yellow onion, chopped
- 1 bunch asparagus, trimmed and halved
- ½ teaspoon saffron powder mixed with 1 tablespoon oil
- ½ tablespoon sweet paprika
- ½ teaspoon cumin, ground
- ½ teaspoon chana masala
- 1 and ½ cups coconut cream
- A pinch of salt and black pepper
- 1 tablespoon cilantro, chopped

Directions:
1. In your instant pot, combine the salmon with the onion and the rest of the ingredients except the cilantro, put the lid on and cook on High for 20 minutes.
2. Release the pressure naturally for 10 minutes, divide the mix into bowls, sprinkle the cilantro on top and serve.
Nutrition: calories 340, fat 9.1, fiber 2, carbs 15.6, protein 7

Cod and Garam Masala Sauce

Preparation time: 5 minutes
Cooking time: 20 minutes
Servings: 4
Ingredients:

- 4 cod fillets, boneless
- 2 tablespoons butter
- 2 yellow onions, chopped
- 2 garlic cloves, minced

- 1 teaspoon turmeric powder
- ½ teaspoon garam masala
- 2 tablespoons lemon juice
- A pinch of salt and black pepper
- 2 tablespoons coriander leaves, chopped

Directions:
1. Set the instant pot on Sauté mode, add the butter, heat it up, add the onion, garlic, turmeric and garam masala, stir and cook for 5 minutes.
2. Add the fish and the other ingredients, toss, put the lid on and cook on High for 15 minutes.
3. Release the pressure fast for 5 minutes, divide the mix between plates and serve.
Nutrition: calories 300, fat 10, fiber 2, carbs 11.5, protein 9

Turmeric Salmon and Lime Sauce

Preparation time: 5 minutes
Cooking time: 20 minutes
Servings: 4
Ingredients:

- 1 pound salmon fillets, boneless and cubed
- 2 tablespoons ghee, melted
- 1 teaspoon turmeric powder
- 2 tablespoons lime juice
- 1 teaspoon lime zest, grated
- 2 garlic cloves, minced
- ½ cup chicken stock
- A pinch of salt and black pepper

Directions:
1. Set the instant pot on Sauté mode, add the ghee, heat it up, add the garlic and turmeric, stir and cook for 3 minutes.
2. Add the fish and the remaining ingredients, put the lid on and cook on Low for 17 minutes.
3. Release the pressure fast for 5 minutes, divide everything between plates and serve.
Nutrition: calories 310, fat 13, fiber 3, carbs 8.6, protein 11

Indian Fennel Halibut

Preparation time: 5 minutes
Cooking time: 15 minutes
Servings: 4
Ingredients:

- 2 teaspoons cumin seeds
- 2 teaspoons fennel seeds
- 2 teaspoons coriander seeds
- 1 teaspoon turmeric powder
- 4 cloves
- ½ teaspoon chili powder
- 4 halibut fillets, boneless
- 3 tablespoons mustard oil
- ¼ cup chicken stock

Directions:
1. Set your instant pot on Sauté mode, add the oil, heat it up, add the cumin, fennel and the coriander, stir and cook for 2 minutes.
2. Add the halibut and the rest of the ingredients, put the lid on and cook on High for 13 minutes.
3. Release the pressure fast for 5 minutes, divide the mix between plates and serve.
Nutrition: calories 291, fat 12, fiber 3, carbs 11.6, protein 7

Ginger Cod Masala

Preparation time: 10 minutes
Cooking time: 15 minutes
Servings: 2
Ingredients:

- 1 pound cod fillet, boneless, skinless and cubed
- 2 tablespoons ghee, melted
- ¼ cup coconut cream
- 2 garlic cloves, minced
- 1 yellow onion, chopped
- 1 teaspoon ginger, grated
- 3 tablespoons coriander, chopped
- ½ teaspoon chili powder
- 1 tablespoon lemon juice

Directions:

1. Set your instant pot on Sauté mode, add the ghee, heat it up, add the garlic, onion and ginger and sauté for 3 minutes.
2. Add the fish and the other ingredients, put the lid on and cook on High for 12 minutes.
3. Release the pressure naturally for 10 minutes, divide the mix between plates and serve.

Nutrition: calories 320, fat 12, fiber 2, carbs 14.6, protein 13

White Rice Tuna Pot

Preparation time: 5 minutes
Cooking time: 15 minutes
Servings: 4
Ingredients:

- 3 garlic cloves, minced
- 1 yellow onion, chopped
- 2 green chilies, chopped
- ½ tablespoon turmeric powder
- 2 teaspoons chili powder
- 14 ounces canned tuna, drained and flaked
- 1 tablespoon ghee, melted
- 1 cup white rice, cooked

Directions:

1. In your instant pot, combine the tuna with the onion, ghee and the rest of the ingredients, put the lid on and cook on High for 15 minutes.
2. Release the pressure fast for 5 minutes, divide the mix into bowls and serve.

Nutrition: calories 370, fat 13.9, fiber 3, carbs 23.5, protein 10

Ginger Coconut Tuna

Preparation time: 5 minutes
Cooking time: 15 minutes
Servings: 4
Ingredients:

- 4 tuna fillets, boneless
- 3 garlic cloves, minced
- ½ teaspoon garam masala
- ½ teaspoon dry mango powder
- 1 teaspoon ginger, grayed
- 1 teaspoon turmeric powder
- 1 tablespoon chili paste

- 2 lemongrass sticks, chopped
- 1 tablespoon ginger, grated
- 2 tablespoons olive oil
- 1 cup coconut cream

Directions:

1. Set the instant pot on Sauté mode, add the oil, heat it up, add the garlic, garam masala, mango powder, ginger, and chili paste, stir and cook for 3 minutes.
2. Add the fish and the rest of the ingredients, toss gently, put the lid on and cook on High for 12 minutes.
3. Release the pressure fast for 5 minutes, divide the mix between plates and serve.

Nutrition: calories 311, fat 13, fiber 4, carbs 16.7, protein 10

Fenugreek Trout

Preparation time: 10 minutes
Cooking time: 15 minutes
Servings: 4
Ingredients:

- 1 pound trout fillets, boneless, skinless and cut into chunks
- 2 tablespoons ghee, melted
- 1 cup tomatoes, cubed
- 2 garlic cloves, minced
- 1 yellow onion, chopped
- 2 tablespoons ginger, grated
- 1 teaspoon turmeric powder
- ½ teaspoon chili powder
- ½ teaspoon fenugreek leaves, dried
- A pinch of salt and black pepper
- 1 tablespoon coriander, chopped

Directions:

1. Set your instant pot on Sauté mode, add the ghee, heat it up, add the garlic, onion, ginger, turmeric and chili powder, stir and cook for 3 minutes.
2. Add the rest of the ingredients, toss, put the lid on and cook on Low for 12 minutes
3. Release the pressure naturally for 10 minutes, divide the mix into bowls and serve.

Nutrition: calories 344, fat 12, fiber 3, carbs 33.6, protein 13

Paprika Tuna Curry

Preparation time: 5 minutes
Cooking time: 20 minutes
Servings: 4
Ingredients:

- 1 pound tuna, boneless, skinless and cubed
- 1 teaspoon curry powder
- ½ teaspoon turmeric powder
- 2 garlic cloves, minced
- ½ teaspoon chili powder
- ½ teaspoon smoked paprika
- Juice of 1 lemon
- 2 tablespoons chives, chopped
- A pinch of salt and black pepper
- 1 tablespoon coconut oil
- 1 cup chicken stock

Directions:
1.   Set the instant pot on Sauté mode, add the oil, heat it up, add the curry powder, turmeric, chili powder, the paprika and the garlic, stir and cook for 2 minutes.
2.   Add the tuna and the rest of the ingredients, put the lid on and cook on High for 18 minutes.
3.   Release the pressure fast for 5 minutes, divide the mix between plates and serve.
Nutrition: calories 300, fat 12, fiber 3, carbs 7.6, protein 11

Salmon and Radish Coconut Mix

Preparation time: 5 minutes
Cooking time: 20 minutes
Servings: 4
Ingredients:

- 1 pound salmon, skinless, boneless and cubed
- 1 cup spinach, torn
- ½ tablespoon coconut, grated
- 1 tablespoon coconut oil
- 1 cup radishes, cubed
- 1 white onion, chopped
- ½ cup chicken stock
- 2 garlic cloves, minced
- 1 teaspoon turmeric powder
- ½ teaspoon garam masala

Directions:
1.   Set instant pot on Sauté mode, add the oil, heat it up, add the onion, garlic, turmeric and the garam masala, stir and cook for 5 minutes.
2.   Add the salmon and the rest of the ingredients, put the lid on and cook on High for 15 minutes.
3.   Release the pressure fast for 5 minutes, divide the mix into bowls and serve.
Nutrition: calories 282, fat 10, fiber 2.6, carbs 7.6, protein 6

Tilapia and Radish Saad

Preparation time: 10 minutes
Cooking time: 15 minutes
Servings: 4
Ingredients:

- 1 cup cherry tomatoes, halved
- 1 pound tilapia fillets, boneless, skinless and cubed
- 1 cup radishes, halved
- 2 tablespoons coconut oil
- 1 teaspoon dry mango powder
- ½ teaspoon turmeric powder
- 1 red onion, chopped
- 2 chili peppers, chopped
- 2 teaspoons red pepper flakes
- A pinch of salt and black pepper
- ½ cup chicken stock

Directions:
1.   Set your instant pot on Sauté mode, add the oil, heat it up, add the onion, chili pepper, pepper flakes, mango and turmeric powder, stir and cook for 3 minutes.
2.   Add the fish and the rest of the ingredients, put the lid on and cook on High for 12 minutes.
3.   Release the pressure naturally for 10 minutes, divide the mix between plates and serve.
Nutrition: calories 292, fat 11, fiber 3, carbs 8.6, protein 9

Radish Sea Bass

Preparation time: 10 minutes
Cooking time: 20 minutes
Servings: 6
Ingredients:

- 1 fennel, shredded
- 1 cucumber, sliced
- 1 cup radishes, sliced
- 1 tablespoon sherry vinegar
- 2 tablespoons coconut oil
- 1 tablespoon chives, chopped
- 2 garlic cloves, minced
- 1 pound sea bass fillets, boneless and cubed
- Juice of 1 lemon
- ½ cup coconut cream

Directions:
1.   Set your instant pot on Sauté mode, add the oil, heat it up, add the garlic, and the fennel and sauté for 5 minutes.
2.   Add the cucumber, the fish and the rest of the ingredients, put the lid on and cook on High for 15 minutes.
3.   Release the pressure naturally for 10 minutes, divide the mix between plates and serve.
Nutrition: calories 432, fat 15.5, fiber 3, carbs 33.6, protein 6

Shrimp and Radish Coconut Curry

Preparation time: 5 minutes
Cooking time: 15 minutes
Servings: 4
Ingredients:

- 1 and ½ pound shrimp, peeled and deveined
- 1 cup radishes, sliced
- 1 cup coconut, grated
- ½ cup red onion, chopped
- ¼ teaspoon turmeric powder
- 1 tablespoon coconut oil
- ¼ teaspoon coriander seeds
- ½ tablespoon tamarind paste
- 1 cup water
- Salt to the taste

Directions:

1. Set your instant pot on Sauté mode, add the oil, heat it up, add the onion, turmeric, coriander and the tamarind, stir and cook for 5 minutes.
2. Add the shrimp and the rest of the ingredients, put the lid on and cook on High for 10 minutes.
3. Release the pressure fast for 5 minutes, divide everything into bowls and serve.

Nutrition: calories 242, fat 6, fiber 1, carbs 7.6, protein 8

Garam Masala Shrimp and Okra

Preparation time: 10 minutes
Cooking time: 15 minutes
Servings: 4
Ingredients:

- 1 and ½ pounds shrimp, peeled and deveined
- 1 cup okra, sliced
- 1 red onion, chopped
- 1 tablespoon coconut oil
- 3 garlic cloves, minced
- ½ tablespoon sweet paprika
- ½ teaspoon garam masala
- 1 cup chicken stock
- ½ teaspoon marjoram, dried
- A pinch of salt and black pepper
- 1 tablespoon cilantro, chopped

Directions:

1. Set your instant pot on Sauté mode, add the oil, heat it up, add the onion, garlic, paprika and garam masala, stir and cook for 3 minutes.
2. Add the shrimp and the rest of the ingredients, put the lid on and cook on High for 12 minutes.
3. Release the pressure naturally for 10 minutes, divide the mix into bowls and serve warm.

Nutrition: calories 270, fat 14, fiber 3, carbs 8, protein 10

Shrimp and Sweet Potatoes Pot

Preparation time: 10 minutes
Cooking time: 20 minutes
Servings: 4
Ingredients:

- 1 pound shrimp, peeled and deveined
- 1 pound sweet potatoes, peeled and cubed
- 2 tablespoons ghee, melted
- ½ cup chicken stock
- 1 yellow onion, chopped
- 1 cup tomatoes, cubed
- ½ teaspoon turmeric powder
- ½ teaspoon garam masala
- ½ teaspoon coriander powder
- ½ teaspoon dry mango powder
- 2 tablespoons parsley, chopped
- 1 tablespoon lemon juice

Directions:

4. Set your instant pot on Sauté mode, add the ghee, heat it up, add the onion, turmeric, garam masala, coriander, and mango powder and cook for 5 minutes.
5. Add the shrimp and the rest of the ingredients, put the lid on and cook on High for 15 minutes.
6. Release the pressure naturally for 10 minutes, divide the mix between plates and serve.

Nutrition: calories 348, fat 8.8, fiber 5.9, carbs 38.1, protein 28.5

Tuna and Avocado Mix

Preparation time: 5 minutes
Cooking time: 20 minutes
Servings: 4
Ingredients:

- 1 pound tuna fillets, boneless, skinless and cubed
- 2 tablespoons ghee melted
- 1 avocado, pitted, peeled and cubed
- ½ cup celery, chopped
- ¼ cup red onion, chopped
- 2 teaspoons lemon juice
- 1 teaspoon lemon zest, grated
- 2 tablespoons cilantro, chopped
- Salt and black pepper to the taste
- ½ teaspoon turmeric powder
- ½ teaspoon dried fenugreek leaves

Directions:

1. Set your instant pot on Sauté mode, add the ghee, heat it up, add the onion, celery, turmeric and fenugreek leaves, stir and cook for 5 minutes.
2. Add the tuna and the rest of the ingredients, put the lid on and cook on High for 15 minutes.
3. Release the pressure fast for 5 minutes, divide everything into bowls and serve.

Nutrition: calories 400, fat 13.2, fiber 2, carbs 14.5, protein 11

Tuna and Green Beans

Preparation time: 5 minutes
Cooking time: 20 minutes
Servings: 4
Ingredients:

- 1 pound tuna fillets, boneless, skinless and roughly cubed
- ½ pound green beans, trimmed and halved
- ½ teaspoon turmeric powder
- ½ teaspoon dry mango powder
- ½ teaspoon garam masala
- 2 tablespoons butter, melted
- Salt and black pepper to the taste
- 2 shallots, chopped
- 1 tablespoon parsley, chopped
- Juice of 1 lemon
- ½ cup chicken stock

Directions:
1. Set the instant pot on Sauté mode, add the butter, heat it up, add the shallots and the green beans and sauté for 5 minutes.
2. Add the tuna and sear it for 3 minutes more.
3. Add the rest of the ingredients, put the lid on and cook on High for 12 minutes.
4. Release the pressure fast for 5 minutes, divide everything between plates and serve.
Nutrition: calories 411, fat 14, fiber 3, fiber 15.6, carbs 11

Shrimp and Creamy Corn

Preparation time: 10 minutes
Cooking time: 15 minutes
Servings: 4
Ingredients:

- 2 pounds shrimp, peeled and deveined
- 2 tablespoons lemongrass past
- 10 curry leaves, chopped
- 1 bunch cilantro, chopped
- 1 chili pepper, chopped
- 2 tablespoons vegetable oil
- 1 teaspoon cumin seeds
- 24 ounces coconut milk
- ½ cup heavy cream
- 3 cups corn

Directions:
1. Ina blender, combine the curry leaves with the lemongrass, cilantro and chili and pulse well.
2. Set the instant pot on Sauté mode, add the oil, heat it up, add the lemongrass paste and cook for 2 minutes.
3. Add the shrimp and the other ingredients, put the lid on and cook on Low for 13 minutes.
4. Release the pressure naturally for 10 minutes, divide the mix into bowls and serve.
Nutrition: calories 260, fat 11, fiber 5.5, carbs 11.5, protein 8

Coconut Shrimp and Zucchinis

Preparation time: 10 minutes
Cooking time: 15 minutes
Servings: 4

Ingredients:

- 2 tablespoons ghee, melted
- 3 cardamom pods
- Juice of 1 lime
- 2 zucchinis, cubed
- ½ teaspoon cumin, ground
- 1 tablespoon cilantro, chopped
- ½ teaspoon mustard seeds
- ½ teaspoon turmeric powder
- 1 teaspoon garam masala
- ½ cup corn
- 1 shallot, chopped
- 1 pound shrimp, peeled and deveined
- 2 cups coconut milk
- 2 tablespoons almonds, chopped
- 1 red chili, chopped
- Salt and black pepper to the taste

Directions:
1. Set the instant pot on Sauté mode, add the ghee, heat it up, add the cardamom, cumin, mustard seeds, turmeric, garam masala, the chili and the shallots, stir and cook for 5 minutes.
2. Add the shrimp and the other ingredients, toss, put the lid on and cook on High for 10 minutes.
3. Release the pressure naturally for 10 minutes, divide the mix into bowls and serve.
Nutrition: calories 224, fat 13, fiber 3, carbs 7, protein 11

Chana Masala Tuna and Mushrooms

Preparation time: 10 minutes
Cooking time: 15 minutes
Servings: 4
Ingredients:

- 1 pound tuna fillets, boneless, skinless and cubed
- ½ teaspoon dry fenugreek leaves
- ½ teaspoon dried mango leaves
- ½ teaspoon turmeric powder
- ½ teaspoon chana masala
- 1 cup tomato puree
- 1 tablespoon lime juice
- A pinch of salt and black pepper
- ½ teaspoon curry powder
- 2 cups mushrooms, sliced
- 1 yellow onion, chopped
- 2 tablespoons ghee, melted

Directions:
1. Set your instant pot on Sauté mode, add the ghee, heat it up, add the onion, mushrooms and the other ingredients except the tuna, tomato puree and the lime juice, stir and sauté for 5 minutes.
2. Add the remaining ingredients, put the lid on and cook on High for 10 minutes.
3. Release the pressure naturally for 10 minutes, divide the mix into bowls and serve.
Nutrition: calories 321, fat 12, fiber 3, carbs 6, protein 8

Tilapia Cardamom Masala

Preparation time: 10 minutes
Cooking time: 15 minutes
Servings: 4
Ingredients:
- 1 pound tilapia, boneless, skinless and cubed
- 2 tablespoons sunflower oil
- Juice of 1 lemon
- 1 bay leaf
- 1 tablespoon coriander, ground
- 1 tablespoon cumin, ground
- 1 teaspoon cinnamon powder
- 1 teaspoon ginger, grated
- 1 teaspoon cardamom , ground
- ½ teaspoon nutmeg, ground
- ½ teaspoon allspice
- 1 cup chicken stock

Directions:
1. Set your instant pot on Sauté mode, add the oil, heat it up, add the tilapia and cook for 3 minutes.
2. Add the rest of the ingredients, put the lid on and cook on High for 12 minutes.
3. Release the pressure naturally for 10 minutes, divide the mix into bowls and serve.

Nutrition: calories 331, fat 11, fiber 3, carbs 10.6, protein 9

Spicy Coconut Tilapia

Preparation time: 10 minutes
Cooking time: 15 minutes
Servings: 4
Ingredients:
- 4 tilapia fillets, boneless
- 2 tablespoons ghee, melted
- 1 yellow onion, chopped
- 1 tablespoon garlic, minced
- 1 teaspoon ginger, grated
- 1 green chili, chopped
- 1 teaspoon turmeric powder
- 1 teaspoon red chili powder
- ½ teaspoon garam masala
- 4 tablespoons mustard
- ½ teaspoon cumin seeds, ground
- ½ cup coconut cream

Directions:
1. Set the instant pot on Sauté mode, add the ghee, heat it up, add the fish and sear it for 2 minutes on each side.
2. Add the rest of the ingredients, put the lid on and cook on High for 11 minutes.
3. Release the pressure naturally for 10 minutes, divide the mix between plates and serve.

Nutrition: calories 292, fat 9, fiber 4, carbs 11.7, protein 9

Tilapia Curry

Preparation time: 10 minutes
Cooking time: 20 minutes
Servings: 4

Ingredients:
- 1 pound tilapia, skinless, boneless and cubed
- ½ red onion, chopped
- 2 teaspoons red chili powder
- 2 teaspoons turmeric powder
- ¼ cup coconut, grated
- Salt and black pepper to the taste
- 1 cup coconut milk
- A pinch of asafetida powder
- 2 tablespoons vegetable oil

Directions:
1. Set the pot on Sauté mode, add the oil, heat it up, add the onion and sauté for 2 minutes
2. Add the fish and the rest of the ingredients, put the lid on and cook on High for 18 minutes.
3. Release the pressure naturally for 10 minutes, divide the curry into bowls and serve.

Nutrition: calories 332, fat 8, fiber 2, carbs 6, protein 11

Classic Turmeric Sea Bass

Preparation time: 5 minutes
Cooking time: 20 minutes
Servings: 4
Ingredients:
- 4 sea bass fillets, boneless
- 2 tablespoons chili powder
- ½ teaspoon turmeric powder
- 1 teaspoon ginger paste
- 1 teaspoon garlic, minced
- 1 tablespoon white vinegar
- Salt and black pepper to the taste
- ¼ cup water
- 2 tomatoes, cubed
- 1 tablespoon sunflower oil

Directions:
1. Set the instant pot on Sauté mode, add the oil, heat it up, add the fish and sear it for 2 minutes on each side.
2. Add the rest of the ingredients, put the lid on and cook on High for 18 minutes.
3. Release the pressure fast for 5 minutes, divide everything between plates and serve.

Nutrition: calories 302, fat 11.5, fiber 1, carbs 5, protein 8

Sea Bass and Cumin Lentils

Preparation time: 5 minutes
Cooking time: 20 minutes
Servings: 4
Ingredients:

- 2 tablespoons vegetable oil
- 1 yellow onion, chopped
- 1 carrot, chopped
- 1 red bell pepper, chopped
- 4 garlic cloves, minced
- 1 tablespoon ginger, grated
- 1 tablespoon curry powder
- 2 tomatoes, cubed
- 2 cups veggie stock
- 1 cup red lentils
- Salt and black pepper to the taste
- 1 pound sea bass fillets, boneless, skinless and roughly cubed
- Salt and black pepper to the taste
- 1 teaspoon turmeric powder
- 1 teaspoon coriander, ground
- 1 teaspoon cumin, ground

Directions:
1. Set the instant pot on Sauté mode, add the oil, heat it up, add the onion, carrots, bell pepper, garlic and ginger, stir and cook for 5 minutes.
2. Add the rest of the ingredients, toss, put the lid on and cook on High for 15 minutes.
3. Release the pressure fast for 5 minutes, divide the mix between plates and serve.
Nutrition: calories 322, fat 9, fiber 2, carbs 17.6, protein 7

Yogurt Sea Bass

Preparation time: 10 minutes
Cooking time: 20 minutes
Servings: 4
Ingredients:

- 4 sea bass fillets, boneless
- 5 tablespoons yogurt
- 1 tablespoon vegetable oil
- Salt and black pepper to the taste
- Juice of 1 lemon
- 2 garlic cloves, minced
- 1 tablespoon ginger, grated
- 1 green chili, chopped
- 1 tablespoon tandoori powder
- 1 tablespoon coriander, chopped
- ½ cup heavy cream

Directions:
1. Set your instant pot on Sauté mode, add the oil, heat it up, add the garlic, ginger, chili and tandoori powder, stir and cook for 3 minutes.
2. Add the fish and the rest of the ingredients, put the lid on and cook on High for 17 minutes.
3. Release the pressure naturally for 10 minutes, divide the mix between plates and serve.

Nutrition: calories 340, fat 7, fiber 3, carbs 16.6, protein 8

Cayenne Mussels

Preparation time: 10 minutes
Cooking time: 12 minutes
Servings: 4
Ingredients:

- 2 tablespoons vegetable oil
- 2 tablespoons ginger, grated
- 2 yellow onions, chopped
- Salt and black pepper to the taste
- 1 teaspoon turmeric powder
- 1 tablespoon coriander, ground
- 1 cup fish stock
- ¼ teaspoon cayenne pepper
- ½ cup coconut milk
- 2 pounds mussels, scrubbed
- 2 tablespoons lemon juice
- ¼ cup cilantro, chopped

Directions:
1. Set the instant pot on Sauté mode, add the oil, heat it up, add the ginger, onion, turmeric, coriander and cayenne, stir and cook for 2 minutes.
2. Add the mussels and the other ingredients, put the lid on and cook on High for 10 minutes.
3. Release the pressure naturally for 10 minutes, divide the mix into bowls and serve.
Nutrition: calories 310, fat 22, fiber 2, carbs 7, protein 24

Curry Coconut Clams

Preparation time: 10 minutes
Cooking time: 15 minutes
Servings: 4
Ingredients:

- 2 pounds clams
- 1 and ½ tablespoons vegetable oil
- Salt and black pepper to the taste
- 1 tablespoon ginger, grated
- 1 yellow onion, chopped
- 2 teaspoons sweet paprika
- ½ teaspoon cumin, ground
- 1 teaspoon coriander, ground
- ½ teaspoon cayenne pepper
- ½ cup coconut milk
- 1 tablespoon lime juice

Directions:
1. Set your instant pot on Sauté mode, add the oil, heat it up, add the ginger, onion, paprika, cumin, coriander and the cayenne pepper, stir and cook for 2 minutes.
2. Add the rest of the ingredients, put the lid on and cook on High for 13 minutes.
3. Release the pressure naturally for 10 minutes, divide the mix into bowls and serve.
Nutrition: calories 221, fat 8, fiber 3, carbs 6, protein 7

Hot Coconut Clams

Preparation time: 10 minutes
Cooking time: 15 minutes
Servings: 4
Ingredients:

- 1 and ½ pounds clams, scrubbed
- 2 tablespoons vegetable oil
- 1 teaspoon mustard seeds
- 3 garlic cloves, minced
- 1 tablespoon turmeric powder
- 1 yellow onion , chopped
- 1 teaspoon tamarind paste
- 1/3 cup coconut, grated
- ½ teaspoon red pepper flakes, crushed
- ½ teaspoon hot paprika
- ½ teaspoon coriander, ground
- ½ cup chicken stock

Directions:
1. Set the instant pot on Sauté mode, add the oil, heat it up, add the garlic, onion, turmeric, mustard seeds, and tamarind paste, stir and cook for 2 minutes.
2. Add the clams and the rest of the ingredients, put the lid on and cook on High for 13 minutes.
3. Release the pressure naturally for 10 minutes, divide the mix into bowls and serve.
Nutrition: calories 235, fat 8, fiber 4, carbs 7, protein 9

Crab Tamarind Curry

Preparation time: 10 minutes
Cooking time: 15 minutes
Servings: 4
Ingredients:

- 2 cups crab meat
- 1 teaspoon tamarind paste
- ½ cup chicken stock
- 2 yellow onions, chopped
- 2 tomatoes, cubed
- 2 red chilies, chopped
- 2 tablespoons garlic paste
- 1 tablespoon ginger paste
- 2 tablespoons coriander powder
- 2 tablespoons cumin powder
- 1 cup coconut, grated
- ½ teaspoon red chili powder

Directions:
1. In your instant pot, combine the crab meat with the tamarind paste and the other ingredients, toss, put the lid on and cook on High for 15 minutes.
2. Release the pressure naturally for 10 minutes, divide everything into bowls and serve.
Nutrition: calories 211, fat 8, fiber 4, carbs 8, protein 8

Pandan Crab and Eggplants

Preparation time: 10 minutes
Cooking time: 20 minutes
Servings: 4

Ingredients:

- 1 pound crab meat
- 1 cup chicken stock
- 2 tablespoons vegetable oil
- 4 tablespoons coconut, shredded
- 3 garlic cloves, minced
- 1 teaspoon ginger, grated
- Salt and black pepper to the taste
- 1 eggplant, cubed
- 1 yellow onion, chopped
- 1 tablespoon curry powder
- 8 curry leaves, chopped
- 2 pandan leaves, dried
- 1 tablespoon tamarind paste

Directions:
1. Set the instant pot on Sauté mode, add the oil, heat it up, add the coconut, garlic, ginger, onion, curry powder, stir and cook for 5 minutes.
2. Add the crab and the rest of the ingredients, put the lid on and cook on High for 15 minutes.
3. Release the pressure naturally for 10 minutes, divide the mix between plates and serve.
Nutrition: calories 293, fat 6.7, fiber 3, carbs 9.6, protein 6

Mustard Mahi Mahi

Preparation time: 10 minutes
Cooking time: 17 minutes
Servings: 4
Ingredients:

- 2 pounds mahi mahi, skinless, boneless and cubed
- ¼ teaspoon sweet paprika
- ¼ teaspoon turmeric powder
- Salt and black pepper to the taste
- 1 tablespoon lime juice
- ½ cup chicken stock
- 2 tablespoons vegetable oil
- 1 tablespoon garlic, minced
- 1 teaspoon mustard seeds
- ½ teaspoons mustard powder
- 1 cup tomatoes, cubed
- 1 tablespoon coriander, chopped

Directions:
1. Set the instant pot on Sauté mode, add the oil, heat it up, add the garlic, mustard seeds, mustard powder, paprika and turmeric and cook for 2 minutes.
2. Add the fish and the other ingredients, toss, put the lid on and cook on High for 15 minutes.
3. Release the pressure naturally for 10 minutes, divide the mix between plates and serve.
Nutrition: calories 280, fat 11, fiber 4, carbs 9.5, protein 12

Mahi Mahi Yogurt Tikka
Preparation time: 10 minutes
Cooking time: 20 minutes
Servings: 4
Ingredients:
- 1 pound mahi mahi, boneless, skinless and cubed
- Salt to the taste
- 1 tablespoon ghee, melted
- 1 teaspoon red chili powder
- 1 cup yogurt
- 3 tablespoons garlic, minced

Directions:
1. In your instant pot, mix the fish with salt and the other ingredients, toss, put the lid on and cook on High for 20 minutes.
2. Release the pressure naturally for 10 minutes, divide the mix into bowls, and serve.
Nutrition: calories 290, fat 12, fiber 3, carbs 7, protein 9

Cod and Pepper Paste
Preparation time: 5 minutes
Cooking time: 15 minutes
Servings: 4
Ingredients:
- 1 pound cod fillets, boneless
- 4 pearl onions, peeled
- 2 tablespoons coconut oil, melted
- ½ teaspoon turmeric powder
- 3 garlic cloves, minced
- 1 teaspoon chili powder
- 1 teaspoon black peppercorns
- ½ teaspoon garam masala
- Juice of ½ lime
- Salt to the taste
- ½ cup fish stock

Directions:
1. In a blender, combine the pearl onions with the oil and the other ingredients except the fish, pulse well and transfer this to your instant pot.
2. Add the trout as well, put the lid on and cook on High for 15 minutes.
3. Release the pressure fast for 5 minutes, divide the mix into bowls and serve.
Nutrition: calories 275, fat 14.3, fiber 2, carbs 11, protein 33

Cod and Mint Chutney
Preparation time: 10 minutes
Cooking time: 15 minutes
Servings: 4
Ingredients:
- 4 cod fillets, boneless
- 1 tablespoon olive oil
- Juice of 1 lemon
- ½ teaspoon cumin, ground
- 2 garlic cloves, minced
- 1-inch ginger, grated
- 1 cup cilantro leaves
- ½ cup mint, chopped

Directions:
1. In a blender, combine the oil with the lemon juice, cilantro and the other ingredients except the fish and pulse well.
2. Put the fish in the instant pot, add the chutney mix, toss gently, put the lid on and cook on High for 15 minutes.
3. Release the pressure naturally for 10 minutes, divide the mix between plates and serve.
Nutrition: calories 282, fat 7.7, fiber 3, carbs 6, protein 9

Tomato Cod Pot
Preparation time: 10 minutes
Cooking time: 15 minutes
Servings: 4
Ingredients:
- 1 pound cod fillet, boneless, skinless and cubed
- 2 garlic cloves, minced
- 2 green chilies, chopped
- 1 tablespoon ghee, melted
- 1 cup cherry tomatoes, halved
- ½ teaspoon garam masala
- ½ tablespoon lime juice
- 1 tablespoon coriander powder
- A pinch of salt and black pepper
- ½ cup tomato sauce

Directions:
1. Set your instant pot on Sauté mode, add the ghee, heat it up, add the garlic, chilies, coriander and garam masala, stir and cook for 2 minutes.
2. Add the fish and the rest of the ingredients, put the lid on and cook on High for 13 minutes.
3. Release the pressure naturally for 10 minutes, divide the mix between plates and serve.
Nutrition: calories 270, fat 11.2, fiber 3, carbs 9.6, protein 14

Indian Instant Pot Poultry Recipes

Lemongrass Yogurt Turkey
Preparation time: 10 minutes
Cooking time: 25 minutes
Servings: 4
Ingredients:
- 1 bunch lemongrass, chopped
- 4 garlic cloves, minced
- 1 pound turkey breast, skinless, boneless and cubed
- Juice of ½ lemon
- 1 green chili pepper, chopped
- 1 teaspoon garam masala
- 2 teaspoons turmeric powder
- 5 ounces yogurt
- 1 tablespoon ginger, grated
- A pinch of salt and black pepper
- ¼ cup cilantro, chopped

Directions:
1. In your instant pot, combine the turkey with the lemongrass, garlic and the rest of the ingredients, toss, put the lid on and cook on High for 25 minutes.
2. Release the pressure naturally for 10 minutes, divide everything between plates and serve.
Nutrition: calories 263, fat 12, fiber 3, carbs 6, protein 14

Onion Turkey Yogurt Mix
Preparation time: 10 minutes
Cooking time: 25 minutes
Servings: 4
Ingredients:
- 1 pound turkey breast, skinless, boneless and cubed
- 1 cup green onions, chopped
- ½ cup cashews, chopped
- 1 cup cilantro, chopped
- 1 teaspoon coriander seeds
- 1 teaspoon cumin seeds
- 1 tablespoon ghee, melted
- 2 tablespoons ginger, grated
- ½ cup yogurt
- ½ cup coconut cream
- 2 tablespoons lemon juice

Directions:
1. Set the instant pot on Sauté mode, add the ghee, heat it up, add the onion, coriander, cumin and the ginger, stir and cook for 2 minutes.
2. Add the meat and brown it for 3 minutes more.
3. Add the rest of the ingredients, put the lid on and cook on High for 20 minutes.
4. Release the pressure naturally for 10 minutes, divide everything between plates and serve.
Nutrition: calories 262, fat 18,8, fiber 2, carbs 14.5, protein 9

Turkey Meatballs and Tomato Sauce
Preparation time: 10 minutes
Cooking time: 21 minutes

Servings: 4
Ingredients:
- 2 tablespoons ghee, melted
- 1 big turkey breast, skinless, boneless and minced
- ½ cup chicken stock
- ½ cup tomato sauce
- 1 yellow onion, chopped
- 1 tablespoon lime juice
- Salt and black pepper to the taste
- 3 tablespoons Dijon mustard
- 2 tablespoons sweet paprika
- 1 teaspoon turmeric powder
- ½ teaspoon cumin powder
- ½ teaspoon garam masala
- 1 tablespoon cilantro, chopped

Directions:
1. In a bowl, combine the meat with the lime juice, salt, pepper, turmeric, cumin, garam masala and the cilantro, stir and shape medium meatballs out of this mix.
2. Set the instant pot on Sauté mode, add the ghee, melt it, add the meatballs and brown them for 3 minutes on each side.
3. Add the rest of the ingredients, toss, put the lid on and cook on High for 15 minutes.
4. Release the pressure naturally for 10 minutes, divide the mix between plates, and serve.
Nutrition: calories 280, fat 11.9, fiber 2, carbs 9.5, protein 10

Orange Turkey and Herbed Broccoli
Preparation time: 10 minutes
Cooking time: 25 minutes
Servings: 4
Ingredients:
- 1 pound turkey breast, skinless, boneless and cubed
- 1 cup orange juice
- 1 cup broccoli florets
- ½ teaspoon nutmeg, ground
- ½ teaspoon chana masala
- ½ teaspoon dried fenugreek powder
- ½ teaspoon dried mango powder
- 1 tablespoon oregano, chopped
- A pinch of salt and black pepper
- 1 teaspoon chili powder

Directions:
1. In your instant pot, combine the turkey with the broccoli and the other ingredients, toss gently, put the lid on and cook on High for 25 minutes.
2. Release the pressure naturally for 10 minutes, divide the mix between plates and serve.
Nutrition: calories 320, fat 14.4, fiber 2, carbs 15.6, protein 11

Cinnamon Turkey and Cauliflower
Preparation time: 10 minutes
Cooking time: 25 minutes
Servings: 4
Ingredients:
- 1 pound turkey breast, skinless, boneless and cubed
- 1 cup cauliflower florets
- 2 tablespoons ghee, melted
- ½ teaspoon turmeric, ground
- ½ teaspoon cinnamon powder
- ½ teaspoon garam masala
- ½ teaspoon chili powder
- 1 yellow onion, chopped
- 1 cup chicken stock
- ½ cup cilantro, chopped

Directions:
1. Set your instant pot on Sauté mode, add the ghee, heat it up, add the onion and the turkey and cook for 5 minutes.
2. Add the rest of the ingredients, toss, put the lid on and cook on High for 20 minutes.
3. Release the pressure naturally for 10 minutes, divide mix between plates and serve.
Nutrition: calories 310, fat 13.8, fiber 2, carbs 5.6, protein 11

Carrot Chicken Thighs
Preparation time: 10 minutes
Cooking time: 25 minutes
Servings: 4
Ingredients:
- 4 chicken thighs, bone-in and skinless
- 1 yellow onion, chopped
- 2 tablespoons canola oil
- 2 carrots, sliced
- ½ teaspoon cayenne pepper
- Salt and black pepper to the taste
- 1 tablespoon curry powder
- 4 garlic cloves, minced
- 14 ounces canned tomatoes, chopped
- 1 cup chicken stock
- ½ cup heavy cream
- ¼ cup cilantro, chopped

Directions:
1. Set your instant pot on Sauté mode, add the oil, heat it up, add the onion and the chicken thighs and brown for 5 minutes.
2. Add the rest of the ingredients, put the lid on and cook on High for 20 minutes.
3. Release the pressure naturally for 10 minutes, divide everything between plates and serve.
Nutrition: calories 290, fat 8, fiber 2, carbs 15.3, protein 11

Cardamom Chicken Mix
Preparation time: 10 minutes
Cooking time: 25 minutes
Servings: 4
Ingredients:
- 2 chicken breasts, skinless, boneless and halved
- 1 teaspoon garlic powder
- 1 teaspoon ginger, grated
- ½ cup chicken stock
- ¼ teaspoon cardamom, ground
- 2 tablespoons vegetable oil
- 1 teaspoon sweet paprika

Directions:
1. Set the instant pot on Sauté mode, add the oil, heat it up, add the meat and brown for 5 minutes.
2. Add the rest of the ingredients, toss, put the lid on and cook on High for 20 minutes.
3. Release the pressure naturally for 10 minutes, divide the mix between plates and serve.
Nutrition: calories 292, fat 12, fiber 3, carbs 13.5, protein 12

Masala Bell Chicken
Preparation time: 10 minutes
Cooking time: 20 minutes
Servings: 4
Ingredients:
- 2 chicken breasts, skinless, boneless and cubed
- 1 cup chicken stock
- 2 tablespoons ghee, melted
- 2 red chilies, minced
- 1 teaspoon garam masala
- ½ teaspoon turmeric powder
- 2 red bell pepper, cut into strips
- 1 teaspoon ginger, grated
- 2 teaspoons cilantro, chopped

Directions:
1. Set the instant pot on Sauté mode, add the ghee, heat it up, add the chilies, masala, turmeric, peppers and the ginger, stir and cook for 2 minutes.
2. Add the meat and brown for 3 minutes more.
3. Add the rest of the ingredients, put the lid on and cook on High for 15 minutes.
4. Release the pressure naturally for 10 minutes, divide the mix between plates and serve.
Nutrition: calories 450, fat 15.7, fiber 1, carbs 22.5, protein 12

Onion Chicken and Artichokes
Preparation time: 10 minutes
Cooking time: 20 minutes
Servings: 4
Ingredients:
- 1 pound chicken breast, skinless, boneless and cubed
- 2 artichokes, trimmed and halved
- A pinch of salt and black pepper
- 1 cup chicken stock
- 1 red onion, chopped
- 1 tablespoon ginger, grated
- 1 and ½ teaspoons cumin, ground
- ½ teaspoon dried fenugreek leaves
- ½ teaspoon turmeric powder
- 1 teaspoon cardamom, ground

Directions:
1. In your instant pot, combine the chicken with the stock, onion and the other ingredients, put the lid on and cook on High for 20 minutes.
2. Release the pressure naturally for 10 minutes, divide the mix between plates and serve.
Nutrition: calories 291, fat 7, fiber 2, carbs 6, protein 12

Oregano Chicken and Eggplants
Preparation time: 10 minutes
Cooking time: 20 minutes
Servings: 4
Ingredients:
- 1 pound chicken breast, skinless, boneless and cubed
- 2 eggplants, cubed
- ½ cup chicken stock
- A pinch of salt and black pepper
- 2 tablespoons sunflower oil
- 2 shallots, chopped
- 1 tablespoon red curry paste
- ½ cup tomato sauce
- 1 tablespoon oregano, dried
- 1 teaspoon turmeric powder
- ½ teaspoon garam masala

Directions:
1. Set your instant pot on Sauté mode, add the oil, heat it up, shallots, meat and the curry paste, stir and brown for 5 minutes.
2. Add the eggplants and the rest of the ingredients, put the lid on and cook on High for 15 minutes.
3. Release the pressure naturally for 10 minutes, divide everything between plates and serve.
Nutrition: calories 252, fat 12, fiber 4, carbs 7, protein 13.6

Pepper Turkey Mix
Preparation time: 10 minutes
Cooking time: 20 minutes
Servings: 4
Ingredients:
- 1 turkey breast, skinless, boneless and cubed
- 2 tablespoons ghee, melted
- ½ cup chicken stock
- 1 yellow onion, chopped
- A pinch of salt and black pepper
- 2 cardamom pods, crushed
- 2 black peppercorns, crushed
- ½ teaspoon cumin, ground
- 4 garlic cloves, minced
- 1 tablespoon cilantro, chopped

Directions:
1. In your instant pot, mix the turkey with the ghee and the other ingredients, toss, put the lid on and cook on High for 20 minutes.
2. Release the pressure naturally for 10 minutes, divide everything between plates and serve.
Nutrition: calories 271, fat 14, fiber 5.3, carbs 7, protein 14

Cinnamon Chicken and Rice Mix
Preparation time: 10 minutes
Cooking time: 25 minutes
Servings: 4
Ingredients:

- 1 pound chicken breast, skinless, boneless and cubed
- 2 tablespoons coconut oil, melted
- 1 cup white rice
- 2 cups chicken stock
- 1 yellow onion, chopped
- 1 tablespoon curry powder
- ½ teaspoon chili powder
- ½ teaspoon cumin, ground
- ½ teaspoon garam masala
- A handful cilantro, chopped
- Salt and black pepper to the taste
- ½ pound cherry tomatoes, halved
- 1 tablespoon cinnamon powder

Directions:
1. Set your instant pot on Sauté mode, add the oil, heat it up, add the meat and brown for 5 minutes.
2. Add the rest of the ingredients, put the lid on and cook on High for 20 minutes.
3. Release the pressure naturally for 10 minutes, divide everything between plates, and serve.
Nutrition: calories 263, fat 14, fiber 1.6, carbs 8.8, protein 12

Chili Chicken and Sweet Potatoes
Preparation time: 10 minutes
Cooking time: 25 minutes
Servings: 4
Ingredients:
- 1 pound chicken breast, skinless, boneless and halved
- 1 tablespoon canola oil
- 2 sweet potatoes, peeled and cut into wedges
- Salt and black pepper to the taste
- 1 tablespoon chili powder
- 1 tablespoon ginger, grated
- 1 teaspoon garam masala
- ½ teaspoon coriander powder
- 2 garlic cloves, minced
- ½ cup chicken stock
- 2 green onions, chopped
- 1 tablespoon cilantro, chopped

Directions:
1. Set your instant pot on Sauté mode, add the oil, heat it up, add the meat, ginger, chili powder, garlic and garam masala, stir and cook for 5 minutes.
2. Add the rest of the ingredients, put the lid on and cook on High for 20 minutes.
3. Release the pressure naturally for 10 minutes, divide everything between plates and serve.
Nutrition: calories 263, fat 12, fiber 3, carbs 11.6, protein 14

Turkey with Garam MAsala Potatoes
Preparation time: 10 minutes
Cooking time: 25 minutes
Servings: 4
Ingredients:
- 1 big turkey breast, skinless, boneless and cubed
- 1 tablespoon ghee, melted
- 1 pound baby potatoes, peeled and halved
- 1 teaspoon chili powder
- 1 teaspoon garam masala
- ½ teaspoon dried mango powder
- ½ teaspoon nutmeg, ground
- ½ teaspoon cinnamon powder
- ½ teaspoon sweet paprika
- 1 cup chicken stock
- Salt and black pepper to the taste
- 1 tablespoon coriander, chopped

Directions:
1. Set the instant pot on Sauté mode, add the ghee, heat it up, add the meat, chili powder, and garam masala, toss and brown for 5 minutes.
2. Add the potatoes and the rest of the ingredients, put the lid on and cook on High for 20 minutes.
3. Release the pressure naturally for 10 minutes, divide the mix between plates and serve.
Nutrition: calories 353, fat 13, fiber 2, carbs 15.7, protein 16

Coconut Spiced Chicken
Preparation time: 10 minutes
Cooking time: 25 minutes
Servings: 4
Ingredients:
- 1 pound chicken breast, skinless, boneless and cubed
- 1 yellow onion, chopped
- 2 garlic cloves, minced
- 1 tablespoon canola oil
- ½ cup chicken stock
- ½ cup coconut, shredded
- 2 tomatoes, cubed
- 1 teaspoon turmeric powder
- ½ teaspoon chana masala
- A pinch of salt and black pepper
- 1 teaspoon oregano, dried

Directions:
1. Set your instant pot on Sauté mode, add the oil, heat it up, add the onion, garlic and the meat and brown for 5 minutes
2. Add the rest of the ingredients, toss, put the lid on and cook on High for 20 minutes.
3. Release the pressure naturally for 10 minutes, divide everything between plates and serve.
Nutrition: calories 284, fat 14, fiber 4, carbs 11.7, protein 15

Coriander Chicken and Mango
Preparation time: 10 minutes
Cooking time: 20 minutes
Servings: 4
Ingredients:
- 1 pound chicken breast, skinless, boneless and cubed
- 1 tablespoon ghee, melted
- 1 yellow onion, chopped
- 3 garlic cloves, minced
- 1 cup chicken stock
- 1 mango, peeled and cubed
- Salt and black pepper to the taste
- ½ teaspoon cumin, ground
- ½ teaspoon coriander, ground
- ½ teaspoon cardamom, crushed
- ½ teaspoon dry mango powder
- 1 tablespoon sage, chopped
- 1 tablespoon coriander, chopped

Directions:
1. Set pot on Sauté mode, add the ghee, heat it up, add the onion, garlic, the meat, salt and pepper, stir and brown for 5 minutes.
2. Add the rest of the ingredients, put the lid on and cook on High for 15 minutes.
3. Release the pressure naturally for 10 minutes, divide the mix between plates and serve.
Nutrition: calories 263, fat 13, fiber 2, carbs 8.7, protein 15

Cumin Turkey and Asparagus
Preparation time: 10 minutes
Cooking time: 25 minutes
Servings: 4
Ingredients:
- 1 pound turkey breast, skinless, boneless and cubed
- 1 asparagus bunch, trimmed and halved
- 1 cup cherry tomatoes, cubed
- 1 tablespoon red curry paste
- ½ teaspoon smoked paprika
- ½ teaspoon garam masala
- ½ teaspoon cumin, ground
- 1 cup chicken stock
- ½ teaspoon chili powder
- A pinch of salt and black pepper

Directions:
1. In your instant pot, mix the chicken with the tomatoes and the other ingredients, toss, put the lid on and cook on High for 25 minutes.
2. Release the pressure naturally for 10 minutes, divide everything between plates and serve.
Nutrition: calories 290, fat 13, fiber 2, carbs 9.5, protein 16

Bell Pepper Chicken Mix

Preparation time: 10 minutes
Cooking time: 25 minutes
Servings: 4
Ingredients:
- 1 pound chicken breast, skinless, boneless and cubed
- ½ cup coconut, shredded
- ½ cup coconut cream
- 1 tablespoon ghee, melted
- 1 red bell pepper, chopped
- 1 green bell pepper, chopped
- 1 tomato, cubed
- ¼ cup chicken stock
- A pinch of salt and black pepper
- 1 tablespoon mustard
- 3 garlic cloves, minced

Directions:
1. Set the instant pot on Sauté mode, add the ghee, heat it up, add the meat, garlic and bell peppers and brown for 5 minutes
2. Add the coconut and the rest of the ingredients, put the lid on and cook on High for 20 minutes.
3. Release the pressure naturally for 10 minutes, divide the mix between plates and serve.

Nutrition: calories 290, fat 12, fiber 2, carbs 6,6, protein 15

Chicken, Avocado and Turmeric Rice

Preparation time: 10 minutes
Cooking time: 25 minutes
Servings: 4
Ingredients:
- 1 pound chicken breast, skinless, boneless and sliced
- 1 red onion, sliced
- 1 tablespoon sunflower oil
- 1 avocado, peeled, pitted and cubed
- 3 garlic cloves, minced
- A pinch of salt and black pepper
- 2 cups chicken stock
- 1 cup basmati rice
- 1 tablespoon ginger, grated
- 1 teaspoon turmeric powder
- ½ teaspoon garam masala
- 1 tablespoon cilantro, chopped

Directions:
1. Set the instant pot on Sauté mode, add the oil, heat it up, add the onion, garlic, the meat, ginger, turmeric and garam masala, stir and brown for 5 minutes.
2. Add the rest of the ingredients, put the lid on and cook on High for 20 minutes.
3. Release the pressure naturally for 10 minutes, divide the mix between plates and serve.

Nutrition: calories 253, fat 14, fiber 2, carbs 13.7, protein 16

Cinnamon Turkey and Green Beans

Preparation time: 10 minutes
Cooking time: 25 minutes
Servings: 4
Ingredients:
- 1 turkey breast, skinless, boneless and cubed
- ½ pound green beans, trimmed and halved
- 2 tablespoons vegetable oil
- 2 garlic cloves, minced
- ½ tablespoon cinnamon powder
- ½ teaspoon sweet paprika
- ½ teaspoon garam masala
- ½ teaspoon turmeric powder
- ½ teaspoon cumin, ground
- 1 yellow onion, sliced
- 1 cup chicken stock
- A pinch of salt and black pepper

Directions:
1. In your instant pot, combine the meat with the green beans and the rest of the ingredients, put the lid on and cook on High for 25 minutes.
2. Release the pressure naturally for 10 minutes, divide the mix between plates and serve.

Nutrition: calories 273, fat 13, fiber 3, carbs 11.7, protein 17

Chicken and Cilantro Fennel

Preparation time: 10 minutes
Cooking time: 20 minutes
Servings: 4
Ingredients:
- 1 pound chicken breast, skinless, boneless and sliced
- 2 fennel bulbs, sliced
- ½ teaspoon garam masala
- ½ teaspoon coriander, ground
- ½ teaspoon cumin, ground
- 1 cup chicken stock
- 2 shallots, chopped
- Juice of 1 lime
- 1 tablespoon vegetable oil
- 1 cup tomatoes, cubed
- 1 tablespoon cilantro, chopped

Directions:
1. Set the instant pot on Sauté mode, add the oil, heat it up, add the shallots, fennel and the meat and brown for 5 minutes
2. Add the rest of the ingredients except the cilantro, put the lid on and cook on High for 15 minutes.
3. Release the pressure naturally for 10 minutes, divide the mix between plates and serve with the cilantro sprinkled on top.

Nutrition: calories 276, fat 15, fiber 3, carbs 6.7, protein 16

Turkey and Masala Sauce
Preparation time: 10 minutes
Cooking time: 25 minutes
Servings: 4
Ingredients:
- 1 pound turkey breast, skinless, boneless and sliced
- 2 tablespoons ghee, melted
- ½ teaspoon chili powder
- 2 green chilies, chopped
- ½ teaspoon garam masala
- 1 cup chicken stock
- A pinch of salt and black pepper
- 1 tablespoon cilantro, chopped
- 1 cup lime juice

Directions:
1. Set your instant pot on Sauté mode, add the ghee, heat it up, add the meat, chili powder, chilies and garam masala, stir and brown for 5 minutes.
2. Add the rest of the ingredients, put the lid on and cook on High for 20 minutes.
3. Release the pressure naturally for 10 minutes, divide the mix between plates and serve.
Nutrition: calories 282, fat 15, fiber 2, carbs 11.6, protein 15

Chicken Filet with Chutney
Preparation time: 10 minutes
Cooking time: 25 minutes
Servings: 4
Ingredients:
- 2 chicken breasts, skinless, boneless and cubed
- ½ cup tomato chutney
- 2 green chilies, chopped
- ½ cup chicken stock
- ½ teaspoon sweet paprika
- ½ teaspoon garam masala
- ½ teaspoon cumin, ground
- 6 curry leaves, chopped
- 1 tablespoon sunflower oil
- 1 tablespoon lemon juice
- A pinch of salt and black pepper
- 1 tablespoon parsley, chopped

Directions:
1. Set the instant pot on Sauté mode, add the oil, heat it up, add the meat, chilies, cumin, paprika and garam masala, stir and brown for 5 minutes.
2. Add the rest of the ingredients, put the lid on and cook on High for 20 minutes.
3. Release the pressure naturally for 10 minutes, divide everything between plates and serve.
Nutrition: calories 334, fat 12, fiber 3, carbs 15.5, protein 7

Paprika Chicken and Pineapple
Preparation time: 10 minutes
Cooking time: 25 minutes
Servings: 4
Ingredients:
- 1 pound chicken breast, skinless, boneless and sliced
- 1 tablespoon chili powder
- ½ teaspoon hot paprika
- ½ teaspoon garam masala
- ½ teaspoon dried fenugreek leaves
- 1 cup pineapple, peeled and cubed
- 1 cup chicken stock
- 2 tablespoons tomato sauce
- 1 tablespoon parsley, chopped

Directions:
1. In your instant pot, combine the chicken with the pineapple, chili powder and the other ingredients, toss, put the lid on and cook on High for 25 minutes.
2. Release the pressure naturally for 10 minutes, divide everything between plates and serve.
Nutrition: calories 263, fat 14, fiber 3, carbs 5.7, protein 16

Masala Chicken and Zucchini
Preparation time: 10 minutes
Cooking time: 25 minutes
Servings: 4
Ingredients:
- 1 pound chicken breast, skinless, boneless and cubed
- 2 zucchinis, cubed
- 1 tablespoon canola oil
- ½ teaspoon turmeric powder
- ½ teaspoon garam masala
- ½ teaspoon cumin, ground
- ½ teaspoon chili powder
- A pinch of salt and black pepper
- 2 tablespoons tomato paste
- 1 cup chicken stock
- 1 tablespoon parsley, chopped

Directions:
1. Set your instant pot on Sauté mode, add the oil, heat it up, add the meat, turmeric, garam masala, cumin and chili powder, stir and brown for 5 minutes
2. Add the rest of the ingredients, put the lid on and cook on High for 20 minutes.
3. Release the pressure naturally for 10 minutes, divide the mix between plates and serve.
Nutrition: calories 263, fat 12, fiber 2, carbs 11.7, protein 18

Paprika Chicken Pot
Preparation time: 10 minutes
Cooking time: 20 minutes
Servings: 4
Ingredients:
- 2 chicken breasts, skinless, boneless and cubed
- Salt and black pepper to the taste
- 1 teaspoon fenugreek, dried
- 1 tablespoon coconut oil, melted
- ½ cup heavy cream
- ½ teaspoon turmeric powder
- 1 tablespoon smoked paprika
- 1 cup chicken stock
- 1 tablespoon basil, chopped

Directions:
1. In your instant pot, combine the chicken with salt, pepper, fenugreek and the other ingredients, toss, put the lid on and cook on High for 20 minutes.
2. Release the pressure naturally for 10 minutes, divide the mix between plates and serve.
Nutrition: calories 291, fat 11.7, fiber 3, carbs 6, protein 22.4

Turkey, Cauliflower and Basmati

Preparation time: 10 minutes
Cooking time: 30 minutes
Servings: 4
Ingredients:
- 1 pound turkey breast, skinless, boneless and cubed
- 1 cup cauliflower florets
- 1 cup basmati rice
- ½ teaspoon dried mango powder
- ½ teaspoon coriander, ground
- 2 cups chicken stock
- 1 yellow onion, chopped
- 2 garlic cloves, minced
- 1 tablespoon chili powder
- 1 cup tomato sauce
- A pinch of salt and black pepper
- 1 tablespoon cilantro, chopped

Directions:
1. In your instant pot, combine the meat with the cauliflower and the other ingredients, toss, put the lid on and cook on High for 30 minutes.
2. Release the pressure naturally for 10 minutes, divide the mix between plates and serve.

Nutrition: calories 263, fat 12, fiber 3, carbs 11.7, protein 15

Cocoa Turkey and Kidney Beans

Preparation time: 10 minutes
Cooking time: 25 minutes
Servings: 4
Ingredients:
- 1 pound turkey breast, skinless, boneless and cubed
- 1 cup canned red kidney beans, drained
- 1 cup chicken stock
- ½ teaspoon garam masala
- 2 green chilies, chopped
- ½ teaspoon turmeric powder
- 1 tablespoon cocoa powder
- 1 tablespoon cumin, ground
- A pinch of salt and black pepper
- 1 tablespoon cilantro, chopped

Directions:
1. In your instant pot, combine the meat with the beans, stock and the other ingredients, toss, put the lid on and cook on High for 25 minutes.
2. Release the pressure naturally for 10 minutes, divide everything between plates and serve.

Nutrition: calories 294, fat 14, fiber 2, carbs 9.6, protein 15

Coriander Chicken Meatballs

Preparation time: 10 minutes
Cooking time: 25 minutes
Servings: 4
Ingredients:
- 1 pound chicken breast, skinless, boneless and minced

- 1 egg, whisked
- 2 tablespoons coconut flour
- Salt and black pepper to the taste
- 1 yellow onion, chopped
- 2 garlic cloves, minced
- 1 tablespoon cilantro, chopped
- 1 tablespoon canola oil
- 2 cups coconut cream
- 1 tablespoon green curry paste
- ½ bunch coriander, chopped

Directions:
1. In a bowl, combine the meat with the egg, flour, salt, pepper, onion, garlic and cilantro, stir and shape medium meatballs from this mix.
2. Set your instant pot on Sauté mode, add the oil, heat it up, add the meatballs and brown them for 5 minutes.
3. Add the rest of the ingredients, put the lid on and cook on High for 20 minutes.
4. Release the pressure naturally for 10 minutes, divide the mix into bowls and serve.

Nutrition: calories 321, fat 12, fiber 6.4, carbs 11.7, protein 15

Paprika Turkey Mix

Preparation time: 10 minutes
Cooking time: 25 minutes
Servings: 4
Ingredients:
- 1 pound turkey breast, skinless, boneless and cubed
- 1 teaspoon smoked paprika
- ½ teaspoon hot paprika
- ½ teaspoon dried mango powder
- 1 cup tomatoes, cubed
- 2 tablespoons ghee, melted
- 2 shallots, chopped
- 2 garlic cloves, minced
- 1 cup chicken stock
- 1 tablespoon parsley, chopped

Directions:
1. Set your instant pot on Sauté mode, add the ghee, heat it up, add the meat, smoked and hot paprika, stir and brown for 5 minutes.
2. Add the rest of the ingredients, put the lid on and cook on High for 20 minutes.
3. Release the pressure naturally for 10 minutes, divide everything between plates and serve.

Nutrition: calories 363, fat 12, fiber 5, carbs 5.7, protein 16

Chicken and Masala Carrots

Preparation time: 10 minutes
Cooking time: 25 minutes
Servings: 4
Ingredients:
- 1 tablespoon canola oil
- 1 pound chicken breasts, skinless, boneless and halved
- A pinch of salt and black pepper
- ½ pound baby carrots, peeled
- ½ teaspoon garam masala
- ½ teaspoon nutmeg, ground
- 1 tablespoon lime juice
- ½ teaspoon turmeric powder
- 1 cup chicken stock
- 1 yellow onion, chopped
- 1 tablespoon coriander, chopped

Directions:
1. Set your instant pot on Sauté mode, add the oil, heat it up, add the meat, onion, garam masala and the nutmeg, toss and brown for 5 minutes.
2. Add the carrots and the other ingredients, put the lid on and cook on High for 20 minutes.
3. Release the naturally for 10 minutes, divide between plates and serve.
Nutrition: calories 292, fat 14, fiber 3, carbs 15.7, protein 14

Chicken and Coriander Zucchini

Preparation time: 10 minutes
Cooking time: 25 minutes
Servings: 4
Ingredients:
- 2 pounds chicken breasts, skinless, boneless and cubed
- 1 cup basmati rice
- 2 cups chicken stock
- 2 zucchinis, cubed
- 1 tablespoon hot chili powder
- ½ teaspoon chana masala
- 10 curry leaves, chopped
- 1 tablespoon coriander, chopped
- A pinch of salt and black pepper

Directions:
1. In your instant pot, mix the rice with the meat and the other ingredients, toss, put the lid on and cook on High for 25 minutes.
2. Release the pressure naturally for 10 minutes, divide everything between plates and serve.
Nutrition: calories 312, fat 12, fiber 6.2, carbs 11.6, protein 15

Cream Cheese Turkey and Rice

Preparation time: 10 minutes
Cooking time: 25 minutes
Servings: 4
Ingredients:
- 1 pound turkey breast, skinless, boneless and cubed
- ½ cup brown rice
- 1 cup chicken stock
- 1 and ½ cup cream cheese
- 1 tablespoon turmeric powder
- ½ teaspoon cumin, ground
- ½ teaspoon coriander, ground
- 1 tablespoon chili powder

- 1 tablespoon cilantro, chopped
- A pinch of salt and black pepper

Directions:
1. In your instant pot, combine the meat with the rice, stock and the other ingredients, toss, put the lid on and cook on High for 25 minutes.
2. Release the pressure naturally for 10 minutes, divide between plates and serve.
Nutrition: calories 363, fat 14, fiber 4.5, carbs 15.6, protein 18

Tomato Chicken and Mushrooms

Preparation time: 10 minutes
Cooking time: 25 minutes
Servings: 4
Ingredients:
- 1 pound chicken breast, skinless, boneless and cubed
- 1 cup cherry tomatoes, cubed
- 1 cup mushrooms, sliced
- 2 tablespoons ghee, melted
- ½ cup coconut cream
- 1 yellow onion, chopped
- ½ teaspoon turmeric powder
- ½ teaspoon dried fenugreek powder
- 5 curry leaves, chopped
- ¼ cup cilantro, chopped

Directions:
1. Set the instant pot on Sauté mode, add the ghee, heat it up, add the onion, the mushrooms and the meat and brown for 5 minutes.
2. Add the remaining ingredients, put the lid on and cook on High for 20 minutes.
3. Release the pressure naturally for 10 minutes, divide everything between plates and serve.
Nutrition: calories 362, fat 16, fiber 6.2, carbs 8, protein 16

Turkey and Peppery Corn

Preparation time: 10 minutes
Cooking time: 25 minutes
Servings: 4
Ingredients:
- 1 pound turkey breast, skinless, boneless and cubed
- 1 cup corn
- 1 tablespoon vegetable oil
- 2 teaspoons garam masala
- ½ teaspoon turmeric powder
- 1 yellow onion, sliced
- 1 cup chicken stock
- A pinch of salt and black pepper

Directions:
1. Set the instant pot on Sauté mode, add the oil, heat it up, add the onion and the meat and brown for 5 minutes.
2. Add the rest of the ingredients, put the lid on and cook on High for 20 minutes.
3. Release the pressure naturally for 10 minutes, divide everything between plates and serve.
Nutrition: calories 343, fat 16, fiber 2.6, carbs 14.4, protein 17

Chicken and Chickpeas Mix
Preparation time: 10 minutes
Cooking time: 25 minutes
Servings: 4
Ingredients:
- 2 tablespoons vegetable oil
- 1 cup yellow onion, chopped
- 1 cup canned chickpeas, drained and rinsed
- A pinch of salt and black pepper
- 1 pound chicken breast, skinless, boneless and cubed
- 1 cup chicken stock
- ½ teaspoon turmeric powder
- ½ teaspoon cumin, ground
- ½ teaspoon chili powder
- 2 teaspoons coriander, ground

Directions:
1. Set your instant pot on Sauté mode, add the oil, heat it up, add the onion, the meat, turmeric, cumin, chili and coriander, stir and brown for 5 minutes.
2. Add the rest of the ingredients, put the lid on and cook on High for 20 minutes.
3. Release the pressure naturally for 10 minutes, divide the mix between plates and serve.
Nutrition: calories 291, fat 17, fiber 3, carbs 14.7, protein 16

Turkey and Curried Lentils
Preparation time: 10 minutes
Cooking time: 25 minutes
Servings: 4
Ingredients:
- 3 garlic cloves, minced
- 1 pound turkey breast, skinless, boneless and cubed
- 1 cup canned lentils, drained and rinsed
- 1 tablespoon yellow curry paste
- ½ teaspoon turmeric powder
- ½ teaspoon coriander, ground
- 2 black peppercorns, crushed
- 2 tablespoons vegetable oil
- 2 red chilies, chopped
- 1 cup chicken stock
- 2 tablespoons cilantro, chopped

Directions:
1. Set your instant pot on Sauté mode, add the oil, heat it up, add meat, turmeric, coriander, chilies and black peppercorns, stir and brown for 5 minutes.
2. Add the rest of the ingredients, put the lid on and cook on High for 20 minutes.
3. Release the pressure naturally for 10 minutes, divide everything between plates and serve.
Nutrition: calories 256, fat 9, fiber 1, carbs 14.5, protein 12

Turkey and Fenugreek Chickpeas
Preparation time: 10 minutes
Cooking time: 25 minutes
Servings: 4

Ingredients:
- 1 yellow onion, chopped
- 2 zucchinis, cubed
- 1 pound turkey breast, skinless, boneless and cubed
- 1 cup canned chickpeas, drained and rinsed
- ½ teaspoon garam masala
- ½ teaspoon cumin, ground
- ½ teaspoon dry mango powder
- ½ teaspoon fenugreek leaves, dried
- 2 tablespoons ghee, melted
- 4 garlic cloves, minced
- 1 teaspoon hot paprika
- A pinch of salt and black pepper
- 1 cup chicken stock

Directions:
1. Set your instant pot on Sauté mode, add the ghee, heat it up, add the onion, the meat, garam masala, cumin , mango powder, garlic and fenugreek, stir and brown for 5 minutes.
2. Add the rest of the ingredients, put the lid on and cook on High for 20 minutes.
3. Release the pressure naturally for 10 minutes, divide the mix between plates and serve.
Nutrition: calories 283, fat 11, fiber 2, carbs 14.8, protein 15

Chicken with Masala Cabbage
Preparation time: 10 minutes
Cooking time: 25 minutes
Servings: 4
Ingredients:
- 1 pound chicken breasts, skinless, boneless and cubed
- 1 green cabbage head, shredded
- ½ teaspoon garam masala
- ½ teaspoon turmeric powder
- 1 tablespoon vegetable oil
- 1 yellow onion, chopped
- A pinch of salt and black pepper
- 1 teaspoon red pepper flakes
- 1 cup chicken stock

Directions:
1. Set your instant pot on Sauté mode, add the oil, heat it up, add the meat, garam masala, turmeric and the onion and brown for 5 minutes
2. Add the rest of the ingredients, put the lid on and cook on High for 20 minutes.
3. Release the pressure naturally for 10 minutes, divide everything between plates and serve.
Nutrition: calories 272, fat 14.7, fiber 3, carbs 11.7, protein 14

Coriander Chicken

Preparation time: 10 minutes
Cooking time: 25 minutes
Servings: 4
Ingredients:

- 1 pound chicken breast, skinless, boneless and cubed
- ½ teaspoon garam masala
- 1 teaspoon cumin, ground
- 1 tablespoon ghee, melted
- ½ teaspoon sweet paprika
- 1 teaspoon turmeric powder
- 1 cup chicken stock
- A pinch of salt and black pepper

Directions:

1. Set your instant pot on Sauté mode, add the ghee, heat it up, add the meat and garam masala, stir and brown for 5 minutes
2. Add the rest of the ingredients, put the lid on and cook on High for 20 minutes.
3. Release the pressure naturally for 10 minutes, divide everything between plates and serve.

Nutrition: calories 211, fat 8.9, fiber 5, carbs 6, protein 12

Masala Chicken and Broccoli

Preparation time: 10 minutes
Cooking time: 25 minutes
Servings: 4
Ingredients:

- 1 pound chicken breast, boneless, skinless and cubed
- 1 cup broccoli florets
- 1 tablespoon canola oil
- ½ teaspoon garam masala
- ½ teaspoon cumin, ground
- ½ teaspoon coriander, ground
- 4 curry leaves, chopped
- 1 yellow onion, chopped
- 1 cup chicken stock
- A pinch of salt and black pepper
- 1 tablespoon chives, chopped

Directions:

1. Set the instant pot on Sauté mode, add the oil, heat it up, add the meat, garam masala, cumin, coriander, curry leaves and the onion and brown for 5 minutes.
2. Add the rest of the ingredients except the chives, put the lid on and cook on High for 20 minutes.
3. Release the pressure naturally for 10 minutes, divide everything between plates, sprinkle the chives on top and serve.

Nutrition: calories 293, fat 15, fiber 4, carbs 6, protein 14

Chicken with Broccoli & Beets

Preparation time: 10 minutes
Cooking time: 20 minutes
Servings: 4
Ingredients:

- 2 chicken breasts, skinless, boneless and halved
- 1 beet, peeled and cubed
- 1 cup broccoli florets
- ½ teaspoon turmeric powder
- ½ teaspoon garlic powder
- ½ teaspoon garam masala
- 3 celery stalks, chopped
- 1 cup chicken stock
- 1 tablespoon tomato sauce
- A pinch of salt and black pepper
- 1 teaspoon chili powder
- 1 tablespoon cilantro, chopped

Directions:

1. In your instant pot, combine the meat with the beet, broccoli and the other ingredients, toss, put the lid on and cook on High for 20 minutes
2. Release the pressure naturally for 10 minutes, divide between plates and serve.

Nutrition: calories 223, fat 9, fiber 2, carbs 4, protein 11

Cinnamon Chicken with Avocado

Preparation time: 10 minutes
Cooking time: 20 minutes
Servings: 4
Ingredients:

- 2 chicken breasts, skinless, boneless and cubed
- 2 cucumbers, sliced
- 1 avocado, peeled, pitted and cubed
- 2 tablespoons coconut oil, melted
- 1 tablespoon sweet paprika
- ½ teaspoon turmeric powder
- ½ teaspoon cumin, ground
- 2 black peppercorns, crushed
- 1 cardamom pod, crushed
- 1 cup chicken stock
- 1 yellow onion, chopped
- ½ teaspoon cinnamon powder
- 1 tablespoon cilantro, chopped

Directions:

1. Set instant pot on Sauté mode, add the oil, heat it up, add the meat, paprika, turmeric, cumin, peppercorns, cardamom and the onion, stir and brown for 5 minutes.
2. Add the rest of the ingredients, put the lid on and cook on High for 15 minutes.
3. Release the pressure naturally for 10 minutes, divide the mix between plates and serve.

Nutrition: calories 290, fat 14.1, fiber 2, carbs 14.7, protein 14

Pomegranate Chicken with Cauliflower
Preparation time: 10 minutes
Cooking time: 25 minutes
Servings: 4
Ingredients:
- 1 pound chicken breast, skinless, boneless and sliced
- 1 cup pomegranate seeds
- 1 cup cauliflower florets
- 1 tablespoon sunflower oil
- 1 red onion, chopped
- 1 cup chicken stock
- 1 tablespoon sweet paprika
- 1 teaspoon red chili powder
- ½ teaspoon garam masala
- A pinch of salt and black pepper
- 1 tablespoon cilantro, chopped

Directions:
1. Set the instant pot on Sauté mode, add the oil, heat it up, add the meat, the onion paprika, chili powder, and garam masala, toss and brown for 5 minutes
2. Add the rest of the ingredients, put the lid on and cook on High for 20 minutes.
3. Release the pressure naturally for 10 minutes, divide everything between plates and serve.
Nutrition: calories 263, fat 8, fiber 2, carbs 7, protein 12

Garlic Turkey and Cauliflower Rice
Preparation time: 10 minutes
Cooking time: 20 minutes
Servings: 4
Ingredients:
- 1 pound turkey breasts, skinless, boneless and cubed
- 1 cup cauliflower rice
- 1 cup cherry tomatoes
- ½ cup chicken stock
- 4 garlic cloves, minced
- ½ teaspoon garam masala
- ½ teaspoon curry powder
- 4 curry leaves, chopped
- 1 tablespoon basil, chopped

Directions:
1. In your instant pot, combine the turkey with the cauliflower rice and the other ingredients, toss, put the lid on and cook on High for 20 minutes.
2. Release the pressure naturally for 10 minutes, divide everything between plates and serve.
Nutrition: calories 390, fat 11.8, fiber 2, carbs 7, protein 15

Cayenne Chicken and Tomatoes
Preparation time: 10 minutes
Cooking time: 25 minutes
Servings: 4
Ingredients:
- 2 chicken breasts, skinless, boneless and cubed
- ½ teaspoon cayenne pepper
- ½ teaspoon hot chili powder
- ½ teaspoon garam masala
- 2 garlic cloves, minced
- ½ teaspoon cumin, ground
- 2 tablespoons ghee, melted
- 1 cup tomato, cubed
- 1 yellow onion, chopped
- 1 cup chicken stock

Directions:
1. Set the instant pot on Sauté mode, add the ghee, heat it up, add the meat, cayenne, chili powder, garam masala and the garlic and brown for 5 minutes.
2. Add the other ingredients, put the lid on and cook on High for 20 minutes.
3. Release the pressure naturally for 10 minutes, divide everything between plates and serve.
Nutrition: calories 282, fat 12.5, fiber 2, carbs 15.6, protein 18

Turkey with Yogurt
Preparation time: 10 minutes
Cooking time: 25 minutes
Servings: 4
Ingredients:
- 1 pound turkey breasts, skinless, boneless and cubed
- 1 teaspoon turmeric powder
- ½ teaspoon coriander, ground
- ½ teaspoon nutmeg, ground
- 1 cup yogurt
- 2 teaspoons cumin, ground
- A pinch of salt and black pepper
- ¾ cup coconut cream
- ¼ cup cilantro, chopped

Directions:
1. In your instant pot, mix the turkey with the turmeric, coriander and the rest of the ingredients, put the lid on and cook on High for 25 minutes.
2. Release the pressure naturally for 10 minutes, divide everything into bowls and serve.
Nutrition: calories 285, fat 16, fiber 4, carbs 8, protein 18

Coconut Turkey with Chili Beans
Preparation time: 10 minutes
Cooking time: 25 minutes
Servings: 4
Ingredients:
- 1 pound turkey breasts, skinless, boneless and cubed
- 1 tablespoon coconut oil, melted
- ½ cup coconut, shredded
- 1 and ½ cups chicken stock
- A pinch of salt and black pepper
- 1 teaspoon red chili powder
- ½ teaspoon turmeric powder
- ½ teaspoon chana masala
- 2 green chilies, chopped
- 1 cup black beans, soaked overnight and drained
- 2 tablespoons tomato sauce

Directions:
1. Set your instant pot on Sauté mode, add the oil, heat it up, add the meat, chili powder, turmeric, masala and the chilies and brown for 5 minutes.
2. Add the rest of the ingredients, put the lid on and cook on High for 20 minutes.
3. Release the pressure naturally for 10 minutes, divide everything between plates and serve.
Nutrition: calories 292, fat 17, fiber 2, carbs 7, protein 16

Chicken Wings and Coconut Sauce
Preparation time: 10 minutes
Cooking time: 25 minutes
Servings: 4
Ingredients:
- 1 pound chicken wings, halved
- 1 tablespoon canola oil
- 1 teaspoon turmeric powder
- 1 cup coconut cream
- A pinch of salt and black pepper
- 2 shallots, chopped
- ½ teaspoon garam masala
- ½ teaspoon garlic powder
- 1 tomato, chopped
- ¼ cup cilantro, chopped

Directions:
1. Set your instant pot on Sauté mode, add the oil, heat it up, add the meat, shallots, turmeric, garam masala and garlic powder, stir and brown for 5 minutes.
2. Add the remaining ingredients, put the lid on and cook on High for 20 minutes.
3. Release the pressure naturally for 10 minutes, divide everything between plates and serve.
Nutrition: calories 324, fat 14, fiber 2, carbs 15.9, protein 11

Turkey and Masala Asparagus
Preparation time: 10 minutes
Cooking time: 25 minutes
Servings: 4
Ingredients:
- 2 pounds turkey breast, skinless, boneless and cubed
- 1 asparagus bunch, trimmed and halved
- 1 tablespoon coconut oil, melted
- ½ teaspoon red chili powder
- 2 green chilies, chopped
- ½ teaspoon curry powder
- ½ teaspoon garam masala
- A pinch of salt and black pepper
- 1 teaspoon cayenne pepper
- 1 cup chicken stock
- 1 tablespoon cilantro, chopped

Directions:
1. Set your instant pot on Sauté mode, heat it up, add the turkey, chili powder, chilies, curry powder and garam masala, stir and brown for 5 minutes
2. Add the rest of the ingredients, put the lid on and cook on High for 20 minutes.
3. Release the pressure naturally for 10 minutes, divide everything between plates and serve.
Nutrition: calories 329, fat 9, fiber 4, carbs 16.7, protein 16

Chicken with Coriander Broccoli Sauté
Preparation time: 10 minutes
Cooking time: 25 minutes
Servings: 4
Ingredients:
- 1 yellow onion, chopped
- 2 chicken breast, skinless, boneless and cubed
- 1 cup broccoli florets
- 1 cup coconut cream
- 2 tablespoons vegetable oil
- 1 tablespoon coriander, chopped
- ½ teaspoon turmeric powder
- ½ teaspoon garam masala
- 2 garlic cloves, minced
- A pinch of salt and black pepper

Directions:
1. Set your instant pot on Sauté mode, add the oil, heat it up, add the meat, onion, coriander, turmeric, garam masala and the garlic, toss and brown for 5 minutes.
2. Add the rest of the ingredients, toss, put the lid on and cook on High for 20 minutes.
3. Release the pressure naturally for 10 minutes, divide the mix between plates and serve.
Nutrition: calories 262, fat 12, fiber 4, carbs 7.7, protein 16

Chicken and Mushrooms Curry
Preparation time: 10 minutes
Cooking time: 30 minutes
Servings: 4
Ingredients:
- 1 pound chicken thighs, boneless and skinless
- 1 tablespoon coconut oil, melted
- 1 cup mushrooms, sliced
- 1 tablespoon green curry paste
- ½ teaspoon turmeric powder
- ½ teaspoon garam masala
- 1 zucchini, cubed
- 4 garlic cloves, minced
- 1 red onion, chopped
- ¼ cup parsley, chopped
- 1 cup chicken stock
- ½ cup heavy cream
- A pinch of salt and black pepper

Directions:
1. Set the instant pot on Sauté mode, add the oil, heat it up, add the meat, curry paste, turmeric, garam masala, garlic and the onion, stir and brown for 5 minutes.
2. Add the rest of the ingredients, put the lid on and cook on High for 25 minutes.
3. Release the pressure naturally for 10 minutes, divide everything into bowls and serve.
Nutrition: calories 361, fat 9, fiber 8, carbs 12, protein 8

Chicken and Cumin Basmati

Preparation time: 10 minutes
Cooking time: 30 minutes
Servings: 4
Ingredients:

- 2 endives, trimmed and shredded
- 1 cup basmati rice
- 2 cups chicken stock
- 1 pound chicken breasts, skinless, boneless and cubed
- ½ teaspoon coriander, ground
- ½ teaspoon cumin, ground
- ½ teaspoon turmeric powder
- ½ teaspoon garam masala
- 1 tablespoon chives, chopped
- 2 tablespoons tomato paste

Directions:

1.   In your instant pot, mix the chicken with the endives, rice and the rest of the ingredients, put the lid on and cook on High for 30 minutes.
2.   Release the pressure naturally for 10 minutes, divide everything between plates and serve.

Nutrition: calories 321, fat 12, fiber 2, carbs 15.6, protein 18

Shallot Chicken Wings

Preparation time: 10 minutes
Cooking time: 25 minutes
Servings: 4
Ingredients:

- 2 shallots, chopped
- 1 tablespoon lime zest, grated
- 2 tablespoons lime juice
- 1 pound chicken wings, halved
- 2 tablespoons ghee, melted
- 1 cup coconut cream
- 1 teaspoon turmeric powder
- ½ teaspoon dried fenugreek leaves
- ½ teaspoon garam masala
- 4 garlic cloves, minced
- A pinch of salt and black pepper

Directions:

1.   Set your instant pot on sauté mode, add the ghee, heat it up, add the shallots, the meat and turmeric, toss and brown for 5 minutes.
2.   Add the rest of the ingredients, put the lid on and cook on High for 20 minutes.
3.   Release the pressure naturally for 10 minutes, divide everything between plates and serve.

Nutrition: calories 331, fat 11, fiber 3, carbs 14.7, protein 18

Zucchini Turkey Bowls

Preparation time: 10 minutes
Cooking time: 25 minutes
Servings: 4
Ingredients:

- 2 tablespoons ghee, melted
- 1 eggplant, cubed

- 1 zucchini, cubed
- ½ cup chicken stock
- 2 tomatoes, cubed
- 1 big turkey breast, skinless, boneless and cubed
- A pinch of salt and black pepper
- 1 cup pomegranate seeds
- 1 tablespoon lemon juice
- ½ teaspoon chana masala
- ½ teaspoon coriander, ground
- ½ teaspoon cumin, ground
- 1 cup walnuts, chopped
- 1 bunch cilantro, chopped

Directions:

1.   Set your instant pot on sauté mode, add the ghee, heat it up, add the meat, chana masala, coriander and the cumin, stir and brown for 5 minutes.
2.   Add the rest of the ingredients, put the lid on and cook on High for 20 minutes.
3.   Release the pressure naturally for 10 minutes, divide everything into bowls and serve.

Nutrition: calories 352, fat 12, fiber 2, carbs 7, protein 17

Rice Turkey and Brussels Sprouts

Preparation time: 10 minutes
Cooking time: 25 minutes
Servings: 4
Ingredients:

- 1 pound turkey breasts, skinless, boneless and cubed
- 1 cup Brussels sprouts, trimmed and halved
- 1 cup basmati rice
- 2 and ½ cups chicken stock
- 1 teaspoon turmeric powder
- ½ teaspoon red chili powder
- 1 teaspoon dried mango powder
- 1 tablespoon canola oil
- A pinch of salt and black pepper

Directions:

1.   Set your instant pot on sauté mode, add the oil, heat it up, add the meat, turmeric, chili powder and mango powder, stir and brown for 5 minutes.
2.   Add the rest of the ingredients, put the lid on and cook on High for 20 minutes.
3.   Release the pressure naturally for 10 minutes, divide everything between plates and serve.

Nutrition: calories 287, fat 9, fiber 3, carbs 13.7, protein 16

Creamy Turkey and Peas Mix

Preparation time: 10 minutes
Cooking time: 30 minutes
Servings: 4
Ingredients:
- 1 pound turkey breast, skinless, boneless and cubed
- 2 tablespoons ghee, melted
- 1 cup peas
- 1 cup chicken stock
- ½ cup heavy cream
- A pinch of salt and black pepper
- 1 tablespoon sweet paprika
- 1 tablespoon chili powder
- ½ teaspoon turmeric powder
- ½ teaspoon cumin, ground
- ½ teaspoon coriander, ground
- 1 tablespoon cilantro, chopped

Directions:
1. Set the instant pot on Sauté mode, add the ghee, heat it up, add the m eat, paprika, chili, turmeric, cumin and coriander, stir and brown for 5 minutes.
2. Add the remaining ingredients, toss, put the lid on and cook on High for 25 minutes.
3. Release the pressure naturally for 10 minutes, divide the mix between plates and serve.

Nutrition: calories 271, fat 11, fiber 2, carbs 15.7, protein 14

Chicken with Chili Onions

Preparation time: 10 minutes
Cooking time: 30 minutes
Servings: 4
Ingredients:
- 2 pounds turkey breast, skinless, boneless and cubed
- 1 cup chicken stock
- 2 red onions, sliced
- 2 shallots, chopped
- 2 tablespoons canola oil
- ½ cup coconut cream
- ½ tablespoon chili powder
- ½ teaspoon garam masala
- ½ teaspoon dried fenugreek leaves
- A pinch of salt and black pepper
- 2 tablespoons cilantro, chopped

Directions:
1. Set your instant pot on Sauté mode, add the oil, heat it up, add the onions, shallots, the meat, chili powder and garam masala, stir and brown for 5 minutes.
2. Add the rest of the ingredients, put the lid on and cook on High for 25 minutes.
3. Release the pressure naturally for 10 minutes, divide the mix between plates and serve.

Nutrition: calories 321, fat 12, fiber 6.2, carbs 11.5, protein 17

Nutmeg Masala Turkey

Preparation time: 10 minutes
Cooking time: 30 minutes
Servings: 4
Ingredients:
- 1 pound turkey breasts, skinless, boneless and cubed
- 2 teaspoons garam masala
- 2 tablespoons sunflower oil
- ½ pound gold potatoes, peeled and cut into wedges
- 1 teaspoon nutmeg, ground
- 2 tablespoons ginger, grated
- 2 teaspoons garlic, minced
- ½ teaspoon cumin, ground
- 1 tablespoon basil, chopped
- 1 cup chicken stock

Directions:
1. Set your instant pot on sauté mode, add the oil, heat it up, add the meat and the garam masala, stir and brown for 5 minutes
2. Add the potatoes and the nutmeg, toss and cook for 5 minutes more.
3. Add the rest of the ingredients, put the lid on and cook on High for 20 minutes.
4. Release the pressure naturally for 10 minutes, divide everything between plates and serve.

Nutrition: calories 321, fat 11.6, fiber 3, carbs 22.8, protein 16

Basmati Chicken and Mango

Preparation time: 10 minutes
Cooking time: 30 minutes
Servings: 4
Ingredients:
- 2 chicken breasts, skinless, boneless and cubed
- 1 mango, peeled, pitted and cubed
- 1 cup basmati rice
- 2 cups chicken stock
- 1 yellow onion, chopped
- 4 garlic cloves, minced
- A pinch of salt and black pepper
- 1 teaspoon red chili powder
- 2 red chilies, chopped
- 1 teaspoon turmeric powder

Directions:
1. In your instant pot, mix the chicken with the mango, the rice with and the rest of the ingredients, put the lid on and cook on High for 30 minutes.
2. Release the pressure naturally for 10 minutes, divide everything into bowls and serve.

Nutrition: calories 291, fat 14, fiber 3, carbs 11.6, protein 13

Coconut Turkey & Carrots

Preparation time: 10 minutes
Cooking time: 30 minutes
Servings: 4
Ingredients:

- 1 tablespoon canola oil
- 1 pound turkey breast, skinless, boneless and cubed
- ½ cup coconut, shredded
- 1 cup basmati rice
- 1 yellow onion, chopped
- 2 carrots, grated
- 4 garlic cloves, minced
- 1 cup coconut milk
- A pinch of salt and black pepper
- 1 tablespoon sweet paprika

Directions:

1. Set the instant pot on Sauté mode, add the oil, heat it up, add the meat, onion, garlic and the carrots, stir and cook for 10 minutes.
2. Add the rest of the ingredients, put the lid on and cook on High for 20 minutes.
3. Release the pressure naturally for 10 minutes, divide everything between plates and serve.

Nutrition: calories 291, fat 17, fiber 2, carbs 11.7, protein 14

Indian Instant Pot Meat Recipes

Cilantro Beef Curry
Preparation time: 10 minutes
Cooking time: 30 minutes
Servings: 4
Ingredients:
- 2 pounds beef stew meat, cubed
- ¼ cup cilantro, chopped
- 1 yellow onion, chopped
- 3 garlic cloves, minced
- ½ cup tomatoes, crushed
- Salt and black pepper to the taste
- 1 tablespoon garam masala
- 1 teaspoon turmeric powder
- ½ teaspoon coriander, ground
- ½ teaspoon cumin, ground
- ½ teaspoon cayenne pepper
- 1 teaspoon brown sugar
- 1 tablespoon vegetable oil
- ½ teaspoon lemon zest, grated
- 1 cup beef stock

Directions:
1. Set the instant pot on Sauté mode, add the oil, heat it up, add the meat, onion, garlic, masala, turmeric and coriander, stir and brown for 10 minutes.
2. Add the rest of the ingredients, toss, put the lid on and cook on High for 20 minutes.
3. Release the pressure naturally for 10 minutes, divide the mix into bowls and serve.
Nutrition: calories 481, fat 17.9, fiber 1.2, carbs 5.7, protein 70.3

Coconut Ribs Curry
Preparation time: 10 minutes
Cooking time: 35 minutes
Servings: 4
Ingredients:
- 2 pounds beef ribs
- 1 yellow onion, chopped
- 1 teaspoon garam masala
- 2 tablespoons tomato paste
- 4 garlic cloves, minced
- 1 tablespoon red curry paste
- 14 ounces coconut cream
- 3 cups beef stock
- 1 tablespoon fish sauce
- 1 pound cauliflower florets
- ½ cup basil, chopped
- 2 bay leaves
- 1 tablespoon sunflower oil
- Salt and black pepper to the taste

Directions:
1. Set the instant pot on Sauté mode, add the oil, heat it up, add the ribs, onion, garlic, curry paste, and the garam masala, stir and brown for 5 minutes.
2. Add the remaining ingredients, put the lid don and cook on High for 30 minutes.
3. Release the pressure naturally for 10 minutes, divide everything into bowls and serve.

Nutrition: calories 761, fat 42, fiber 6.1, protein 17.6, protein 76.5

Creamy Coconut Pork
Preparation time: 10 minutes
Cooking time: 30 minutes
Servings: 6
Ingredients:
- 2 pounds pork stew meat, cubed
- 2 cups beef stock
- 4 garlic cloves, minced
- 1 leek, sliced
- ½ cup coconut, shredded
- 1 teaspoon garam masala
- ½ teaspoon cumin, ground
- 1 teaspoon sage, dried
- ½ cup heavy cream
- 1 tablespoon coconut oil
- Salt and black pepper to the taste

Directions:
1. Set the instant pot on Sauté mode, add the oil, heat it up, add the meat, garlic and the leek and brown for 5 minutes.
2. Add the rest of the ingredients, toss, put the lid on and cook on High for 25 minutes.
3. Release the pressure naturally for 10 minutes, divide everything into bowls and serve.
Nutrition: calories 377, fat 15.7, fiber 6.7, carbs 22.3, protein 14.3

Madras Tomato Beef
Preparation time: 10 minutes
Cooking time: 30 minutes
Servings: 4
Ingredients:
- 1 tablespoon cumin, ground
- 2 tablespoons coriander, ground
- 1 teaspoon turmeric powder
- 1 teaspoon chili powder
- Salt and black pepper to the taste
- 2 teaspoons ginger, grated
- 2 garlic cloves, minced
- 2 tablespoons lemon juice
- 2 pounds beef stew meat, cubed
- 2 tablespoons canola oil
- 1 cup beef stock
- 2 tablespoons tomato paste
- 1 tablespoon mint, chopped

Directions:
1. Set the instant pot on Sauté mode, add the oil, heat it up, add the meat, garlic, ginger, chili powder, turmeric, coriander and the cumin, stir and brown for 5 minutes.
2. Add the rest of the ingredients, put the lid on and cook on High for 25 minutes.
3. Release the pressure naturally for 10 minutes, divide the mix into bowls and serve.
Nutrition: calories 399, fat 16.6, fiber 7.7, carbs 26.5, protein 12.7

Ginger Beef Curry

Preparation time: 10 minutes
Cooking time: 35 minutes
Servings: 4
Ingredients:
- 2 tablespoons vegetable oil
- 1 yellow onion, chopped
- 12 curry leaves, chopped
- 6 garlic cloves, minced
- 4 teaspoons ginger, grated
- 1 tablespoon tomato paste
- 2 teaspoons coriander, ground
- 1 cup water
- 1 teaspoon garam masala
- ½ teaspoon turmeric powder
- 4 star anise
- Salt and black pepper to the taste
- 2 pounds beef short ribs, cut into medium pieces

Directions:
1. Set the instant pot on Sauté mode, add the oil, heat it up, add the onion, garlic, curry leaves, ginger and the meat and brown for 5 minutes.
2. Add the rest of the ingredients, toss, put the lid on and cook on High for 30 minutes.
3. Release the pressure naturally for 10 minutes, divide the mix into bowls and serve.

Nutrition: calories 353, fat 14.4, fiber 4.5, carbs 22.3, protein 46

Beef with Cardamom Veggies

Preparation time: 10 minutes
Cooking time: 25 minutes
Servings: 6
Ingredients:
- 2 pound beef stew meat, cut into strips
- 2 yellow onions, chopped
- 2 tomatoes, cubed
- 2 tablespoons ginger paste
- 2 tablespoons garlic paste
- 3 green chilies, chopped
- 2 tablespoons coriander seeds
- 4 tablespoons fennel seeds
- 8 cloves
- 6 cardamom pods
- 1 tablespoon black peppercorns, crushed
- 10 curry leaves, chopped
- 1 cup coconut, shredded
- 1 tablespoon mustard seeds
- 2 tablespoons sunflower oil

Directions:
1. Set the instant pot on Sauté mode, add the oil, heat it up, add the meat, onions, garlic and ginger paste, stir and brown for 5 minutes.
2. Add the rest of the ingredients, put the lid on and cook on High for 20 minutes.
3. Release the pressure naturally for 10 minutes, divide the mix into bowls and serve.

Nutrition: calories 344, fat 12.4. fiber 6.6, carbs 19.9, protein 25

Onion Beef in Yogurt

Preparation time: 10 minutes
Cooking time: 30 minutes
Servings: 4
Ingredients:
- 1 pound beef stew meat, cubed
- 4 garlic cloves, minced
- 2 cups yellow onion, chopped
- 1 tablespoon ginger, grated
- 1 cup yogurt
- 2 bay leaves
- 1 teaspoon sweet paprika
- 2 tablespoons curry powder
- 1 teaspoon garam masala
- 2 tablespoons lemon juice
- Salt and black pepper to the taste

Directions:
1. In your instant pot, combine the beef with the garlic and the other ingredients, toss, put the lid on and cook on High for 30 minutes.
2. Release the pressure naturally for 10 minutes, divide the mix into bowls and serve.

Nutrition: calories 388, fat 15.5, fiber 5.67, carbs 25.5. protein 22

Ginger Beef Mix

Preparation time: 10 minutes
Cooking time: 30 minutes
Servings: 4
Ingredients:
- 2 pounds beef stew meat, cubed
- 1 tablespoon garlic, minced
- 1-inch ginger, grated
- 2 cups red onion, chopped
- 2 tablespoons lemon juice
- 2 teaspoons coriander powder
- 2 teaspoons meat masala
- 2 teaspoons chili powder
- 1 teaspoon turmeric powder
- ½ cup water
- Salt to the taste

Directions:
1. In your instant pot, combine the meat with the garlic, ginger and the other ingredients, toss, put the lid on and cook on High for 30 minutes.
2. Release the pressure naturally for 10 minutes, divide everything into bowls and serve.

Nutrition: calories 388, fat 14.5, fiber 5.5, carbs 22, protein 17

Beef and Lentils Curry

Preparation time: 10 minutes
Cooking time: 35 minutes
Servings: 4
Ingredients:

- ¼ cup vegetable oil
- 1 tablespoon coriander, ground
- 1 teaspoon cumin seeds
- 1 yellow onion, chopped
- 4 garlic cloves, minced
- 1 tablespoon ginger, grated
- 2 pounds beef stew meat, cubed
- 14 ounces canned tomatoes, chopped
- 1 teaspoon turmeric powder
- 2 cups water
- ½ cup green lentils, rinsed
- 1 green chili, chopped
- Salt and black pepper to the taste

Directions:
1. Set the instant pot on Sauté mode, add the oil, heat it up, add the meat, ginger, garlic and onion, stir and brown for 5 minutes.
2. Add the coriander, cumin and the other ingredients, toss, put the lid on and cook on High for 30 minutes.
3. Release the pressure naturally for 10 minutes, divide the mix into bowls and serve.
Nutrition: calories 372, fat 15.5, fiber 6.6, carbs 19.8, protein 22

Curry Pork with Lentils

Preparation time: 10 minutes
Cooking time: 30 minutes
Servings: 4
Ingredients:

- 1 pound pork stew meat, cubed
- ½ cup curry paste
- 2 teaspoons vegetable oil
- 2 garlic cloves, minced
- 1 yellow onion, chopped
- 1 cup red lentils
- 2 teaspoons ginger, grated
- 1 and ½ cups beef stock
- 1 cup coconut milk
- 2 tablespoons coriander, chopped

Directions:
1. Set the instant pot on Sauté mode, add the oil, heat it up, add the meat, onion and the garlic and sauté for 5 minutes.
2. Add the rest of the ingredients, put the lid on and cook on High for 25 minutes.
3. Release the pressure naturally for 10 minutes, divide the mix into bowls and serve.
Nutrition: calories 356, fat 16.5, fiber 4.5, carbs 22, protein 4.65

Ground Beef Masala

Preparation time: 10 minutes
Cooking time: 20 minutes
Servings: 4
Ingredients:

- 2 pounds beef, ground
- 1 red onion, chopped
- 10 garlic cloves, minced
- 2 tablespoons cumin powder
- 2 green chilies, chopped
- 1 tablespoon coriander, ground
- 1 tomato, cubed
- ½ cup dill, chopped
- 1 potato, peeled and cubed
- Salt and black pepper to the taste
- ¼ cup beef stock

Directions:
1. In your instant pot, combine the beef with the onion, garlic and the other ingredients, toss, put the lid on and cook on High for 20 minutes.
2. Release the pressure naturally for 10 minutes, divide the mix between plates and serve..
Nutrition: calories 254, fat 12, fiber 2, carbs 14.6, protein 16

Chili Beef and Peas

Preparation time: 10 minutes
Cooking time: 20 minutes
Servings: 4
Ingredients:

- 2 pounds beef meat, ground
- 2 tablespoons canola oil
- 2 garlic cloves, minced
- 1-inch ginger, grated
- 1 chili pepper, minced
- 1 teaspoon garam masala
- 2 tomatoes, cubed
- Salt and black pepper to the taste
- ½ cup peas
- ¼ cup cilantro, chopped
- ¼ cup beef stock

Directions:
1. Set the instant pot on Sauté mode, add the oil, heat it up, add the garlic, chili pepper and the meat and brown for 5 minutes.
2. Add the rest of the ingredients, toss, put the lid on and cook on High for 15 minutes.
3. Release the pressure naturally for 10 minutes, divide the mix between plates and serve.
Nutrition: calories 343, fat 15, fiber 3, carbs 14.6, protein 20

Coconut Masala Beef
Preparation time: 10 minutes
Cooking time: 25 minutes
Servings: 4
Ingredients:
- 2 pounds beef stew meat, cubed
- 2 tablespoons canola oil
- 1 teaspoon garam masala
- ½ teaspoon coriander, ground
- 2 and ½ tablespoons curry powder
- 2 yellow onions, chopped
- Salt and black pepper to the taste
- 2 garlic cloves, minced
- 10 ounces coconut milk
- 2 tablespoons cilantro, chopped

Directions:
1. Set your instant pot on Sauté mode, add the oil, heat it up, add the meat, garam masala, coriander, onions and garlic and brown for 5 minutes.
2. Add the rest of the ingredients, put the lid on and cook on High for 20 minutes.
3. Release the pressure naturally for 10 minutes, divide everything between plates and serve.
Nutrition: calories 363, fat 16, fiber 3, carbs 15.6, protein 16

Saag and Paprika Beef Gosht
Preparation time: 10 minutes
Cooking time: 30 minutes
Servings: 4
Ingredients:
- 1 and ½ pound beef, cubed
- 2 tablespoons ghee, melted
- 1 yellow onion, chopped
- 1 tablespoon ginger, grated
- 1 teaspoon coriander, ground
- 1 teaspoon cumin, ground
- 1 teaspoon sweet paprika
- ½ teaspoon turmeric powder
- ½ teaspoon cloves, ground
- ½ teaspoon cinnamon powder
- ½ teaspoon garam masala
- 2 tomatoes, cubed
- 1 tablespoon tomato paste
- 2 cups beef stock
- 2 tablespoons yogurt
- 1 bay leaf
- 10 ounces spinach, torn

Directions:
1. Set your instant pot on Sauté mode, add the ghee, heat it up, add the meat, on ion, ginger, coriander, cumin, paprika and turmeric, stir and brown for 5 minutes.
2. Add the rest of the ingredients except the cilantro, put the lid on and cook on High for 25 minutes.
3. Release the pressure naturally for 10 minutes, divide the mix between plates and serve.
Nutrition: calories 354, fat 14, fiber 4, carbs 15.6, protein 15

Cumin Beef
Preparation time: 10 minutes
Cooking time: 30 minutes

Servings: 4
Ingredients:
- 2 pounds beef stew meat, cubed
- 1 yellow onion, chopped
- 2 tablespoons canola oil
- A pinch of salt and black pepper
- 1 cup beef stock
- 6 garlic cloves, chopped
- 2 green chilies, minced
- 1 teaspoon coriander, ground
- ½ teaspoon cumin, ground
- ½ teaspoon allspice, ground
- 1 teaspoon chili powder
- ½ teaspoon hot paprika
- ½ cup beef stock
- 1 tablespoon parsley, chopped

Directions:
1. Set your instant pot on Sauté mode, add the oil, heat it up, add the meat, on ion, garlic, and the chilies, stir and brown for 5 minutes.
2. Add the rest of the ingredients except the parsley, put the lid on and cook on High for 25 minutes.
3. Release the pressure naturally for 10 minutes, divide the mix between plates and serve with the parsley sprinkled on top,
Nutrition: calories 363, fat 12, fiber 4, carbs 22.6, protein 16

Beef and Beans Curry
Preparation time: 10 minutes
Cooking time: 35 minutes
Servings: 4
Ingredients:
- 1 and ½ pound beef, cubed
- 1 yellow onion, chopped
- 2 garlic cloves, minced
- 1 tablespoon ginger, grated
- 2 teaspoons cumin, ground
- 2 teaspoons coriander, ground
- 2 tablespoons canola oil
- 1 teaspoon turmeric powder
- ½ teaspoon cardamom powder
- 12 ounces canned tomatoes, cubed
- 1 and ½ cups beef stock
- 2 carrots, chopped
- Salt and black pepper to the taste
- 1 cup green beans, trimmed and halve d
- 1 cup cauliflower florets
- 1/3 cup yogurt

Directions:
1. Set your instant pot on Sauté mode, add the oil, heat it up, add the meat, onion, garlic , ginger, cumin, coriander, turmeric and cardamom, stir and brown for 5 minutes.
2. Add the rest of the ingredients, put the lid on and cook on High for 30 minutes.
3. Release the pressure naturally for 10 minutes, divide the mix between plates and serve.
Nutrition: calories 363, fat 14, fiber 6.4, carbs 22.6, protein 18

Beef with Eggplant Curry

Preparation time: 10 minutes
Cooking time: 35 minutes
Servings: 4
Ingredients:

- 2 pounds beef roast, cubed
- 1 tablespoon ghee, melted
- 1 yellow onion, chopped
- 2 tablespoons cumin, ground
- 4 garlic cloves, minced
- 2 tablespoons mustard seeds
- 1 tablespoon turmeric powder
- 1 tablespoon garam masala
- 1 teaspoon chili powder
- 8 curry leaves, chopped
- 2 cups beef stock
- ½ pound butternut squash, peeled and cubed
- 1 eggplant, cubed
- ½ cup coriander, chopped
- ½ cup coconut cream

Directions:
1.   Set the instant pot on Sauté mode, add the ghee, heat it up, add the meat, onion, cumin, garlic, mustard seeds, turmeric, garam masala and chili powder, stir and brown for 5 minutes.
2.   Add the rest of the ingredients, put the lid on and cook on High for 30 minutes.
3.   Release the pressure naturally for 10 minutes, divide the mix into bowls and serve.
Nutrition: calories 354, fat 14, fiber 4, carbs 32.6, protein 17

Cinnamon Beef and Pumpkin

Preparation time: 10 minutes
Cooking time: 30 minutes
Servings: 4
Ingredients:

- 2 tablespoons ghee, melted
- 2 pounds beef stew meat, cubed
- 1 teaspoon cinnamon powder
- ½ teaspoon ginger, grated
- Salt and black pepper to the taste
- ½ teaspoon red pepper, crushed
- 4 shallots, chopped
- ½ cup beef stock
- 4 garlic cloves, minced
- 14 ounces canned tomatoes, cubed
- 4 cups pumpkin, peeled and cubed
- ¼ cup cilantro, chopped

Directions:
1.   Set the instant pot on Sauté mode, add the ghee, heat it up, add the meat, cinnamon, ginger, pepper, shallots and the garlic and brown for 5 minutes.
2.   Add the rest of the ingredients, put the lid on and cook on High for 25 minutes.
3.   Release the pressure naturally for 10 minutes, divide the mix into bowls and serve.

Nutrition: calories 283, fat 9.5, fiber 4.8, carbs 25.7, protein 25.6

Beef with Masala Scallions

Preparation time: 10 minutes
Cooking time: 35 minutes
Servings: 4
Ingredients:

- 4 scallions, chopped
- 2 tablespoons ghee, melted
- 2 pounds beef stew meat, cubed
- 2 cups beef stock
- 2 garlic cloves, minced
- 1 tablespoon lemon zest, grated
- 1 tablespoon lemon juice
- ½ teaspoon cumin , ground
- ½ teaspoon coriander, ground
- ½ teaspoon garam masala
- A pinch of salt and black pepper
- 2 tablespoons cilantro, chopped

Directions:
1.   Set your instant pot on Sauté mode, add the ghee, heat it up, add the scallions, meat, garlic, lemon juice and lemon zest, stir and brown for 5 minutes.
2.   Add the rest of the ingredients, put the lid on and cook on High for 30 minutes.
3.   Release the pressure naturally for 10 minutes, divide the mix between plates and serve.
Nutrition: calories 263, fat 14, fiber 5, carbs 7.5, protein 15

Creamy Beef and Rice

Preparation time: 10 minutes
Cooking time: 30 minutes
Servings: 4
Ingredients:

- 2 pounds beef stew meat, cubed
- ½ teaspoon turmeric powder
- ½ teaspoon garam masala
- 3 ounces cream cheese
- 1 tablespoon canola oil
- 1 red onion, chopped
- 1 cup basmati rice
- 1 and ½ cups beef stock
- 1 tablespoon parsley, chopped
- A pinch of salt and black pepper

Directions:
1.   Set your instant pot on Sauté mode, add the oil, heat it up, add the meat, onion, turmeric and garam masala and brown for 5 minutes.
2.   Add the rest of the ingredients, toss, put the lid on and cook on High for 25 minutes.
3.   Release the pressure naturally for 10 minutes, divide everything into bowls and serve.
Nutrition: calories 283, fat 14, fiber 3, carbs 22.7, protein 17

Beef with Cardamom Zucchini
Preparation time: 10 minutes
Cooking time: 30 minutes
Servings: 4
Ingredients:
- 2 tablespoons chili paste
- 1 pound beef stew meat, cubed
- 1 cup beef stock
- 1 tablespoon ghee, melted
- ½ teaspoon turmeric powder
- ½ teaspoon garam masala
- ½ teaspoon allspice, ground
- ½ teaspoon cardamom, ground
- 1 tablespoon cinnamon powder
- ¼ teaspoon red pepper flakes
- A pinch of salt and black pepper
- 3 zucchinis, cubed

Directions:
1. Set your instant pot on Sauté mode, add the ghee, heat it up, add the meat, chili paste, turmeric, garam masala, allspice, cardamom and cinnamon, stir and brown for 5 minutes.
2. Add the rest of the ingredients, toss. put the lid on and cook on High for 25 minutes.
3. Release the pressure naturally for 10 minutes, divide the mix between plates and serve.
Nutrition: calories 276, fat 14, fiber 3, carbs 15.7, protein 20

Masala Cinnamon Beef
Preparation time: 10 minutes
Cooking time: 30 minutes
Servings: 4
Ingredients:
- 2 pounds beef stew meat, cubed
- 1 tablespoon canola oil
- ½ cup lime juice
- 1 yellow onion, chopped
- ¼ cup beef stock
- 1 tablespoon cumin, ground
- ½ teaspoon garam masala
- 2 teaspoons sweet paprika
- 1 and ½ teaspoons cinnamon powder
- 1 tablespoon coriander, chopped

Directions:
1. Set your instant pot on Sauté mode, heat it up, add the meat, onion, cumin, garam masala, paprika and cinnamon, stir and brown for 5 minutes.
2. Add the rest of the ingredients, toss, put the lid on and cook on High for 25 minutes.
3. Release the pressure naturally for 10 minutes, divide the mix between plates and serve.
Nutrition: calories 287, fat 16, fiber 4, carbs 15.6, protein 20

Beef and Cumin Beets
Preparation time: 10 minutes
Cooking time: 40 minutes
Servings: 4

Ingredients:
- 2 pounds beef roast, cubed
- 1 cup beef stock
- 1 beet, peeled and cubed
- 1 yellow onion, chopped
- 3 garlic cloves, chopped
- Salt and black pepper to the taste
- ½ teaspoon turmeric powder
- ½ teaspoon cumin, ground
- ½ teaspoon allspice, ground
- 1 cup tomato puree
- 1 tablespoon coriander, chopped

Directions:
1. In your instant pot, mix the beef with the stock, the beet and the other ingredients, toss, put the lid on and cook on High for 40 minutes.
2. Release the pressure naturally for 10 minutes, divide the mix into bowls and serve.
Nutrition: calories 284, fat 11.8, fiber 3, carbs 22.6, protein 17

Yogurt Lamb Curry
Preparation time: 10 minutes
Cooking time: 30 minutes
Servings: 6
Ingredients:
- 2 pounds lamb meat, cubed
- 4 cloves
- 2 bay leaves
- 2 tablespoons vegetable oil
- 2 yellow onions, chopped
- 1 teaspoon cardamom, ground
- 1 tablespoon ginger, grated
- 1 teaspoon cinnamon powder
- 1 tablespoon garlic, minced
- ½ teaspoon turmeric powder
- 2 teaspoons garam masala
- 2 teaspoons coriander, ground
- ½ cup tomato puree
- ½ cup yogurt
- 2 cups water

Directions:
1. Set your instant pot on Sauté mode, add the oil, heat it up, add the meat, cloves, bay leaves, onions, garlic, ginger, cardamom and the cinnamon, stir and brown for 5 minutes.
2. Add the rest of the ingredients, toss, put the lid on and cook on High for 25 minutes.
3. Release the pressure naturally for 10 minutes, divide the mix into bowls and serve.
Nutrition: calories 323, fat 17, fiber 1, carbs 7, protein 33

Cocoa Lamb

Preparation time: 10 minutes
Cooking time: 35 minutes
Servings: 4
Ingredients:

- 1 pound lamb meat, cubed
- 1 teaspoon cumin, ground
- 1 teaspoon sweet paprika
- ½ teaspoon turmeric powder
- 1 tablespoon cocoa powder
- ½ teaspoon garam masala
- 2 tablespoons canola oil
- A pinch of salt and black pepper
- 3 garlic cloves, minced
- 1 cup beef stock
- 1 tablespoon coriander, chopped

Directions:

1. Set your instant pot on Sauté mode, add the oil, heat it up, add the meat, cumin, paprika, turmeric, cocoa and garam masala, stir and brown for 5 minutes.
2. Add the rest of the ingredients, put the lid on and cook on High for 30 minutes.
3. Release the pressure naturally for 10 minutes, divide the lamb mix into bowls and serve.

Nutrition: calories 343, fat 12, fiber 3, carbs 16.7, protein 10

Coconut Lamb with Carrots

Preparation time: 10 minutes
Cooking time: 30 minutes
Servings: 4
Ingredients:

- 2 pounds lamb meat, cubed
- 2 carrots, sliced
- 2 tablespoons vegetable oil
- ½ cup coconut cream
- 1 cup heavy cream
- 3 tablespoons curry powder
- ½ teaspoon garam masala
- ½ teaspoon turmeric powder
- 1 red onion, chopped
- A pinch of salt and black pepper
- 1 tablespoon cilantro, chopped

Directions:

1. Set your instant pot on Sauté mode, add the oil, heat it up, add the meat, curry powder, garam masala, turmeric and the onion, stir and brown for 5 minutes.
2. Add the rest of the ingredients, put the lid on and cook on High for 25 minutes.
3. Release the pressure naturally for 10 minutes, divide the mix into bowls and serve.

Nutrition: calories 333, fat 14.7, fiber 2, carbs 22.6, protein 12

Creamy Lamb with Green Beans

Preparation time: 10 minutes
Cooking time: 35 minutes
Servings: 4

Ingredients:

- 1 pound lamb meat, cubed
- 2 tablespoons ghee, melted
- 1 cup green beans, trimmed and halved
- ½ cup coconut, shredded
- A pinch of salt and black pepper
- 1 yellow onion, chopped
- ½ cup heavy cream
- 1 teaspoon cumin, ground
- ½ teaspoon turmeric powder
- ½ teaspoon garam masala
- 2 garlic cloves, minced
- 2 tablespoons parsley, chopped

Directions:

1. Set your instant pot on Sauté mode, add the ghee, heat it up, add the meat, coconut, the onion, and the garlic, stir and brown for 5 minutes.
2. Add the rest of the ingredients, put the lid on and cook on High for 30 minutes.
3. Release the pressure naturally for 10 minutes, divide the mix between plates and serve.

Nutrition: calories 435, fat 12, fiber 5, carbs 16.7, protein 10

Masala Lamb with Corn

Preparation time: 10 minutes
Cooking time: 30 minutes
Servings: 4
Ingredients:

- 2 pounds lamb shoulder, cubed
- 2 tablespoons ghee, melted
- 1 cup corn
- ½ cup beef stock
- 1 yellow onion, chopped
- Salt and black pepper to the taste
- 2 garlic cloves, minced
- 1 teaspoon cumin powder
- 1 teaspoon ginger powder
- ½ teaspoon turmeric powder
- ½ teaspoon garam masala
- ½ teaspoon allspice, ground
- 1 teaspoon cinnamon powder

Directions:

1. Set the instant pot on Sauté mode, add the ghee, heat it up, add the meat, onion, garlic, cumin, ginger and turmeric, stir and brown for 5 minutes.
2. Add the rest of the ingredients, toss, put the lid on and cook on High for 25 minutes.
3. Release the pressure naturally for 10 minutes, divide mix into bowls and serve.

Nutrition: calories 291, fat 9, fiber 2, carbs 13.6, protein 12

Spiced Lamb & Brussels Sprouts

Preparation time: 10 minutes
Cooking time: 30 minutes
Servings: 4
Ingredients:

- 1 pound lamb shoulder, cubed
- 1 cup Brussels sprouts, trimmed and halved
- 1 yellow onion, chopped
- 2 tomatoes, cubed
- 2 garlic cloves, minced
- 2 tablespoons tomato paste
- 1 tablespoon vegetable oil
- ½ cup beef stock
- 1 teaspoon garam masala
- ½ teaspoon turmeric powder
- ½ teaspoon cinnamon powder
- ½ teaspoon allspice, ground
- A pinch of salt and black pepper
- A handful parsley, chopped

Directions:

1. Set your instant pot on Sauté mode, add the oil, heat it up, add the meat, onion, garlic, garam masala, turmeric, cinnamon and the allspice, stir and brown for 5 minutes.
2. Add the rest of the ingredients except the parsley, put the lid on and cook on High for 25 minutes
3. Release the pressure naturally for 10 minutes, divide everything between plates, sprinkle the parsley on top and serve.

Nutrition: calories 254, fat 12, fiber 3, carbs 8.6, protein 15.6

Beef with Fenugreek Quinoa

Preparation time: 10 minutes
Cooking time: 30 minutes
Servings: 4
Ingredients:

- 1 cup quinoa
- 1 pound beef stew meat, cubed
- 1 yellow onions, chopped
- 2 cups beef stock
- 1 tablespoon chili powder
- ½ teaspoon smoked paprika
- ½ teaspoon turmeric powder
- ½ teaspoon allspice, ground
- ½ teaspoon dried fenugreek powder
- 1 tablespoon coriander, chopped
- A pinch of salt and black pepper

Directions:

1. In your instant pot, combine the meat with the quinoa and the rest of the ingredients, toss, put the lid on and cook on High for 30 minutes.
2. Release the pressure naturally for 10 minutes, divide the mix between plates and serve.

Nutrition: calories 342, fat 10, fiber 11.5, carbs 16.7, protein 11

Chutney Lamb Chops

Preparation time: 10 minutes
Cooking time: 30 minutes
Servings: 4
Ingredients:

- 4 lamb chops
- ¼ cup green chutney
- Juice of 1 lime
- 2 teaspoons chili powder
- 2 tablespoons ginger and garlic paste
- 2 tablespoons vegetable oil
- 1 teaspoon turmeric powder
- 1 teaspoon garam masala
- ½ cup beef stock

Directions:

1. Set the instant pot on Sauté mode, add the oil, heat it up, add the lamb chops, chili powder, ginger paste, turmeric and garam masala, stir and brown for 5 minutes.
2. Add the remaining ingredients, toss, put the lid on and cook on High for 25 minutes.
3. Release the pressure naturally for 10 minutes, divide the mix between plates and serve.

Nutrition: calories 343, fat 15, fiber 4, carbs 23.6, protein 10

Minty Masala Lamb

Preparation time: 10 minutes
Cooking time: 35 minutes
Servings: 4
Ingredients:

- 4 lamb chops
- 2 tablespoons ghee, melted
- 1 tablespoon mint, chopped
- ½ cup beef stock
- 1 teaspoon garam masala
- ½ teaspoon allspice, ground
- ½ teaspoon coriander, ground
- ½ teaspoon dried mango powder
- 3 garlic cloves, minced
- 1 red onion, chopped
- A pinch of salt and black pepper
- ½ bunch cilantro, chopped

Directions:

1. Set your instant pot on Sauté mode, add the ghee, heat it up, add the lamb chops, garam masala, allspice, coriander, mango powder, garlic and the onion and brown for 5 minutes.
2. Add the rest of the ingredients, put the lid on and cook on High for 30 minutes.
3. Release the pressure naturally for 10 minutes, divide the mix between plates and serve.

Nutrition: calories 332, fat 12.5, fiber 4, carbs 5.66, protein 9

Cinnamon Lamb and Cucumber

Preparation time: 10 minutes
Cooking time: 30 minutes
Servings: 4
Ingredients:
- 2 pounds lamb shoulder, cubed
- 1 cucumber, sliced
- 1 yellow onion, chopped
- 3 garlic cloves, minced
- 2 tablespoons ghee, melted
- ½ teaspoon garam masala
- ½ teaspoon turmeric powder
- ½ teaspoon dry fenugreek leaves
- 10 curry leaves, chopped
- ½ teaspoon cinnamon powder
- A pinch of salt and black pepper
- 1 cup beef stock
- 2 tablespoons coriander, chopped

Directions:
1. Set your instant pot on Sauté mode, add the ghee, heat it up, add the meat, onion, garlic, garam masala, turmeric and fenugreek leaves, stir and brown for 5 minutes.
2. Add the rest of the ingredients, put the lid on and cook on High for 25 minutes.
3. Release the pressure naturally for 10 minutes, divide the mix between plates and serve.

Nutrition: calories 274, fat 13.9, fiber 5, carbs 15.6, protein 12

Coriander Lamb with Beets

Preparation time: 10 minutes
Cooking time: 30 minutes
Servings: 4
Ingredients:
- 1 pound lamb shoulder, cubed
- 2 tablespoons ghee, melted
- 2 beets, peeled and cubed
- A pinch of salt and black pepper
- 1 teaspoon turmeric powder
- 1 teaspoon cinnamon powder
- 1 tablespoon ginger, grated
- 2 garlic cloves, minced
- ½ cup beef stock
- 1 teaspoon coriander, chopped

Directions:
1. Set your instant pot on Sauté mode, add the ghee, heat it up, add the meat, turmeric, cinnamon, ginger and the garlic and brown for 5 minutes.
2. Add the rest of the ingredients, put the lid on and cook on High for 25 minutes.
3. Release the pressure naturally for 10 minutes, divide everything between plates and serve.

Nutrition: calories 332, fat 11.9, fiber 3, carbs 22.6, protein 10

Mustard Pork Chops

Preparation time: 10 minutes
Cooking time: 25 minutes
Servings: 4

Ingredients:
- 4 pork chops
- 1 tablespoon canola oil
- 1 tablespoon cumin, ground
- 1 tablespoon brown sugar
- 2 green chilies, minced
- 1 teaspoon cloves, ground
- 1 teaspoon coriander seeds
- ½ teaspoon curry powder
- ½ teaspoon cardamom powder
- ½ teaspoon onion powder
- ½ teaspoon black peppercorns
- ½ teaspoon mustard seeds
- ¼ teaspoon garlic powder
- Salt and black pepper to the taste
- ½ cup beef stock

Directions:
1. Set your instant pot on Sauté mode, add the oil, heat it up, add pork chops and brown them for 5 minutes.
2. Add the rest of the ingredients, put the lid on and cook on High for 20 minutes.
3. Release the pressure naturally for 10 minutes, divide everything between plates and serve.

Nutrition: calories 320, fat 11, fiber 3, carbs 22.6, protein 15

Pork Chops with Spinach

Preparation time: 10 minutes
Cooking time: 25 minutes
Servings: 4
Ingredients:
- 4 pork chops
- 2 tablespoons ghee, melted
- 2 garlic cloves, minced
- 2 tablespoons lime juice
- ½ teaspoon sweet paprika
- ½ teaspoon chili powder
- ½ teaspoon turmeric powder
- 1 teaspoon allspice, ground
- 1 cup baby spinach
- 1 yellow onion, chopped
- ½ cup beef stock
- Salt and black pepper to the taste
- 1 tablespoon parsley, chopped

Directions:
1. Set your instant pot on Sauté mode, add the ghee, heat it up, add the pork chops, garlic, onion, paprika, chili powder and turmeric, stir and brown for 5 minutes.
2. Add the rest of the ingredients except the parsley, put the lid on and cook on High for 20 minutes.
3. Release the pressure naturally for 10 minutes, divide everything between plates and serve with the parsley sprinkled on top.

Nutrition: calories 310, fat 14.5, fiber 3, carbs 22.8, protein 12

Pork and Tomato Chutney

Preparation time: 10 minutes
Cooking time: 30 minutes
Servings: 4
Ingredients:
- 1 pound pork stew meat, cubed
- 2 tablespoons sunflower oil
- ½ teaspoon coriander, ground
- ½ teaspoon garam masala
- 2 teaspoons chili powder
- 1 cup tomato chutney
- 2 garlic cloves, minced
- Salt and black pepper to the taste
- 1 bunch coriander, chopped

Directions:
1. Set the instant pot on Sauté mode, add the oil, heat it up, add the meat and brown for 5 minutes.
2. Add the coriander, garam masala and the other ingredients, toss, put the lid on and cook on High for 25 minutes.
3. Release the pressure naturally for 10 minutes, divide the mix into bowls and serve.
Nutrition: calories 248, fat 11, fiber 3, carbs 12.6, protein 15

Cocoa Pork Chops and Green Beans

Preparation time: 10 minutes
Cooking time: 25 minutes
Servings: 4
Ingredients:
- 4 pork chops
- 1 tablespoon cocoa powder
- 2 tablespoons coconut oil, melted
- 1 cup green beans, trimmed and halved
- 1 cup beef stock
- 2 teaspoons sweet paprika
- 1 teaspoon turmeric powder
- ½ teaspoon garam masala
- ½ teaspoon fenugreek leaves, dried
- 5 curry leaves, chopped
- A pinch of salt and black pepper

Directions:
1. Set the instant pot on Sauté mode, add the oil, heat it up, add the pork chops and the cocoa powder, toss and brown for 5 minutes.
2. Add the rest of the ingredients, toss, put the lid on and cook on High for 20 minutes.
3. Release the pressure naturally for 10 minutes, divide everything between plates and serve.
Nutrition: calories 333, fat 11.9, fiber 3, carbs 6.7, protein 14

Pork with Cinnamon Carrots Mix

Preparation time: 10 minutes
Cooking time: 25 minutes
Servings: 4
Ingredients:
- 4 pork chops
- 2 tablespoons canola oil
- 2 carrots, sliced
- 1 tablespoon cinnamon powder
- ½ teaspoon turmeric powder
- ½ teaspoon garam masala
- A pinch of salt and black pepper
- 2 garlic cloves, minced
- 1 yellow onion, chopped
- 1 cup beef stock
- ¼ cup tomato sauce
- 1 tablespoon parsley, chopped

Directions:
1. Set your instant pot on Sauté mode, add the oil, heat it up, add the pork chops, cinnamon, turmeric, garam masala, onion and the garlic and brown for 5 minutes
2. Add the rest of the ingredients, put the lid on and cook on High for 20 minutes.
3. Release the pressure naturally for 10 minutes, divide the mix between plates and serve.
Nutrition: calories 327, fat 14, fiber 4, carbs 13.6, protein 16

Onion Pork Chops

Preparation time: 10 minutes
Cooking time: 25 minutes
Servings: 4
Ingredients:
- 4 pork chops
- 2 tablespoons ghee, melted
- 2 cups red onions, chopped
- 1 tablespoon ginger, grated
- 6 garlic cloves, minced
- 2 tablespoons coriander, ground
- 1 teaspoon chili powder
- ½ teaspoon meat masala
- 15 ounces tomato sauce
- 2 tablespoons honey
- Salt and black pepper to the taste

Directions:
1. Set your instant pot on Sauté mode, add the ghee, heat it up, add the pork chops, onions, ginger, garlic and the meat masala, toss and brown for 5 minutes.
2. Add the rest of the ingredients except the sesame seeds, put the lid on and cook on High for 20 minutes.
3. Release the pressure naturally for 10 minutes, divide mix between plates and serve.
Nutrition: calories 436, fat 12, fiber 2, carbs 22.7, protein 15

Cashew Pork with Broccoli

Preparation time: 10 minutes
Cooking time: 30 minutes
Servings: 4
Ingredients:

- 2 pounds pork loin, cubed
- 1 cup beef stock
- 2 cups broccoli florets
- 1 yellow onion, chopped
- 2 tablespoons ghee, melted
- ¼ teaspoon red pepper, crushed
- ½ cup green onions, chopped
- 1 tablespoon sugar
- 1 tablespoon ginger, grated
- 4 garlic cloves, minced
- 2 tablespoons soy sauce
- ½ cup cashews, chopped

Directions:
1. Set the instant pot on Sauté mode, add the ghee, heat it up, add the meat, the onion, red pepper, green onions, ginger and garlic and brown for 5 minutes.
2. Add the rest of the ingredients, put the lid on and cook on High for 25 minutes.
3. Release the pressure naturally for 10 minutes, divide the mix between plates and serve.
Nutrition: calories 473, fat 12, fiber 4, carbs 15.7, protein 17

Masala Pork Chops and Cauliflower

Preparation time: 10 minutes
Cooking time: 25 minutes
Servings: 4
Ingredients:

- 1 cup beef stock
- 1 tablespoon peppercorns, crushed
- 1 cup cauliflower florets
- 1 teaspoon turmeric powder
- 4 pork chops
- 4 garlic cloves, minced
- 1 yellow onion, chopped
- 2 tablespoons canola oil
- ½ teaspoon garam masala
- A pinch of salt and black pepper

Directions:
1. Set your instant pot on sauté mode, add the oil, heat it up, add the garlic, onion, the meat and the garam masala, stir and brown for 5 minutes.
2. Add the rest of the ingredients, put the lid on and cook on High for 20 minutes.
3. Release the pressure naturally for 10 minutes, divide the mix between plates and serve.
Nutrition: calories 244, fat 12, fiber 2, carbs 15.5, protein 16

Onion Pork with Almonds

Preparation time: 10 minutes
Cooking time: 25 minutes
Servings: 4
Ingredients:

- 4 pork chops
- 2 tablespoons almonds, chopped
- ½ cup beef stock
- 3 garlic cloves, minced
- 1 yellow onion, chopped
- 1 bunch coriander, chopped
- ½ teaspoon turmeric powder
- ½ teaspoon meat masala
- A pinch of salt and black pepper

Directions:
1. In your instant pot, combine the pork chops with the almonds, the stock and the other ingredients, toss, put the lid on and cook on High for 25 minutes.
2. Release the pressure naturally for 10 minutes, divide the mix between plates and serve.
Nutrition: calories 354, fat 14, fiber 3, carbs 17.6, protein 17

Nutmeg Pork Chops

Preparation time: 10 minutes
Cooking time: 30 minutes
Servings: 6
Ingredients:

- 6 pork chops
- 2 tablespoons ghee, melted
- 1 teaspoon mustard seeds
- 1 teaspoon coriander seeds
- ½ teaspoon cumin, ground
- ½ teaspoon nutmeg, ground
- ½ teaspoon turmeric powder
- A pinch of salt and black pepper
- 1 tablespoon smoked paprika
- 2 tablespoons Dijon mustard
- 1 cup beef stock
- 1 tablespoon cilantro, chopped

Directions:
1. Set your instant pot on Sauté mode, add the ghee, heat it up, add the pork chops, mustard seeds, coriander seeds, cumin and turmeric, toss and brown for 5 minutes
2. Add the remaining ingredients, toss, put the lid on and cook on High for 25 minutes.
3. Release the pressure naturally for 10 minutes, divide the mix between plates and serve.
Nutrition: calories 263, fat 14, fiber 6.6, carbs 22.6, protein 20

Coriander Pork with Potatoes

Preparation time: 10 minutes
Cooking time: 25 minutes
Servings: 4
Ingredients:

- 4 pork chops
- 2 tablespoons vegetable oil
- ½ pound gold potatoes, peeled and cubed
- 1 teaspoon sweet paprika
- ½ teaspoon chili powder
- ½ teaspoon nutmeg, ground
- ½ teaspoon chana masala
- ½ teaspoon coriander, ground
- A pinch of salt and black pepper
- 1 teaspoon onion powder
- 1 yellow onion, chopped
- 1 cup beef stock
- ½ teaspoon cayenne pepper

Directions:
1.   Set the instant pot on Sauté mode, add the oil, heat it up, add the meat, paprika, chili powder and the masala, stir and brown for 5 minutes.
2.   Add the potatoes, nutmeg and the other ingredients, toss, put the lid on and cook on High for 20 minutes.
3.   Release the pressure naturally for 10 minutes, divide the pork chops and potatoes mix between plates and serve.
Nutrition: calories 283, fat 13, fiber 4, carbs 15.6, protein 16

Pandi Onion Stew

Preparation time: 10 minutes
Cooking time: 35 minutes
Servings: 4
Ingredients:

- 3 teaspoons cumin seeds
- 2 teaspoons red pepper, crushed
- 1 teaspoon mustard seeds
- 1 teaspoon fenugreek seeds
- ½ teaspoon haldi powder
- 2 cloves
- 2 tablespoons vegetable oil
- 2 curry leaves, chopped
- 1 tablespoon coriander seeds
- 2 pounds pork stew meat, cubed
- 1 teaspoon chili powder
- 4 garlic cloves, minced
- 2 yellow onions, chopped
- 1 tablespoon ginger, grated
- 2 green chilies, chopped
- 1 tablespoon coriander leaves, chopped
- 1 cup beef stock

Directions:
1.   Set your instant pot on Sauté mode, add the oil, heat it up, add cumin, red pepper, mustard seeds, fenugreek seeds, cloves, curry leaves, haldi powder, coriander and the pork stew meat, toss and brown for 5 minutes.
2.   Add the rest of the ingredients, put the lid on and cook on High for 30 minutes.
3.   Release the pressure naturally for 10 minutes, divide the mix between plates and serve.

Nutrition: calories 353, fat 14, fiber 6.7, carbs 16.6, protein 18

Pork Indaad

Preparation time: 10 minutes
Cooking time: 30 minutes
Servings: 4
Ingredients:

- 1 pound pork loin, cubed
- 1 tablespoon vegetable oil
- 1 teaspoon white vinegar
- 4 cloves
- 1 tablespoon mint, chopped
- 2 teaspoons sugar
- Salt and black pepper to the taste
- 1 cinnamon stick
- ½ tablespoon cumin, ground
- 2 red chilies, chopped
- 10 peppercorns
- 1 teaspoon turmeric powder
- 1 tablespoon tamarind paste
- 2 yellow onions, chopped
- ½ cup beef stock

Directions:
1.   Set your instant pot on Sauté mode, add the oil, heat it up, add the meat, cloves, cumin, chilies, peppercorns and the turmeric and brown for 5 minutes.
2.   Add the rest of the ingredients, put the lid on and cook on High for 25 minutes.
3.   Release the pressure naturally for 10 minutes, divide everything into bowls and serve.
Nutrition: calories 364, fat 14, fiber 3, carbs 17.6, protein 17

Paprika Pork Mix

Preparation time: 10 minutes
Cooking time: 35 minutes
Servings: 4
Ingredients:

- 2 tablespoons canola oil
- 1 pound pork stew meat, cubed
- 3 red chilies, chopped
- 1 teaspoon smoked paprika
- ½ teaspoon chili powder
- ½ teaspoon cumin, ground
- ½ teaspoon garam masala
- A pinch of salt and black pepper
- 1 red bell pepper, roughly chopped
- 1 green bell pepper, roughly chopped
- 3 garlic cloves, minced
- 1 cup beef stock
- 1 tablespoon coriander, chopped

Directions:
1.   Set your instant pot on Sauté mode, add the oil, heat it up, add the meat, chilies, paprika, chili powder and garam masala, stir and brown for 5 minutes.
2.   Add all the other ingredients except the parsley, put the lid on and cook on High for 30 minutes.
3.   Release the pressure naturally for 10 minutes, divide the mix into bowls and serve.
Nutrition: calories 373, fat 13, fiber 2, carbs 156, protein 15

Orange Fenugreek Pork Mix

Preparation time: 10 minutes
Cooking time: 35 minutes
Servings: 4
Ingredients:
- 1 pound pork shoulder, cubed
- 3 garlic cloves, minced
- ½ cup orange juice
- ½ teaspoon garam masala
- ½ teaspoon turmeric powder
- ½ teaspoon cumin, ground
- ½ teaspoon fenugreek leaves, dried
- 1 bay leaf
- A pinch of salt and black pepper
- 1 tablespoon ginger, grated
- ½ cup beef stock

Directions:
1. In your instant pot, combine the pork with the garlic, orange juice and all the other ingredients, put the lid on and cook on High for 35 minutes.
2. Release the pressure naturally for 10 minutes, divide the mix between plates and serve.
Nutrition: calories 314, fat 14, fiber 6.2, carbs 13.6, protein 16

Carrots Pork Mix

Preparation time: 10 minutes
Cooking time: 35 minutes
Servings: 4
Ingredients:
- 1 cup basmati rice
- 2 pounds pork stew meat, cubed
- 3 cups water
- 2 carrots, sliced
- 1 yellow onion, chopped
- ½ teaspoon turmeric powder
- 1 tablespoon ginger paste
- 4 bay leaves
- 2 tablespoons sweet paprika
- 2 tablespoons ghee, melted
- Salt and black pepper to the taste
- ¼ cup mint, chopped

Directions:
1. Set the instant pot on Sauté mode, add the ghee, heat it up, add the meat, the onion, turmeric, ginger and the paprika, toss, and brown for 5 minutes.
2. Add the rest of the ingredients, put the lid on and cook on High for 30 minutes.
3. Release the pressure naturally for 10 minutes, divide the mix between plates and serve.
Nutrition: calories 264, fat 14, fiber 5.6, carbs 15.8, protein 12

Cocoa Pork and Tomatoes

Preparation time: 10 minutes
Cooking time: 30 minutes
Servings: 4
Ingredients:
- 4 pork chops
- 1 cup cherry tomatoes, halved
- A pinch of salt and black pepper
- 2 tablespoons cocoa powder
- 1 teaspoon chili powder
- ½ teaspoon cumin, ground
- ½ teaspoon allspice, ground

- ½ teaspoon coriander, ground
- ½ teaspoon garam masala
- 1 cup beef stock
- 1 tablespoon parsley, chopped

Directions:
1. In your instant pot, combine the pork chops with the tomatoes and with the rest of the ingredients, put the lid on and cook on High for 30 minutes.
2. Release the pressure naturally for 10 minutes, divide the mix between plates and serve.
Nutrition: calories 300, fat 9, fiber 2, carbs 15.6, protein 12

Pork Chili Cheese Soup

Preparation time: 10 minutes
Cooking time: 35 minutes
Servings: 4
Ingredients:
- 2 pounds pork shoulder, cubed
- 4 gold potatoes, peeled and cut into wedges
- 10 dried chilies, minced
- A pinch of salt and black pepper
- 3 tomatoes, cubed
- 10 green onions, chopped
- 2 tablespoons ghee, melted
- ½ teaspoon turmeric powder
- 2 cups beef stock

Directions:
1. Set your instant pot on Sauté mode, add the ghee, heat it up, add the meat, chilies and the turmeric and brown for 5 minutes.
2. Add the rest of the ingredients, put the lid on and cook on High for 30 minutes.
3. Release the pressure naturally for 10 minutes, divide everything into bowls and serve.
Nutrition: calories 334, fat 11, fiber 3, carbs 11.7, protein 15

Ginger Pork with Bamboo

Preparation time: 10 minutes
Cooking time: 30 minutes
Servings: 4
Ingredients:
- 2 pounds pork shoulder, cubed
- 2 tablespoons vegetable oil
- 1 cup bamboo shoots
- Salt and black pepper to the taste
- 2 yellow onions, chopped
- 1 tablespoon ginger, grated
- 1 tablespoon chili powder
- A bunch coriander, chopped
- 1 cup beef stock

Directions:
1. Set your instant pot on Sauté mode, add the oil, heat it up, add the pork, onions, ginger and chili powder, stir and brown for 5 minutes.
2. Add the rest of the ingredients, put the lid on and cook on High for 25 minutes.
3. Release the pressure naturally for 10 minutes, divide the mix into bowls and serve.
Nutrition: calories 273, fat 14, fiber 2, carbs 14.5, protein 15

Pork Kaleez Ankiti

Preparation time: 10 minutes
Cooking time: 30 minutes
Servings: 4
Ingredients:
- 2 pounds pork stew meat, cubed
- 1 teaspoon garam masala
- 2 yellow onions, roughly chopped
- 6 garlic cloves, minced
- 1-inch ginger, grated
- 2 green chilies, chopped
- Juice of 1 lime
- 10 bay leaves
- 1 teaspoon vinegar
- 1 cup beef stock
- Salt and black pepper to the taste

Directions:
1. In your instant pot, mix the pork with the garam masala, onion, garlic ad the other ingredients, put the lid on and cook on High for 30 minutes.
2. Release the pressure naturally for 10 minutes, divide everything into bowls and serve.

Nutrition: calories 292, fat 12, fiber 3, carbs 7, protein 16

Pork Potatoes Mix

Preparation time: 10 minutes
Cooking time: 30 minutes
Servings: 4
Ingredients:
- 2 pounds pork stew meat, cubed
- 2 tablespoons vegetable oil
- 2 yellow onions, chopped
- 3 red chilies, chopped
- 2 green chilies, chopped
- 1 teaspoon garlic, minced
- 2 potatoes, peeled and cut into wedges
- Salt and black pepper to the taste
- ½ teaspoon ginger, grated
- ¼ teaspoon turmeric powder
- 2 tomatoes, cubed
- 1 tablespoon white vinegar

Directions:
1. Set the instant pot on Sauté mode, add the oil, heat it up, add the onions, all the chilies, garlic, ginger and the meat and brown for 5 minutes.
2. Add the rest of the ingredients, put the lid on and cook on High for 25 minutes.
3. Release the pressure naturally for 10 minutes, divide everything between plates and serve.

Nutrition: calories 357, fat 14, fiber 6.5, carbs 14.7, protein 17

Coconut Meatballs

Preparation time: 10 minutes
Cooking time: 30 minutes
Servings: 4
Ingredients:
- ½ cup coconut cream

- 1 tablespoon ghee, melted
- 2 tablespoons coconut flour
- 2 eggs, whisked
- 2 pounds pork meat, ground
- ½ teaspoon sweet paprika
- ½ teaspoon turmeric powder
- 1 yellow onion, minced
- Salt and black pepper to the taste
- 2 pounds pork meat, ground
- ½ cup beef stock
- 1 tablespoon parsley, chopped

Directions:
1. In a bowl, mix the pork with the flour and the other ingredients except the oil, stock and the cream, stir well and shape medium meatballs out of this mix.
2. Set the instant pot on Sauté mode, add the ghee, heat it up, add the meatballs and brown for 5 minutes.
3. Add the cream and the stock, toss, put the lid on and cook on High for 25 minutes.
4. Release the pressure naturally for 10 minutes, divide the mix between plates and serve.

Nutrition: calories 374, fat 12, fiber 4, carbs 15.7, protein 16

Garlic Pork

Preparation time: 10 minutes
Cooking time: 30 minutes
Servings: 4
Ingredients:
- 2 pounds pork stew meat, cubed
- 2 tablespoons vegetable oil
- 2 garlic cloves, minced
- 1 cup beef stock
- 2 tablespoons brown sugar
- 2 tablespoons tamarind paste
- 3 shallots, chopped
- 1 teaspoon fish sauce
- 1 tablespoon soy sauce
- 1 red chili, chopped
- ½ teaspoon turmeric powder
- 1 tablespoon cilantro, chopped

Directions:
1. Set the instant pot on Sauté mode, add the oil, heat it up, add the meat, garlic, shallots, red chili and the turmeric, stir and brown for 5 minutes.
2. Add the rest of the ingredients, toss, put the lid on and cook on High for 25 minutes.
3. Release the pressure naturally for 10 minutes, divide the mix between plates and serve.

Nutrition: calories 269, fat 12, fiber 3, carbs 5, protein 16

Paprika BBQ Ribs

Preparation time: 10 minutes
Cooking time: 30 minutes
Servings: 4
Ingredients:

- 2 tablespoons fennel seeds
- 2 tablespoon cumin seeds
- 1 teaspoon black peppercorns
- 2 tablespoons sunflower oil
- 1 tablespoon smoked paprika
- Salt and black pepper to the taste
- 2 tablespoons tomato Sauce
- 1 tablespoon hot chili sauce
- 1 teaspoon chili powder
- 2 tablespoons honey
- 1 tablespoon soy sauce
- 2 racks of ribs
- 1 cup beef stock

Directions:
1. Set the instant pot on Sauté mode, add the oil, heat it up, add the fennel, cumin, black peppercorns, paprika and chili sauce, stir and cook for 2 minutes.
2. Add the rack of ribs, toss and brown for 3 minutes more.
3. Add the rest of the ingredients, put the lid on and cook on High for 25 minutes.
4. Release the pressure naturally for 10 minutes, divide everything between plates and serve.
Nutrition: calories 293, fat 14, fiber 4, carbs 12.6, protein 18

Spicy Pork and Artichokes

Preparation time: 10 minutes
Cooking time: 30 minutes
Servings: 4
Ingredients:

- 1 red onion, chopped
- 1 tablespoon ghee, melted
- ½ teaspoon turmeric powder
- ½ teaspoon garam masala
- ½ teaspoon chili powder
- ½ teaspoon hot paprika
- 2 artichokes, trimmed and quartered
- 2 tablespoons lemon juice
- A pinch of salt and black pepper
- 2 pounds pork stew meat, cubed
- 1 cup beef stock

Directions:
1. Set the instant pot on Sauté mode, add the ghee, heat it up, add the onion, turmeric, garam masala, chili powder, paprika and the meat and brown for 5 minutes.
2. Add the rest of the ingredients, put the lid on and cook on High for 25 minutes.
3. Release the pressure naturally for 10 minutes, divide the mix between plates and serve.
Nutrition: calories 263, fat 12, fiber 3, carbs 12.4, protein 13

Beef and Creamy Turmeric Potatoes

Preparation time: 10 minutes
Cooking time: 30 minutes
Servings: 4
Ingredients:

- 1 pound beef stew meat, cubed
- 2 gold potatoes, peeled and cubed
- 1 cup beef stock
- ½ cup heavy cream
- 1 yellow onion, chopped
- 2 tablespoons ghee, melted
- 1 teaspoon chili powder
- ½ teaspoon turmeric powder
- ½ teaspoon cumin, ground
- ½ teaspoon coriander seeds
- 1 tablespoon parsley, chopped
- A pinch of salt and black pepper

Directions:
1. Set your instant pot on Sauté mode, add the ghee, heat it up, add the meat, the onion, chili powder, turmeric, cumin and coriander, toss and brown for 5 minutes.
2. Add the rest of the ingredients except the parsley, put the lid on and cook on High for 25 minutes.
3. Release the pressure naturally for 10 minutes, divide the mix between plates, sprinkle the parsley on top and serve.
Nutrition: calories 263, fat 14, fiber 3, carbs 11.57, protein 19

Indian Instant Pot Vegetable Recipes

Coriander Artichokes
Preparation time: 10 minutes
Cooking time: 20 minutes
Servings: 4
Ingredients:
- 5 garlic cloves, minced
- 1 tablespoon ginger, grated
- 2 tablespoons vegetable oil
- 1 yellow onion, chopped
- 3 tomatoes, cubed
- 1 teaspoon cumin seeds, ground
- 1 teaspoon coriander, ground
- ½ teaspoon garam masala
- ½ teaspoon turmeric powder
- 3 tablespoons yogurt
- 1 tablespoon lime juice
- 4 artichokes, trimmed and halved
- 1 cup water

Directions:
1. Set the instant pot on Sauté mode, add the oil, heat it up, add the garlic, ginger and the onion and sauté for 5 minutes.
2. Add the rest of the ingredients, put the lid on and cook on High for 15 minutes.
3. Release the pressure naturally for 10 minutes, divide everything between plates and serve.
Nutrition: calories 188, fat 7.7, fiber 10.9, carbs 27.5, protein 7.6

Turmeric Artichokes
Preparation time: 5 minutes
Cooking time: 15 minutes
Servings: 4
Ingredients:
- 10 ounces canned artichoke hearts, drained and halved
- A pinch of salt and black pepper
- ¼ cup chicken stock
- 2 tablespoons ghee, melted
- 1 teaspoon turmeric powder
- ½ teaspoon cumin, ground
- ½ teaspoon fenugreek leaves, dried

Directions:
4. Set the instant pot on Sauté mode, add the ghee, heat it up, add the artichokes and sauté for 2 minutes.
5. Add the rest of the ingredients, put the lid on and cook on High for 13 minutes.
6. Release the pressure fast for 5 minutes, divide the artichokes mix between plates and serve.
Nutrition: calories 94, fat 6.7, fiber 4.1, carbs 8.3, protein 2.6

Creamy Artichokes and Coconut
Preparation time: 5 minutes
Cooking time: 20 minutes
Servings: 4
Ingredients:
- 4 artichokes, trimmed and halved
- 1 cup coconut cream
- ½ teaspoon turmeric powder
- ½ teaspoon cumin, ground
- ½ teaspoon sweet paprika
- 1 teaspoon onion powder

Directions:
3. In your instant pot, combine the artichokes with the cream, turmeric and the other ingredients, put the lid on and cook on High for 20 minutes.
4. Release the pressure fast for 5 minutes, divide the mix between plates and serve.
Nutrition: calories 219, fat 14.7, fiber 10.3, carbs 21.3, protein 6.8

Nutmeg Asparagus
Preparation time: 5 minutes
Cooking time: 12 minutes
Servings: 4
Ingredients:
- 1 bunch asparagus, trimmed and halved
- ½ teaspoon garam masala
- ½ teaspoon nutmeg, ground
- ½ teaspoon turmeric powder
- 1 bay leaf
- 1 cup chicken stock
- 1 tablespoon chili powder
- 2 garlic cloves, chopped

Directions:
6. In your instant pot, combine the asparagus with the rest of the ingredients, put the lid on and cook on High for 12 minutes.
7. Release the pressure fast for 5 minutes, divide the mix between plates and serve.
Nutrition: calories 17, fat 0.6, fiber 1.2, carbs 2.8, protein 1

Masala Artichokes and Rice
Preparation time: 5 minutes
Cooking time: 20 minutes
Servings: 4
Ingredients:
- 1 cup canned artichoke hearts, drained and quartered
- 2 tablespoons ghee, melted
- 1 yellow onion, chopped
- ½ cup basmati rice
- 1 cup chicken stock
- ½ teaspoon turmeric powder
- ½ teaspoon garam masala
- A pinch of salt and black pepper
- 1 tablespoon smoked paprika
- 1 tablespoon cilantro, chopped

Directions:
3. Set the instant pot on Sauté mode, add the ghee, heat it up, add the onion, turmeric, garam masala and the paprika, stir and sauté for 5 minutes.
4. Add the rest of the ingredients, toss, put the lid on and cook on High for 15 minutes.
5. Release the pressure fast for 5 minutes, divide the mix between plates and serve.
Nutrition: calories 217, fat 7.1, fiber 8.2, carbs 35.2, protein 6.4

Garam Masala Asparagus

Preparation time: 5 minutes
Cooking time: 10 minutes
Servings: 4
Ingredients:

- 1 tablespoon vegetable oil
- ½ teaspoon pepper flakes, crushed
- 1 bunch asparagus, trimmed and halved
- 2 tablespoons almonds, chopped
- ½ tablespoon chili powder
- ½ teaspoon garam masala
- ½ teaspoon coriander, ground
- A pinch of salt and black pepper
- 1 cup chicken stock

Directions:
1. Set the instant pot on Sauté mode, add the oil, heat it up, add the pepper flakes, almonds, chili powder, garam masala and the coriander, stir and cook for 2 minutes.
2. Add the remaining ingredients, toss, put the lid on and cook on High for 8 minutes.
3. Release the pressure fast for 5 minutes, divide the asparagus between plates and serve.
Nutrition: calories 56, fat 5.2, fiber 1, carbs 2, protein 1.3

Ginger Asparagus

Preparation time: 5 minutes
Cooking time: 10 minutes
Servings: 4
Ingredients:

- 1 bunch asparagus, trimmed and halved
- 2 tablespoons vegetable oil
- 1 tablespoon ginger, grated
- ½ teaspoon chili powder
- 1 teaspoon coriander, ground
- A pinch of salt and black pepper
- 1 cup chicken stock

Directions:
1. In your instant pot, mix the asparagus with the oil, ginger and the rest of the ingredients, put the lid on and cook on High for 10 minutes.
2. Release the pressure fast for 5 minutes, divide everything between plates and serve.
Nutrition: calories 72, fat 7.1, fiber 0.6, carbs 2, protein 0.7

Cinnamon Green Beans

Preparation time: 10 minutes
Cooking time: 15 minutes
Servings: 4
Ingredients:

- 1 pound green beans, trimmed and halved
- 1 tablespoon vegetable oil
- A pinch of salt and black pepper
- 1 teaspoon sweet paprika
- 1 teaspoon turmeric powder
- 1 teaspoon cinnamon powder
- ½ teaspoon garam masala

- 1 cup chicken stock

Directions:
4. In your instant pot, combine the green beans with the oil, salt, pepper and the other ingredients, toss, put the lid on and cook on High for 15 minutes.
5. Release the pressure naturally for 10 minutes, divide the mix between plates and serve.
Nutrition: calories 71, fat 3.8, fiber 4.2, carbs 9, protein 2.4

Fenugreek Beans & Orange Sauce

Preparation time: 5 minutes
Cooking time: 15 minutes
Servings: 4
Ingredients:

- 1 pound green beans, trimmed and halved
- 2 teaspoons orange zest, grated
- 1 cup orange juice
- 1 teaspoon chili powder
- ½ teaspoon garam masala
- ½ teaspoon turmeric powder
- ½ teaspoon dried fenugreek leaves
- A pinch of salt and black pepper

Directions:
1. In your instant pot, combine the green beans with the orange zest and the other ingredients, put the lid on and cook on High for 15 minutes.
2. Release the pressure fast for 5 minutes, divide the mix between plates and serve.
Nutrition: calories 69, fat 0.4, fiber 4.5, carbs 15.6, protein 2.7

Coconut Chili Beets

Preparation time: 10 minutes
Cooking time: 20 minutes
Servings: 4
Ingredients:

- 1 cup chicken stock
- 4 beets, peeled and roughly cubed
- 2 shallots, chopped
- ½ cup coconut cream
- 1 teaspoon chili powder
- 1 teaspoon turmeric powder
- A pinch of salt and black pepper
- 1 tablespoon dill, chopped

Directions:
3. In your instant pot, combine the beets with the stock, shallots and the rest of the ingredients, put the lid on and cook on High for 20 minutes.
4. Release the pressure naturally for 10 minutes, divide everything between plates and serve.
Nutrition: calories 125, fat 7.7, fiber 3.1, carbs 13.8, protein 3

Creamy Brussels Sprouts

Preparation time: 10 minutes
Cooking time: 20 minutes
Servings: 4
Ingredients:

- 1 pound Brussels sprouts, trimmed and halved
- 1 cup heavy cream
- 4 garlic cloves, minced
- 1 tablespoon chili powder
- 1 tablespoon sweet paprika
- 5 curry leaves, chopped
- ½ teaspoon garam masala
- A pinch of salt and black pepper
- 1 tablespoon cilantro, chopped

Directions:

1. In your instant pot, mix the Brussels sprouts with the cream, garlic and the rest of the ingredients, put the lid on and cook on High for 20 minutes.
2. Release the pressure naturally for 10 minutes, divide the mix between plates and serve.

Nutrition: calories 176, fat 12.4, fiber 6.5, carbs 15.6, protein 5.5

Walnuts Allspice Bell Peppers

Preparation time: 10 minutes
Cooking time: 20 minutes
Servings: 4
Ingredients:

- 1 pound red bell peppers, cut into wedges
- ½ cup coconut cream
- ½ teaspoon dry mango powder
- ½ teaspoon allspice, ground
- ½ teaspoon turmeric powder
- 1 bay leaf
- 1 tablespoon walnuts, chopped

Directions:

1. In your instant pot, mix the bell peppers with the cream, mango powder and the rest of the ingredients, put the lid on and cook on High for 20 minutes.
2. Release the pressure naturally for 10 minutes, divide the mix into bowls and serve.

Nutrition: calories 93, fat 8.4, fiber 1.3, carbs 4.6, protein 1.5

Cilantro Minty Peppers

Preparation time: 10 minutes
Cooking time: 20 minutes
Servings: 4
Ingredients:

- 1 red bell peppers, cut into wedges
- 1 tablespoon chili powder
- ½ teaspoon garam masala
- ½ teaspoon nutmeg, ground
- ¼ cup veggie stock
- 3 garlic cloves, minced
- 1 tablespoon mint, chopped
- 1 tablespoon cilantro, chopped

Directions:

1. In your instant pot, combine the bell peppers with the chili powder, garam masala and the rest of the ingredients, put the lid on and cook on High for 20 minutes.
2. Release the pressure naturally for 10 minutes, divide the mix between plates and serve.

Nutrition: calories 22, fat 0.6, fiber 1.3, carbs 4.4, protein 0.8

Bell Peppers and Masala Potatoes

Preparation time: 10 minutes
Cooking time: 20 minutes
Servings: 4
Ingredients:

- 1 pound mixed bell peppers, cut into wedges
- 2 sweet potatoes, peeled and cut into wedges
- ½ cup chicken stock
- 1 teaspoon chili powder
- ½ teaspoon garam masala
- ½ teaspoon coriander, ground
- ½ teaspoon cumin, ground
- 1 tablespoon olive oil

Directions:

1. In your instant pot, combine the bell peppers with the potatoes, the stock and the rest of the ingredients, put the lid on and cook on High for 20 minutes.
2. Release the pressure naturally for 10 minutes, divide the mix between plates and serve.

Nutrition: calories 132, fat 4, fiber 3.7, carbs 23.7, protein 1.7

Fenugreek Peppers Mix

Preparation time: 5 minutes
Cooking time: 20 minutes
Servings: 4
Ingredients:

- 1 pound mixed bell peppers, cut into wedges
- 1 teaspoon coriander, ground
- ½ teaspoon sweet paprika
- ½ teaspoon chana masala
- ½ teaspoon fenugreek leaves, dried
- 1 teaspoon mustard seeds
- 1 teaspoon chili powder
- ½ teaspoon cumin, ground
- Salt and black pepper to the taste
- 1 cup heavy cream

Directions:

1. In your instant pot, combine the bell peppers with the coriander, mustard seeds and the rest of the ingredients, put the lid on and cook on High for 20 minutes.
2. Release the pressure naturally for 5 minutes, divide the mix between plates and serve.

Nutrition: calories 122, fat 11.7, fiber 1, carbs 4.3, protein 1.4

Beets with Yogurt

Preparation time: 10 minutes
Cooking time: 25 minutes
Servings: 4
Ingredients:
- 1 pound beets, peeled and cubed
- Juice of 1 lime
- 1 cup yogurt
- ½ teaspoon turmeric powder
- ½ teaspoon dried mango powder
- ½ teaspoon fenugreek leaves, dried
- A pinch of salt and black pepper

Directions:
1. In your instant pot, combine the beets with the lime juice and the rest of the ingredients, put the lid on and cook on High for 25 minutes.
2. Release the pressure naturally for 10 minutes, divide the mix between plates and serve.

Nutrition: calories 99, fat 1, fiber 2.5, carbs 17, protein 5.6

Dill Potatoes

Preparation time: 10 minutes
Cooking time: 20 minutes
Servings: 4
Ingredients:
- 2 pounds sweet potatoes, peeled and cut into wedges
- 1 cup yogurt
- 1 tablespoon dill, chopped
- 1 teaspoon turmeric powder
- ½ teaspoon garam masala
- ½ teaspoon chili powder
- A pinch of salt and black pepper

Directions:
1. In your instant pot, mix the potatoes with the yogurt, dill and the rest of the ingredients, toss, put the lid on and cook on High for 20 minutes.
2. Release the pressure naturally for 10 minutes, divide the mix between plates and serve.

Nutrition: calories 316, fat 1.3, fiber 9.7, carbs 68.5, protein 7.2

Creamy Potatoes

Preparation time: 10 minutes
Cooking time: 30 minutes
Servings: 4
Ingredients:
- 1 pound gold potatoes, peeled and roughly cubed
- 1 tablespoon coconut oil, melted
- 2 shallots, chopped
- ½ teaspoon cumin, ground
- ½ teaspoon coriander, ground
- ½ teaspoon chili powder
- ½ teaspoon turmeric powder
- 1 cup coconut cream
- A pinch of salt and black pepper
- 2 tablespoons cilantro, chopped

Directions:
1. Set the instant pot on Sauté mode, add the oil, heat it up, add the shallots, stir and sauté for 5 minutes.
2. Add the potatoes and the rest of the ingredients, put the lid on and cook on High for 25 minutes.
3. Release the pressure naturally for 10 minutes, divide the mix between plates and serve.

Nutrition: calories 250, fat 17.9, fiber 4.6, carbs 22.8, protein 3.1

Gold Potato Masala

Preparation time: 10 minutes
Cooking time: 25 minutes
Servings: 4
Ingredients:
- 1 pound gold potatoes, peeled and roughly cubed
- 1 teaspoon garam masala
- ½ teaspoon turmeric powder
- ½ teaspoon coriander, ground
- 1 tablespoon ghee, melted
- 4 garlic cloves, minced
- 1 cup beef stock
- A pinch of salt and black pepper
- 1 tablespoon coriander, chopped

Directions:
1. Set your instant pot on Sauté mode, add the ghee, heat it up, add the garlic, garam masala, turmeric and the ground coriander, stir and cook for 5 minutes.
2. Add the potatoes and the rest of the ingredients, put the lid on and cook on High for 20 minutes more.
3. Release the pressure naturally for 10 minutes, divide the mix between plates and serve.

Nutrition: calories 113, fat 3.4, fiber 3.2, carbs 19.4, protein 2.4

Fenugreek Zucchini

Preparation time: 10 minutes
Cooking time: 20 minutes
Servings: 4
Ingredients:
- 2 tablespoons ghee, melted
- 1 teaspoon turmeric powder
- ½ teaspoon garam masala
- ½ teaspoon dried fenugreek leaves
- 4 zucchinis, sliced
- 1 red onion, chopped
- 1 cup chicken stock
- A pinch of salt and black pepper
- 1 tablespoon dill, chopped

Directions:
1. Set the instant pot on Sauté mode, add the ghee, heat it up, add the onion, stir and sauté for 5 minutes.
2. Add the zucchinis and the rest of the ingredients, put the lid on and cook on High for 15 minutes.
3. Release the pressure naturally for 10 minutes, divide the mix between plates and serve.

Nutrition: calories 106, fat 7, fiber 3.1, carbs 10.4, protein 3.2

Turmeric Zucchinis

Preparation time: 10 minutes
Cooking time: 15 minutes
Servings: 4
Ingredients:
- 4 zucchinis, sliced
- ½ teaspoon turmeric powder
- 1 teaspoon chili powder
- ¼ cup chicken stock
- 1 tablespoon chili powder
- ½ teaspoon cayenne pepper
- ½ teaspoon garam masala

Directions:
4. In your instant pot, mix the zucchinis with the turmeric, the stock and the rest of the ingredients, put the lid on and cook on High for 15 minutes.
5. Release the pressure naturally for 10 minutes, divide the mix between plates and serve.
Nutrition: calories 42, fat 0.9, fiber 3.1, carbs 8.3, protein 2.8

Sweet Potato and Zucchini

Preparation time: 10 minutes
Cooking time: 20 minutes
Servings: 4
Ingredients:
- 2 sweet potatoes, peeled and roughly cubed
- 2 zucchinis, roughly cubed
- 2 tablespoons ghee, melted
- 1 teaspoon garam masala
- ½ teaspoon turmeric powder
- ½ teaspoon cumin, ground
- ½ teaspoon nutmeg, ground
- A pinch of salt and black pepper
- ½ cup chicken stock
- 1 tablespoon parsley, chopped

Directions:
1. In your instant pot, mix the potatoes with the zucchinis, the melted ghee and the rest of the ingredients, put the lid on and cook on High for 20 minutes.
2. Release the pressure naturally for 10 minutes, divide the mix between plates and serve.
Nutrition: calories 165, fat 7, fiber 4.4, carbs 24.8, protein 2.6

Spinach Turmeric Mix

Preparation time: 5 minutes
Cooking time: 12 minutes
Servings: 4
Ingredients:
- 1 pound spinach leaves
- 1 tablespoon coconut oil, melted
- 2 shallots, chopped
- ½ teaspoon turmeric powder
- ½ teaspoon garam masala
- ½ teaspoon coriander, ground
- 1 tablespoon tomato sauce
- A pinch of salt and black pepper
- ¼ cup chicken stock
- 1 tablespoon parsley, chopped

Directions:
1. Set the instant pot on Sauté mode, add the oil, heat it up, add the shallots, stir and sauté for 2 minutes.

2. Add the spinach, turmeric and the other ingredients, toss, put the lid on and cook on High for 10 minutes.
3. Release the pressure naturally for 5 minutes, divide the mix between plates and serve.
Nutrition: calories 62, fat 3.9, fiber 2.7, carbs 5.5, protein 3.5

Nutmeg Okra

Preparation time: 10 minutes
Cooking time: 20 minutes
Servings: 4
Ingredients:
- 1 pound okra, trimmed
- ½ cup chicken stock
- 1 tablespoon ghee, melted
- 1 red onion, chopped
- ½ teaspoon nutmeg, ground
- ½ teaspoon garam masala
- ½ teaspoon chili powder
- ½ teaspoon coriander, ground
- A pinch of salt and black pepper
- 1 tablespoon sweet paprika
- 2 tablespoon cilantro, chopped

Directions:
1. Set the instant pot on Sauté mode, add the ghee, heat it up, add the onion and sauté for 4 minutes.
2. Add the okra, the nutmeg and the rest of the ingredients, put the lid on and cook on High for 16 minutes.
3. Release the pressure naturally for 10 minutes, divide the mix between plates and serve.
Nutrition: calories 93, fat 3.9, fiber 5.1, carbs 12.4, protein 2.9

Coriander Broccoli and Onions

Preparation time: 10 minutes
Cooking time: 20 minutes
Servings: 4
Ingredients:
- 1 pound broccoli florets
- 1 tablespoon sunflower oil
- 1 yellow onion, chopped
- 2 spring onions, chopped
- 1 teaspoon turmeric powder
- ½ teaspoon chili powder
- ½ teaspoon garam masala
- 2 garlic cloves, minced
- 1 cup chicken stock
- A pinch of salt and black pepper
- 1 tablespoon coriander, chopped

Directions:
1. Set the instant pot on Sauté mode, add the oil, heat it up, add the onion and spring onions, stir and sauté for 5 minutes.
2. Add the broccoli, turmeric and the rest of the ingredients except the dill, put the lid on and cook on High for 15 minutes.
3. Release the pressure naturally for 10 minutes, divide the mix between plates and serve.
Nutrition: calories 91, fat 4.2, fiber 4, carbs 11.9, protein 4

Creamy Masala Cauliflower

Preparation time: 10 minutes
Cooking time: 20 minutes
Servings: 4
Ingredients:

- 1 pound cauliflower florets
- 1 teaspoon nutmeg, ground
- ½ teaspoon garam masala
- 1 cup coconut cream
- 1 tablespoon chili powder
- A pinch of salt and black pepper
- 1 tablespoon cilantro, chopped

Directions:
1. In your instant pot, combine the cauliflower with the nutmeg, garam masala and the other ingredients, toss, put the lid on and cook on High for 20 minutes.
2. Release the pressure naturally for 10 minutes, divide the mix between plates and serve.
Nutrition: calories 122, fat 2.5, fiber4. 2, carbs 5, protein 3.56

Cumin Spinach and Potato

Preparation time: 10 minutes
Cooking time: 20 minutes
Servings: 4
Ingredients:

- 1 pound gold potatoes, peeled and roughly cubed
- 1 cup baby spinach
- ½ cup chicken stock
- 1 teaspoon turmeric powder
- 1 teaspoon cumin, ground
- ½ teaspoon hot paprika
- 1 teaspoon chili powder
- A pinch of salt and black pepper
- 1 tablespoon dill, chopped

Directions:
1. In your instant pot, mix the potatoes with the spinach, the stock and the rest of the ingredients, put the lid on and cook on High for 20 minutes.
2. Release the pressure naturally for 10 minutes, divide the mix between plates and serve.
Nutrition: calories 130, fat 7.2, fiber 2, carbs 4, protein 4.6

Cinnamon Potato

Preparation time: 10 minutes
Cooking time: 20 minutes
Servings: 4
Ingredients:

- 1 yellow onion, chopped
- 2 tablespoons vegetable oil
- 3 garlic cloves, minced
- 2 pounds gold potatoes, peeled and cubed
- 1 tablespoon cinnamon powder
- ½ teaspoon garam masala
- ½ teaspoon dried mango powder
- A pinch of salt and black pepper
- 1 cup chicken stock

- 1 tablespoon cilantro, chopped

Directions:
1. Set the instant pot on Sauté mode, add the oil, heat it up, add the onion, garlic, garam masala and mango powder, stir and sauté for 5 minutes.
2. Add the potatoes and the rest of the ingredients, put the lid on and cook on High for 15 minutes.
3. Release the pressure naturally for 10 minutes, divide the mix between plates and serve.
Nutrition: calories 210, fat 5.2, fiber 2, carbs 7.5, protein 4.7

Masala & Coconut Fennel Pot

Preparation time: 10 minutes
Cooking time: 20 minutes
Servings: 4
Ingredients:

- 2 fennel bulbs, trimmed and sliced
- 2 tablespoons ghee, melted
- ½ cup coconut, shredded
- 1 cup coconut cream
- A pinch of salt and black pepper
- 1 teaspoon garam masala
- ½ teaspoon turmeric powder
- 1 tablespoon dill, chopped

Directions:
1. Set the instant pot on Sauté mode, add the ghee, heat it up, add the fennel and the coconut and cook for 5 minutes.
2. Add the rest of the ingredients, put the lid on and cook on High for 15 minutes.
3. Release the pressure naturally for 10 minutes, divide the mix between plates and serve.
Nutrition: calories 114, fat 4.2, fiber 2, carbs 4.4, protein 4

Masala Curry Endives

Preparation time: 10 minutes
Cooking time: 15 minutes
Servings: 4
Ingredients:

- 4 endives, trimmed and halved
- 1 tablespoon garam masala
- 1 cup chicken stock
- 1 teaspoon chili powder
- 4 curry leaves, chopped
- A pinch of salt and black pepper
- ½ teaspoon nutmeg, ground

Directions:
1. In your instant pot, combine the endives with the garam masala, the stock and the rest of the ingredients, put the lid on and cook on High for 15 minutes.
2. Release the pressure naturally for 10 minutes, divide the mix between plates and serve.
Nutrition: calories 144, fat 3.2, fiber 1, carbs 5.3, protein 4

Lime Spinach and Okra

Preparation time: 5 minutes
Cooking time: 20 minutes
Servings: 4
Ingredients:
- 1 cup baby spinach
- 2 cups okra, trimmed
- 1 cup chicken stock
- 1 tablespoon sweet paprika
- 1 tablespoon lemon juice
- 1 tablespoon lime juice
- A pinch of salt and black pepper
- 1 teaspoon turmeric powder
- ½ teaspoon cumin, ground
- 2 tablespoons parsley, chopped

Directions:
1. In your instant pot, mix the okra with the spinach, the stock and the rest of the ingredients, put the lid on and cook on High for 20 minutes.
2. Release the pressure fast for 5 minutes, divide the mix between plates and serve.

Nutrition: calories 171, fat 3.1, fiber 4.1, carbs 8.4, protein 3.5

Creamy Potato and Apples Mix

Preparation time: 10 minutes
Cooking time: 20 minutes
Servings: 4
Ingredients:
- 2 sweet potatoes, peeled and cut into wedges
- 2 green apples, peeled, cored and cut into wedges
- 1 tablespoon chili powder
- 1 teaspoon coriander, ground
- 1 teaspoon mustard seeds
- 1 teaspoon cumin, ground
- 2 cups coconut cream
- A pinch of salt and black pepper
- 1 tablespoon cilantro, chopped

Directions:
1. In your instant pot, combine the potatoes with the apples, chili powder and the rest of the ingredients, toss, put the lid on and cook on High for 20 minutes.
2. Release the pressure naturally for 10 minutes, divide the mix between plates and serve.

Nutrition: calories 200, fat 7, fiber 3.2, carbs 11.4, protein 6.6

Eggplant Masala

Preparation time: 5 minutes
Cooking time: 20 minutes
Servings: 4
Ingredients:
- 1 pound eggplant, roughly cubed
- 1 yellow onion, chopped
- 2 garlic cloves, minced
- 1 tablespoon vegetable oil
- A pinch of salt and black pepper
- 1 tablespoon sweet paprika
- 1 teaspoon cumin, ground
- 1 teaspoon garam masala
- 2 black peppercorns, crushed
- 1 teaspoon mustard seeds
- 1 teaspoon turmeric powder
- 1 cup tomato sauce

Directions:
1. Set the instant pot on Sauté mode, add the oil, heat it up, add the onion, garlic, cumin, garam masala, peppercorns and the mustard seeds, stir and cook for 5 minutes.
2. Add the eggplant and the rest of the ingredients, put the lid on and cook on High for 15 minutes.
3. Release the pressure fast for 5 minutes, divide the mix between plates and serve.

Nutrition: calories 99, fat 4.4, fiber 6.5, carbs 14.9, protein 2.9

Spiced Eggplant Mix

Preparation time: 10 minutes
Cooking time: 12 minutes
Servings: 4
Ingredients:
- 1 pound eggplant, cubed
- 1 teaspoon cumin, ground
- 1 teaspoon dried fenugreek leaves
- 4 curry leaves, chopped
- 1 teaspoon turmeric powder
- 1 teaspoon dried mango powder
- 1 teaspoon nutmeg, ground
- 1 tablespoon canola oil
- 1 red onion, chopped
- 1 cup chicken stock
- 1 teaspoon chili powder
- A pinch of salt and black pepper

Directions:
1. Set the instant pot on Sauté mode, add the oil, heat it up, add the onion, cumin, fenugreek, curry leaves, turmeric, mango powder and the nutmeg, stir and cook for 2 minutes.
2. Add the eggplant and the rest of the ingredients, put the lid on and cook on High for 10 minutes.
3. Release the pressure naturally for 10 minutes, divide the mix between plates and serve.

Nutrition: calories 105, fat 3.5, fiber 3.2, carbs 8.3, protein 2.4

Coriander Zucchinis and Eggplants
Preparation time: 10 minutes
Cooking time: 20 minutes
Servings: 4
Ingredients:
- 1 pound eggplant, roughly cubed
- 2 zucchinis, sliced
- 2 tablespoons sweet paprika
- 1 teaspoon mustard seeds
- 2 black peppercorns, crushed
- 1 teaspoon turmeric powder
- 1 teaspoon coriander, ground
- A pinch of salt and black pepper
- ½ cup chicken stock
- ¼ cup lime juice
- 1 tablespoon lime zest, grated
- 1 tablespoon cilantro, chopped

Directions:
1. In your instant pot, mix the eggplants with the zucchinis and the rest of the ingredients except the cilantro, put the lid on and cook on High for 20 minutes.
2. Release the pressure naturally for 10 minutes, divide the mix between plates, sprinkle the cilantro on top and serve.
Nutrition: calories 128, fat 3.3, fiber 1.2, carbs 9.4, protein 2.5

Creamy Eggplants
Preparation time: 10 minutes
Cooking time: 15 minutes
Servings: 4
Ingredients:
- 2 eggplants, roughly cubed
- 1 cup coconut, shredded
- 1 cup coconut cream
- 2 tablespoons lime juice
- 1 bunch coriander, chopped
- ½ cup chicken stock
- 1 tablespoon ginger, grated

Directions:
1. In your instant pot, combine the eggplants with the coconut, the cream and the rest of the ingredients, put the lid on and cook on High for 15 minutes.
2. Release the pressure naturally for 10 minutes, divide the mix between plates and serve.
Nutrition: calories 126, fat 5.4, fiber 2, carbs 11.4, protein 2.6

Coconut Masala Tomatoes
Preparation time: 10 minutes
Cooking time: 15 minutes
Servings: 4
Ingredients:
- 1 pound cherry tomatoes, halved
- 2 garlic cloves, chopped
- 2 spring onions, chopped
- 1 tablespoon vegetable oil
- 1 teaspoon turmeric powder
- 1 teaspoon garam masala
- ½ cup coconut, shredded
- 1 red chili pepper, chopped
- ¾ cup veggie stock
- 1 tablespoon cilantro, chopped

Directions:
1. Set your instant pot on Sauté mode, add the oil, heat it up, add the garlic, spring onions, the chili and the coconut, stir and cook for 3 minutes.
2. Add the tomatoes and the rest of the ingredients, put the lid on and cook on High for 12 minutes.
3. Release the pressure naturally for 10 minutes, divide the mix between plates and serve.
Nutrition: calories 136, fat 3.4, fiber 2, carbs 9.4, protein 2.7

Zucchini and Chili Cauliflower
Preparation time: 10 minutes
Cooking time: 15 minutes
Servings: 4
Ingredients:
- cup cauliflower florets
- 1 zucchini, roughly cubed
- 1 red onion, chopped
- 1 cup chicken stock
- 1 tablespoon vegetable oil
- 1 teaspoon chili powder
- ½ teaspoon turmeric powder
- ½ teaspoon garam masala
- 1 teaspoon hot paprika
- A pinch of salt and black pepper
- ½ teaspoon coriander, ground

Directions:
1. Set your instant pot on Sauté mode, add the oil, heat it up, add the onion, chili powder, turmeric, garam masala and the paprika, stir and cook for 2 minutes.
2. Add the cauliflower and the rest of the ingredients, put the lid on and cook on High for 13 minutes.
3. Release the pressure naturally for 10 minutes, divide the mix into bowls and serve.
Nutrition: calories 61, fat 3.8, fiber 2.1, carbs 6.3, protein 1.7

Mango Turmeric Kale
Preparation time: 5 minutes
Cooking time: 15 minutes
Servings: 4
Ingredients:
- 3 garlic cloves, chopped
- 1 tablespoon coconut oil, melted
- 1 teaspoon turmeric powder
- ½ teaspoon cumin, ground
- ½ teaspoon dried mango powder
- 1 pound kale, trimmed
- 1 tablespoon lime zest, grated
- 1 tablespoon lime juice
- ½ cup chicken stock

Directions:
1. Set the instant pot on Sauté mode, add the oil, heat it up, add the garlic, turmeric, cumin and mango powder, stir and sauté for 2 minutes.
2. Add the rest of the ingredients, put the lid on and cook on High for 13 minutes.
3. Release the pressure fast for 5 minutes, divide the mix between plates and serve.
Nutrition: calories 109, fat 4.4, fiber 2, carbs 5.3, protein 1.2

Cocoa Zucchinis

Preparation time: 10 minutes
Cooking time: 20 minutes
Servings: 6
Ingredients:

- 1 pound zucchinis, sliced
- 1 pound red bell peppers, cut into strips
- 1 yellow onion, chopped
- 1 tablespoon vegetable oil
- 1 tablespoon cocoa powder
- ½ teaspoon turmeric powder
- ½ teaspoon garam masala
- ½ teaspoon chili powder
- 1 cup chicken stock
- 4 garlic cloves, chopped
- A pinch of salt and black pepper
- ¼ teaspoon red pepper flakes, crushed

Directions:

1. Set the instant pot on Sauté mode, add the oil, heat it up, add the onion, cocoa powder, turmeric, garam masala and chili powder, stir and cook for 5 minutes.
2. Add the rest of the ingredients, toss, put the lid on and cook on High for 15 minutes.
3. Release the pressure naturally for 10 minutes, divide the mix into bowls and serve.

Nutrition: calories 119, fat 4.2, fiber 2, carbs 6.4, protein 1.5

Orange Masala Zucchinis

Preparation time: 10 minutes
Cooking time: 20 minutes
Servings: 4
Ingredients:

- A pinch of salt and black pepper
- ½ teaspoon cayenne pepper
- 2 zucchinis, sliced
- 1 cup orange juice
- 1 red onion, chopped
- 1 tablespoon vegetable oil
- 1 teaspoon turmeric powder
- ½ teaspoon garam masala
- ½ teaspoon cumin, ground
- 1 teaspoon chili powder

Directions:

3. Set the instant pot on Sauté mode, add the oil, heat it up, add the onion, the turmeric, garam masala, cumin and chili powder and sauté for 5 minutes.
4. Add the rest of the ingredients, put the lid on and cook on High for 15 minutes.
5. Release the pressure naturally for 10 minutes, stir the mix, divide it between plates and serve.

Nutrition: calories 91, fat 4, fiber 2.2, carbs 13.3, protein 2.1

Cherry Tomatoes and Citric Rice

Preparation time: 10 minutes
Cooking time: 20 minutes
Servings: 4

Ingredients:

- 1 cup basmati rice
- 2 cups chicken stock
- 2 garlic cloves, minced
- 2 cups cherry tomatoes, halved
- 1 tablespoon orange juice
- 1 tablespoon orange zest, grated
- 2 tablespoon vegetable oil
- 1 yellow onion, chopped
- 1 teaspoon cumin, ground
- ½ teaspoon turmeric powder
- ½ teaspoon garam masala
- 2 tablespoons cilantro, chopped

Directions:

1. Set your instant pot on Sauté mode, add the oil, heat it up, add the onion, garlic and the tomatoes and cook for 5 minutes.
2. Add rest of the ingredients, put the lid on and cook on High for 15 minutes.
3. Release the pressure naturally for 10 minutes, divide the mix between plates and serve.

Nutrition: calories 200, fat 8.1, fiber 4, carbs 11.6, protein 3.7

Allspice Zucchinis

Preparation time: 5 minutes
Cooking time: 20 minutes
Servings: 4
Ingredients:

- 2 tablespoons ghee, melted
- 1 pound zucchinis, roughly cubed
- 1 yellow onion, chopped
- 2 garlic cloves, minced
- 1 teaspoon turmeric powder
- ½ teaspoon garam masala
- ½ teaspoon nutmeg, ground
- ½ teaspoon ginger, grated
- ½ teaspoon allspice, ground

Directions:

1. Set your instant pot on Sauté mode, add the ghee, heat it up, add onion and garlic, stir and sauté for 5 minutes.
2. Add the zucchinis and the rest of the ingredients, toss, put the lid on and cook on High for 15 minutes.
3. Release the pressure fast for 5 minutes, divide the mix between plates and serve.

Nutrition: calories 110, fat 4.7, fiber 2.3, carbs 7.8, protein 1.6

Ginger Zucchinis and Carrots

Preparation time: 5 minutes
Cooking time: 20 minutes
Servings: 4
Ingredients:
- 1 pound carrots, sliced
- 2 zucchinis, sliced
- 1 cup chicken stock
- ½ teaspoon dried mango powder
- 1 teaspoon chili powder
- 1 teaspoon sweet paprika
- ½ teaspoon ginger, grated
- 3 garlic cloves, minced
- 2 tablespoons ghee, melted
- 1 yellow onion, chopped
- 1 teaspoon cardamom, ground
- A pinch of salt and black pepper

Directions:
4. Set the instant pot on sauté mode, add the ghee, heat it up, add the onion, garlic, mango powder, chili powder and the paprika, and sauté for 5 minutes.
5. Add the remaining ingredients, put the lid on and cook on High for 15 minutes.
6. Release the pressure fast for 5 minutes, stir the mix, divide between plates and serve.
Nutrition: calories 100, fat 5.8, fiber 2.4, carbs 8.6, protein 1.8

Onion Potato and Carrots

Preparation time: 10 minutes
Cooking time: 20 minutes
Servings: 4
Ingredients:
- 2 spring onions, chopped
- 2 carrots, grated
- 1 pound gold potatoes, peeled and cubed
- A pinch of salt and black pepper
- 1 teaspoon chili powder
- ½ teaspoon garam masala
- 1 teaspoon cumin, ground
- ¼ cup coconut cream

Directions:
4. In your instant pot, combine the potatoes with the carrots and the other ingredients, toss, put the lid on and cook on High for 20 minutes.
5. Release the pressure naturally for 10 minutes, divide the mix between plates and serve.
Nutrition: calories 129, fat 3.8, fiber 4.6, carbs 23.1, protein 2.4

Turmeric Beets

Preparation time: 10 minutes
Cooking time: 20 minutes
Servings: 4
Ingredients:
- 2 tablespoons sunflower oil
- 1 teaspoon cardamom, crushed
- 1 pound beets, peeled and roughly cubed
- ½ teaspoon chili powder

- 1 cup chicken stock
- 1 teaspoon turmeric powder
- ½ teaspoon garam masala
- A pinch of salt and black pepper
- ½ cup currants, chopped

Directions:
4. Set your instant pot on Sauté mode, add the oil, heat it up, add the currants, cardamom, chili powder, turmeric powder and garam masala, stir and cook for 5 minutes.
5. Add the rest of the ingredients, stir, put the lid on and cook on High for 15 minutes.
6. Release the pressure naturally for 10 minutes, divide the mix between plates and serve.
Nutrition: calories 127, fat 7.5, fiber 3.3, carbs 14.3, protein 2.4

Minty Masala Tomatoes

Preparation time: 10 minutes
Cooking time: 20 minutes
Servings: 4
Ingredients:
- 1 tablespoon sunflower oil
- 1 pound cherry tomatoes, halved
- 2 shallots, chopped
- 1 tablespoon lime zest, grated
- 1 teaspoon lime juice
- 1 teaspoon garam masala
- 1 teaspoon cumin, ground
- 1 teaspoon coriander, ground
- A pinch of salt and black pepper
- 1 cup chicken stock
- 2 tablespoons mint leaves, chopped

Directions:
1. Set the instant pot on Sauté mode, add the shallots, garam masala, cumin and coriander, stir and sauté for 5 minutes.
2. Add the tomatoes and the rest of the ingredients, toss, put the lid on and cook on High for 15 minutes.
3. Release the pressure naturally for 10 minutes, divide between plates and serve.
Nutrition: calories 110, fat 3.8, fiber 3.3, carbs 7.7, protein 1.8

Onion Spinach and Broccoli

Preparation time: 10 minutes
Cooking time: 20 minutes
Servings: 4
Ingredients:

- 2 garlic cloves, minced
- 2 tablespoons vegetable oil
- 1 cup baby spinach
- 1 yellow onion, chopped
- 1 cup broccoli florets
- 1 teaspoon red pepper flakes, crushed
- 1 teaspoon cumin, ground
- 1 teaspoon garam masala
- 1 teaspoon coriander, ground
- A pinch of salt and black pepper
- 2 tablespoons lemon juice

Directions:
4. Set your instant pot on sauté mode, add the oil, heat it up, add the onion, garlic, pepper flakes, cumin and garam masala, stir and sauté for 5 minutes.
5. Add the rest of the ingredients, toss, put the lid on and cook on High for 15 minutes.
6. Release the pressure naturally for 10 minutes, divide the mix between plates and serve.
Nutrition: calories 88, fat 7.2, fiber 1.6, carbs 5.5, protein 1.5

Fenugreek Beets and Onions

Preparation time: 10 minutes
Cooking time: 20 minutes
Servings: 4
Ingredients:

- 1 tablespoon sunflower oil
- 2 beets, peeled and roughly cubed
- 2 yellow onions, chopped
- 1 cup chicken stock
- 1 teaspoon garam masala
- 1 teaspoon chili powder
- ½ teaspoon fenugreek seeds
- 1 teaspoon mustard seeds
- 2 garlic cloves, minced

- 1 and ½ tablespoons thyme, chopped
- A pinch of salt and black pepper

Directions:
1. Set your instant pot on Sauté mode, add the oil, heat up, add the onions, garlic, garam masala, chili powder, fenugreek seeds and mustard seeds, stir and cook for 5 minutes.
2. Add the rest of the ingredients, toss, put the lid on and cook on High for 15 minutes.
3. Release the pressure naturally for 10 minutes, divide the mix between plates and serve.
Nutrition: calories 105, fat 4.6, fiber 3.4, carbs 7.6, protein 2.4

Cumin Potato and Cream

Preparation time: 10 minutes
Cooking time: 20 minutes
Servings: 4
Ingredients:

- 1 cup heavy cream
- ½ cup yellow onion, chopped
- 2 tablespoons ghee, melted
- 4 potatoes, peeled and cut into wedges
- A pinch of salt and black pepper
- 1 teaspoon cumin, ground
- 4 curry leaves, chopped
- 1 teaspoon garam masala
- 1 teaspoon turmeric powder
- 1 tablespoon basil, chopped

Directions:
4. Set your instant pot on Sauté mode, add the ghee, heat it up, add the onion, cumin, curry leaves, garam masala and the turmeric, stir and sauté for 5 minutes.
5. Add the potatoes, and the rest of the ingredients, toss, put the lid on and cook on High for 15 minutes.
6. Release the pressure naturally for 10 minutes, divide the mix between plates and serve.
Nutrition: calories 323, fat 18.1, fiber 6.3, carbs 37.4, protein 4.8

Indian Instant Pot Dessert Recipes

Milky Pistachios Halwa
Preparation time: 10 minutes
Cooking time: 15 minutes
Servings: 8
Ingredients:
- 2 pounds carrots, grated
- 2 cinnamon sticks
- 1 cup sugar
- 1 cup ghee, melted
- 1 cup condensed milk
- 1 tablespoon almonds, chopped
- 1 tablespoon pistachios, chopped

Directions:
4. In your instant pot, combine the carrots with the cinnamon and the other ingredients, toss, put the lid on and cook on High for 15 minutes.
5. Release the pressure naturally for 10 minutes, divide the mix into bowls and serve.
Nutrition: calories 496, fat 29.4, fiber 3.2, carbs 57.7, protein 4.3

Cardamom Mango Shrikhand
Preparation time: 10 minutes
Cooking time: 20 minutes
Servings: 4
Ingredients:
- 1 cup yogurt
- 1 teaspoon cardamom powder
- 1 mango, peeled and chopped
- ½ teaspoon saffron powder
- ¾ cup sugar
- ½ cup mango puree
- Juice of 1 lemon
- 1 tablespoon mint
- 2 teaspoons chaat masala

Directions:
1. In your instant pot, combine the yogurt with the cardamom, the mango and the other ingredients, toss, put the lid on and cook on High for 20 minutes.
2. Release the pressure naturally for 10 minutes, blend the mix using an immersion blender, divide into bowls and serve.
Nutrition: calories 252, fat 1.3, fiber 2, carbs 58.3, protein 4.6

Milky Payasam
Preparation time: 10 minutes
Cooking time: 30 minutes
Servings: 4
Ingredients:
- 1 cup white rice
- 2 cups milk
- 1 teaspoon cardamom powder
- 3 tablespoons sugar
- 1 tablespoon ghee, melted
- 1 tablespoon cashews, chopped
- 1 tablespoon raisins, chopped

Directions:
1. In your instant pot, combine the rice with the milk, cardamom and the other ingredients, toss, put the lid on and cook on Low for 30 minutes.
2. Release the pressure naturally for 10 minutes, divide the mix into bowls and serve.
Nutrition: calories 312, fat 7, fiber 0.9, carbs 54.8, protein 7.8

Pistachio Phirni
Preparation time: 10 minutes
Cooking time: 20 minutes
Servings: 4
Ingredients:
- 2 cups milk
- 1 tablespoon pistachios, chopped
- 1 tablespoon gram rice flour
- 1 teaspoon cardamom powder
- 1 tablespoon sugar

Directions:
1. In your instant pot, combine the milk with the pistachios and the other ingredients, toss, put the lid on and cook on High for 20 minutes.
2. Release the pressure naturally for 10 minutes, divide the mix into bowls, cool down completely and serve.
Nutrition: calories 88, fat 3, fiber 0.3, carbs 11.6, protein 4.4

Indian Almond Kulfi
Preparation time: 10 minutes
Cooking time: 20 minutes
Servings: 4
Ingredients:
- 1 quart milk
- ½ teaspoon saffron powder
- ½ cup sugar
- 12 almonds, blanched and chopped
- 4 green cardamoms
- 2 tablespoons pistachios, chopped

Directions:
1. In your instant pot, combine the milk with the saffron and the other ingredients, toss, put the lid on and cook on High for 20 minutes.
2. Release the pressure naturally for 10 minutes, divide the mix into moulds and freeze before serving.
Nutrition: calories 250, fat 7.8, fiber 0.9, carbs 39, protein 9.3

Vermicelli Kheer
Preparation time: 10 minutes
Cooking time: 25 minutes
Servings: 4
Ingredients:
- ½ cup red rice vermicelli
- 1 tablespoon butter
- 2 and ½ cups milk
- 1 tablespoon almonds, chopped
- ¼ teaspoon cardamom powder
- ½ teaspoon saffron powder
- 3 tablespoons sugar

Directions:
1. In your instant pot, combine the rice vermicelli with the butter and the other ingredients, toss, put the lid on and cook on High for 25 minutes.
2. Release the pressure naturally for 10 minutes, divide everything into bowls and serve.
Nutrition: calories 156, fat 6.3, fiber 0.5, carbs 20.7, protein 5.2

Cardamom Kiwi and Oranges

Preparation time: 5 minutes
Cooking time: 10 minutes
Servings: 4
Ingredients:
- 1 quart milk
- 1 teaspoon saffron powder
- 1 teaspoon cardamom powder
- 1 tablespoon almonds, chopped
- ½ cup kiwi, peeled and cubed
- ½ cup grapes, halved
- ½ cup apples, peeled, cored and cubed
- ½ cup orange, peeled and cut into segments
- 2 tablespoons sugar

Directions:
1. In your instant pot, combine the milk with the saffron and the other ingredients, toss, put the lid on and cook on High for 10 minutes.
2. Release the pressure fast for 5 minutes, divide the mix into bowls and serve cold.

Nutrition: calories 201, fat 6, fiber 2.3, carbs 30.5, protein 9

Wheat Cashew Kheer

Preparation time: 10 minutes
Cooking time: 20 minutes
Servings: 4
Ingredients:
- 1 cup broken wheat
- 1 tablespoon ghee, melted
- 1 tablespoon raisins
- 2 cardamom pods
- 1 tablespoon sugar
- ½ cup gram cashew nut
- ½ quart milk

Directions:
1. In your instant pot, combine the wheat with the ghee and the other ingredients, stir, put the lid on and cook on High for 20 minutes.
2. Release the pressure naturally for 10 minutes, divide the mix into bowls and serve.

Nutrition: calories 227, fat 15.2, fiber 0.6, carbs 16.3, protein 7.6

Rice Ada Pradhaman

Preparation time: 10 minutes
Cooking time: 20 minutes
Servings: 4
Ingredients:
- 1 cup rice flat pasta
- 1 cup palm jaggery
- 2 cups coconut milk
- 1 teaspoon cardamom powder
- 1 tablespoon coconut, shredded
- 1 tablespoon cashews, chopped
- 1 tablespoon raisins
- 1 tablespoon ghee, melted

Directions:
1. In your instant pot, combine the rice with the jaggery and the other ingredients, toss, put the lid on and cook on High for 20 minutes.
2. Release the pressure naturally for 10 minutes, divide the mix into bowls and serve.

Nutrition: calories 400, fat 34.7, fiber 4.3, carbs 22.9, protein 4.5

Pistachio Parfait

Preparation time: 10 minutes
Cooking time: 20 minutes
Servings: 4
Ingredients:
- 1 tablespoon pistachios, chopped
- 2 eggs, whisked
- 1 tablespoon sugar
- 2 cups double cream
- 1 cup raspberries
- 1 tablespoon lemon juice

Directions:
1. In your instant pot, combine the pistachios with the eggs, sugar and the other ingredients, toss, put the lid on and cook on High for 20 minutes.
2. Release the pressure naturally for 10 minutes, divide the mix into bowls and serve cold.

Nutrition: calories 272, fat 25.1, fiber 2.1, carbs 8.8, protein 4.6

Saffron Zucchini Pudding

Preparation time: 10 minutes
Cooking time: 20 minutes
Servings: 4
Ingredients:
- 3 cups zucchinis, grated
- 1 cup caster sugar
- 2 eggs, whisked
- 2 tablespoons ghee, melted
- 1 cup milk
- ½ teaspoon saffron powder

Directions:
1. In your instant pot, combine the zucchinis with the sugar and the other ingredients, toss, put the lid on and cook on High for 20 minutes.
2. Release the pressure naturally for 10 minutes, divide the pudding into bowls and serve cold.

Nutrition: calories 252, fat 5.5, fiber 2, carb 11.6, protein 3.6

Turmeric Pear Coconut Bowls

Preparation time: 10 minutes
Cooking time: 20 minutes
Servings: 4
Ingredients:
- 2 tablespoons almonds, chopped
- 1 tablespoon raisins
- 1 teaspoon turmeric powder
- 1 teaspoon vanilla extract
- 2 cups pears, cored and cubed
- 1 cup coconut cream

Directions:
1. In your instant pot, combine the almonds with the pears and the other ingredients, toss, put the lid on and cook on High for 20 minutes.
2. Release the pressure naturally for 10 minutes, divide the dessert into bowls and serve.

Nutrition: calories 220, fat 11.4, fiber 4.2, carbs 9.4, protein 2.4

Banana and Rice Pudding

Preparation time: 10 minutes
Cooking time: 30 minutes
Servings: 4
Ingredients:

- 2 egg, whisked
- 3 tablespoons sugar
- 2 tablespoons ghee, melted
- 1 cup white rice
- 2 and ½ cups milk
- 2 bananas, peeled and mashed
- 1 teaspoon saffron powder

Directions:
1.   In your instant pot, mix the rice with the milk, the eggs and the other ingredients, whisk, put the lid on and cook on High for 30 minutes.
2.   Release the pressure naturally for 10 minutes, divide the pudding into bowls and serve.
Nutrition: calories 262, fat 11.7, fiber 5.2, carbs 14.5, protein 2.8

Cinnamon Apples

Preparation time: 10 minutes
Cooking time: 15 minutes
Servings: 4
Ingredients:

- 2 teaspoons turmeric powder
- ½ teaspoon cinnamon powder
- 4 apples, cored and cut into chunks
- 2 tablespoons sugar
- ½ cup milk

Directions:
1.   In your instant pot, mix the apples with the cinnamon, turmeric and the rest of the ingredients, put the lid on and cook on High for 15 minutes.
2.   Release the pressure naturally for 10 minutes, divide the mix into bowls and serve.
Nutrition: calories 220, fat 9.2, fiber 4.2, carbs 14.4, protein 3.6

Raisins Rice

Preparation time: 10 minutes
Cooking time: 25 minutes
Servings: 4
Ingredients:

- 1 cup grapes, halved
- ½ cup white rice
- 2 cups milk
- ¼ cup raisins
- 2 tablespoons sugar
- ½ teaspoon lime juice
- 1 teaspoon vanilla extract

Directions:
1.   In your instant pot, combine grapes with the rice, milk and the other ingredients, toss, put the lid on and cook on High for 25 minutes.
2.   Release the pressure naturally for 10 minutes, divide the mix into bowls and serve.
Nutrition: calories 262, fat 12.2, fiber 4.2, carbs 11.4, protein 3.5

Cocoa Milky Grapes

Preparation time: 5 minutes
Cooking time: 15 minutes
Servings: 4
Ingredients:

- 1 cup grapes, halved
- 1 tablespoon cocoa powder
- 1 cup milk
- 1 tablespoon sugar
- ½ teaspoon cardamom, ground

Directions:
1.   In your instant pot, combine the grapes with the cocoa and the other ingredients, toss, put the lid on and cook on High for 15 minutes.
2.   Release the pressure fast for 5 minutes, divide the mix into bowls and serve.
Nutrition: calories 272, fat 11.2, fiber 4.3, carbs 13.4, protein 2.5

Cranberries with Milky Pistachios

Preparation time: 10 minutes
Cooking time: 20 minutes
Servings: 4
Ingredients:

- 4 ounces cranberries, chopped
- 2 cups milk
- 2 tablespoons pistachios, chopped
- 4 tablespoons sugar
- 1 teaspoon ginger powder
- 1 teaspoon cinnamon powder
- ½ teaspoon turmeric powder
- 2 cups water

Directions:
1.   In a bowl, combine the cranberries with the milk, pistachios and the other ingredients, whisk well and divide into 4 ramekins.
2.   Add the water to the instant pot, add the steamer basket inside, add the ramekins inside, put the lid on and cook on High for 20 minutes.
3.   Release the pressure naturally for 10 minutes, and serve the dessert cold.
Nutrition: calories 134, fat 3.4, fiber 1.3, carbs 21.6, protein 4.4

Carrots Sugary Pudding

Preparation time: 10 minutes
Cooking time: 20 minutes
Serving: 4
Ingredients:

- 1 pound carrots, grated
- 2 eggs, whisked
- 2 cups milk
- ¾ cup sugar
- 1 teaspoon cinnamon powder
- 1 teaspoon turmeric powder
- ½ teaspoon saffron powder
- 1 cup water

Directions:
1.   In a bowl, mix the carrots with the eggs and the other ingredients except the water, whisk well and transfer to a pudding mould.
2.   Add the water to the instant pot, add the steamer basket, put the pudding pan inside, put the lid on and cook on High for 20 minutes.
3.   Release the pressure naturally for 10 minutes, cool the pudding down and serve.
Nutrition: calories 200, fat 8.5, fiber 3.2, carbs 11.5, protein 4.6

Apples Quinoa Cardamom Pudding
Preparation time: 10 minutes
Cooking time: 20 minutes
Servings: 4
Ingredients:
- 2 cups milk
- ½ cup quinoa
- 2 apples, cored, peeled and cubed
- ½ cup sugar
- 1 teaspoon turmeric powder
- ½ teaspoon cardamom powder
- 1 teaspoon cinnamon powder

Directions:
1. In your instant pot, mix the quinoa with the milk and the other ingredients, toss, put the lid on and cook on High for 20 minutes.
2. Release the pressure naturally for 10 minutes, divide the pudding into bowls and serve.
Nutrition: calories 272, fat 7.6, fiber 2, carbs 11.4, protein 2.5

Almond & Rice Pudding
Preparation time: 10 minutes
Cooking time: 20 minutes
Servings: 4
Ingredients:
- ¼ cup almonds, chopped
- 1 cup rice
- 2 eggs, whisked
- 2 cups milk
- 3 tablespoons sugar
- 1 teaspoon turmeric powder
- 1 teaspoon cinnamon powder
- 1 teaspoon vanilla extract

Directions:
1. In your instant pot, mix the rice with the almonds, the eggs and the other ingredients, whisk, put the lid on and cook on High for 20 minutes.
2. Release the pressure naturally for 10 minutes, divide the pudding into bowls and serve.
Nutrition: calories 334, fat 8, fiber 1.5, carbs 53.9, protein 11.4

Coconut and White Cinnamon Rice
Preparation time: 10 minutes
Cooking time: 20 minutes
Servings: 4
Ingredients:
- 1 cup white rice
- 1 cup coconut cream
- 1 cup milk
- 1 tablespoon cinnamon powder
- ½ cup sugar
- 1 teaspoon saffron powder

Directions:
1. In your instant pot, combine the rice with the cream and the other ingredients, whisk, put the lid on and cook on High for 20 minutes.

2. Release the pressure naturally for 10 minutes, divide everything into bowls and serve.
Nutrition: calories 431, fat 15.9, fiber 1.9, carbs 68.3, protein 6.7

Saffron Coconut Cream
Preparation time: 10 minutes
Cooking time: 15 minutes
Servings: 4
Ingredients:
- 1 cup heavy cream
- 1 cup coconut cream
- ½ teaspoon saffron powder
- 1 teaspoon vanilla extract
- 4 tablespoons sugar
- Zest of 1 lime, grated
- 1 tablespoon lime juice
- 1 cup water

Directions:
1. In a bowl, mix the cream with the coconut cream and the other ingredients except the water, whisk well and divide into 4 ramekins.
2. Add the water to the instant pot, add the steamer basket, put the ramekins inside, put the lid on and cook on High for 15 minutes.
3. Release the pressure naturally for 10 minutes and serve the mix cold.
Nutrition: calories 292, fat 25.4, fiber 1.4, carbs 17.2, protein 2

Milky Raisins Pudding
Preparation time: 10 minutes
Cooking time: 20 minutes
Servings: 4
Ingredients:
- 1 cup white rice
- 2 cups milk
- ½ cup raisins
- 4 tablespoons sugar
- ½ teaspoon vanilla extract
- ½ teaspoon turmeric powder

Directions:
1. In your instant pot, combine the rice with the milk, raisins and the other ingredients, whisk, put the lid on and cook on High for 20 minutes.
2. Release the pressure naturally for 10 minutes, and serve the pudding cold.
Nutrition: calories 270, fat 6.4, fiber 2.4, carbs 11.5, protein 4.2

Cardamom Banana and Avocado Mix
Preparation time: 5 minutes
Cooking time: 10 minutes
Servings: 4
Ingredients:
- 2 bananas, peeled and sliced
- 1 avocado, peeled, pitted and cut into wedges
- 1 teaspoon vanilla extract
- ½ teaspoon cardamom, ground
- ½ teaspoon turmeric powder
- 1 tablespoon cinnamon powder
- 1 cup milk
- 2 tablespoons sugar

Directions:
1. In your instant pot, mix the bananas with the avocado and the other ingredients, toss, put the lid on and cook on High for 10 minutes.
2. Release the pressure fast for 5 minutes, divide the mix into bowls and serve cold.
Nutrition: calories 282, fat 5.4, fiber 2.3, carbs 11.4, protein 4.6

Masala Grapes and Bananas
Preparation time: 5 minutes
Cooking time: 10 minutes
Servings: 4
Ingredients:
- 1 cup grapes, halved
- 2 bananas, peeled and sliced
- Juice of ½ lemon
- 1 tablespoon lemon zest, grated
- 1 cup coconut cream
- ½ teaspoon turmeric powder
- ½ teaspoon chana masala
- ½ teaspoon vanilla extract

Directions:
1. In your instant pot, mix grapes with the bananas and the other ingredients, toss, put the lid on and cook on High for 10 minutes.
2. Release the pressure fast for 5 minutes, divide the mix into bowls and serve.
Nutrition: calories 162, fat 4.2, fiber 2.1, carbs 7.4, protein 1.6

Saffron Cauliflower Rice Pudding
Preparation time: 10 minutes
Cooking time: 15 minutes
Servings: 4
Ingredients:
- 1 cup cauliflower rice
- 1 tablespoon raisins
- 1 tablespoon pistachios, chopped
- 2 cups milk
- ½ teaspoon saffron powder
- 3 tablespoon sugar
- 1 teaspoon vanilla extract
- 1 tablespoon cinnamon powder

Directions:

1. In your instant pot, mix the cauliflower rice with the raisins, the pistachios and the rest of the ingredients, put the lid on and cook on High for 15 minutes.
2. Release the pressure naturally for 10 minutes, divide the mix into bowls and serve.
Nutrition: calories 124, fat 3.4, fiber 0.2, carbs 18.9, protein 5.3

Sweet Wheat Bowls
Preparation time: 10 minutes
Cooking time: 20 minutes
Servings: 4
Ingredients:
- 1 cup broken wheat
- 2 cups milk
- 3 tablespoons sugar
- 1 tablespoon lemon juice
- ½ teaspoon turmeric powder
- 1 teaspoon lemon zest, grated

Directions:
1. In your instant pot, combine the wheat with the milk and the other ingredients, whisk, put the lid on and cook on High for 20 minutes.
2. Release the pressure naturally for 10 minutes, divide the mix into bowls and serve.
Nutrition: calories 195, fat 2.6, fiber 0.1, carbs 15.4, protein 4.1

Sweet Potatoes Vanilla Pudding
Preparation time: 10 minutes
Cooking time: 20 minutes
Servings: 4
Ingredients:
- 1 cup sweet potatoes, peeled and grated
- 1 egg, whisked
- 2 cups milk
- 3 tablespoons sugar
- 1 cup coconut cream
- 1 teaspoon vanilla extract
- 1 teaspoon saffron powder
- ½ teaspoon cardamom, ground

Directions:
1. In your instant pot, combine the potatoes with the egg and the other ingredients, whisk, put the lid on and cook on High for 20 minutes.
2. Release the pressure naturally for 10 minutes, divide the pudding into bowls and serve.
Nutrition: calories 297, fat 18, fiber 2.9, carbs 29.2, protein 7.4

Cashew Apples Bowls

Preparation time: 10 minutes
Cooking time: 15 minutes
Servings: 4
Ingredients:
- 1 cup cashew milk
- 1 tablespoon lime zest, grated
- 1 tablespoon lime juice
- 2 apples, cored and cubed
- 1 teaspoon vanilla extract
- 1 cup water

Directions:
1. In your instant pot, combine the apples with the milk and the other ingredients, toss, put the lid on and cook on High for 15 minutes.
2. Release the pressure naturally for 10 minutes, divide into bowls and serve.
Nutrition: calories 92, fat 1.5, fiber 2.9, carbs 18.4, protein 2.3

Sugary Orange Cream

Preparation time: 10 minutes
Cooking time: 20 minutes
Servings: 4
Ingredients:
- Juice of 1 orange
- 1 pound orange, peeled and cut into segments
- 1 tablespoon lime zest, grated
- 4 tablespoons sugar
- 1 cup heavy cream

Directions:
1. In your instant pot, mix the oranges with the orange juice and the rest of the ingredients, put the lid on and cook on High for 20 minutes.
2. Release the pressure naturally for 10 minutes, blend the mix using an immersion blender, divide into bowls and serve cold.
Nutrition: calories 162, fat 9.1, fiber 3.2, carbs 11.3, protein 2.6

Raspberries and Milky Rice

Preparation time: 10 minutes
Cooking time: 20 minutes
Servings: 4
Ingredients:
- 1 cup raspberries, chopped
- Zest of 1 lemon
- 1 cup white rice
- 2 cups milk
- 3 tablespoons sugar
- 1 teaspoon saffron powder
- 1 teaspoon vanilla extract

Directions:
1. In your instant pot, combine the raspberries with the rice and the other ingredients, whisk, put the lid on and cook on High for 20 minutes.
2. Release the pressure naturally for 10 minutes and serve cold.
Nutrition: calories 240, fat 7.1, fiber 4.2, carbs 11.4, protein 3.3

Cardamom Carrot Cream

Preparation time: 10 minutes
Cooking time: 20 minutes

Servings: 4
Ingredients:
- 1 pound carrots, peeled and grated
- 2 tablespoons lime juice
- 1 cup sugar
- 2 cups heavy cream
- 1 teaspoon turmeric powder
- ½ teaspoon cardamom powder
- 1 teaspoon cinnamon powder

Directions:
1. In your instant pot, combine the carrots with the lime juice and the other ingredients, whisk, put the lid on and cook on High for 20 minutes.
2. Release the pressure naturally for 10 minutes, blend the mix using an immersion blender, divide into bowls and serve cold.
Nutrition: calories 224, fat 9.2, fiber 2.2, carbs 8.4, protein 3.5

Cardamom Pears Smoothie

Preparation time: 10 minutes
Cooking time: 15 minutes
Servings: 4
Ingredients:
- 4 pears, cored, peeled and chopped
- 1 cup heavy cream
- 1 cup milk
- 1 teaspoon cardamom, ground
- ½ teaspoon turmeric powder
- 1 teaspoon vanilla extract

Directions:
1. In your instant pot, mix the pears with the cream and the rest of the ingredients, put the lid on and cook on High for 15 minutes.
2. Release the pressure naturally for 10 minutes, blend using an immersion blender, divide into bowls and serve.
Nutrition: calories 229, fat 5.2, fiber 3.2, carbs 11.4, protein 5.7

Saffron Cauliflower Rice

Preparation time: 10 minutes
Cooking time: 15 minutes
Servings: 4
Ingredients:
- 2 cups cauliflower rice
- ½ teaspoon saffron powder
- 2 tablespoons caster sugar
- 1 tablespoon ginger, grated
- 2 cups milk
- 1 teaspoon vanilla extract

Directions:
1. In your instant pot, mix the rice with the saffron powder and the rest of the ingredients, whisk, put the lid on and cook on High for 15 minutes.
2. Release the pressure naturally for 10 minutes, divide the rice mix in to bowls and serve.
Nutrition: calories 91, fat 10.9, fiber 4.3, carbs 40.1, protein 8.3

Zesty Blackberries Bowls
Preparation time: 10 minutes
Cooking time: 15 minutes
Servings: 4
Ingredients:
- 3 cups blackberries
- 1 teaspoon turmeric powder
- 2 tablespoons lime zest, grated
- 2 tablespoons sugar
- 1 and ½ cups milk
- 1 teaspoon vanilla extract

Directions:
1. In your instant pot, mix the berries with the turmeric, lime zest and the other ingredients, toss, put the lid on and cook on High for 15 minutes.
2. Release the pressure naturally for 10 minutes, divide the mix into bowls and serve cold.
Nutrition: calories 120, fat 1.3, fiber 6.4, carbs 25.1, protein 3.3

Apple Milky Quinoa Mix
Preparation time: 10 minutes
Cooking time: 15 minutes
Servings: 4
Ingredients:
- 2 cups apples, cored and cubed
- 2 tablespoons lemon juice
- 1 cup quinoa
- 2 cups milk
- ½ teaspoon cardamom powder
- ¾ cup sugar
- 1 teaspoon vanilla extract

Directions:
1. In your instant pot, mix the quinoa with the apples and the rest of the ingredients, put the lid on and cook on High for 15 minutes.
2. Release the pressure naturally for 10 minutes, divide the mix into bowls and serve.
Nutrition: calories 252, fat 4.1, fiber 3.2, carbs 7.4, protein 2.5

Saffron Avocado Cream
Preparation time: 5 minutes
Cooking time: 10 minutes
Servings: 4
Ingredients:
- 2 avocados, peeled, pitted and cut into wedges
- 1 teaspoon saffron powder
- 1 cup heavy cream
- 2 tablespoons lime juice
- 3 tablespoons sugar

Directions:
1. In your instant pot, mix the avocados with the saffron and the other ingredients, whisk, put the lid on and cook on High for 10 minutes.
2. Release the pressure fast for 5 minutes, blend the mix using an immersion blender, divide into bowls and serve.
Nutrition: calories 210, fat 11.2, fiber 2.2, carbs 8.5, protein 2.5

Milky Apricots Rice
Preparation time: 10 minutes
Cooking time: 25 minutes
Servings: 4
Ingredients:
- 2 cups apricots, cubed
- 1 cup white rice
- 2 cups milk
- 4 tablespoons sugar
- 1 tablespoon almonds, chopped
- 2 tablespoons ghee, melted
- 1 teaspoon turmeric powder

Directions:
1. In your instant pot, mix the apricots with the rice and the rest of the ingredients, put the lid on and cook on High for 25 minutes.
2. Release the pressure naturally for 10 minutes, divide everything into bowls and serve cold.
Nutrition: calories 258, fat 5.4, fiber 1, carbs 7.5, protein 2

Zucchinis Cardamom Rice
Preparation time: 10 minutes
Cooking time: 15 minutes
Servings: 4
Ingredients:
- 2 cups zucchinis, grated
- 1 cup heavy cream
- 1 cup milk
- ½ teaspoon saffron powder
- ½ teaspoon cardamom powder
- 4 tablespoons sugar
- 1 teaspoon vanilla extract

Directions:
1. In your instant pot, mix the zucchinis with the cream, the milk and with the rest of the ingredients, put the lid on and cook on High for 15 minutes.
2. Release the pressure naturally for 10 minutes, divide the mix into bowls and serve.
Nutrition: calories 252, fat 7.2, fiber 2, carbs 8.4, protein 1.4

Dates Quinoa
Preparation time: 10 minutes
Cooking time: 20 minutes
Servings: 4
Ingredients:
- 1 cup quinoa
- 2 cups milk
- ½ cup dates, pitted
- ½ teaspoon turmeric powder
- ½ teaspoon saffron powder
- 1 teaspoon cinnamon powder
- 1 teaspoon vanilla extract

Directions:
1. In your instant pot, mix the quinoa with the milk and the other ingredients, whisk, put the lid on and cook on High for 20 minutes.
2. Release the pressure naturally for 10 minutes, divide the mix into bowls and serve cold.
Nutrition: calories 210, fat 6.1, fiber 2, carbs 8.4, protein 3.6

Coconut Banana Pot

Preparation time: 10 minutes
Cooking time: 15 minutes
Servings: 4
Ingredients:
- 2 bananas, peeled and sliced
- ½ teaspoon cinnamon powder
- 1 cup yogurt
- 2 tablespoons sugar
- 2 tablespoons coconut flakes

Directions:
1. In your instant pot, combine the bananas with the cinnamon and the rest of the ingredients, put the lid on and cook on High for 15 minutes.
2. Release the pressure naturally for 10 minutes, divide the mix into bowls and serve.

Nutrition: calories 127, fat 1.8, fiber 1.8, carbs 24.2, protein 4.2

Cardamom Walnuts Cream

Preparation time: 10 minutes
Cooking time: 20 minutes
Servings: 4
Ingredients:
- 1 cup milk
- 1 cup heavy cream
- 3 eggs, whisked
- 1 teaspoon vanilla extract
- 3 tablespoons sugar
- 2 cups walnuts, chopped
- 1 teaspoon cardamom powder
- 1 teaspoon turmeric powder
- 1 teaspoon cinnamon powder

Directions:
1. In your instant pot, combine the milk with the cream and the other ingredients, stir, put the lid on and cook on High for 20 minutes.
2. Release the pressure naturally for 10 minutes, blend using an immersion blender, divide into bowls and serve cold.

Nutrition: calories 608, fat 52.6, fiber 4.5, carbs 20.1, protein 21.9

Coconut Strawberry Mix

Preparation time: 10 minutes
Cooking time: 20 minutes
Servings: 4
Ingredients:
- 1 cup coconut cream
- 1 cup strawberries, chopped
- 3 tablespoons sugar
- 1 cup milk
- 1 teaspoon vanilla extract
- 2 eggs, whisked
- 2 cups water

Directions:
1. In a bowl, mix the cream with the strawberries and the other ingredients except the water, blend

using an immersion blender, and divide into 4 ramekins.
2. Add the water to the instant pot, add the steamer basket, put the ramekins inside, put the lid on and cook on High for 20 minutes.
3. Release the pressure naturally for 10 minutes, and serve the dessert cold.

Nutrition: calories 248, fat 17.9, fiber 2, carbs 18.4, protein 6.4

Pineapple Pudding

Preparation time: 10 minutes
Cooking time: 20 minutes
Servings: 4
Ingredients:
- 2 cups milk
- 1 cup white rice
- ½ cup pineapple, peeled and cubed
- 1 teaspoon saffron powder
- ½ teaspoon cardamom powder
- ½ cup sugar
- ½ teaspoon vanilla extract

Directions:
1. In your instant pot, mix the rice with the pineapple and the other ingredients, put the lid on and cook on High for 20 minutes.
2. Release the pressure naturally for 10 minutes, divide the pudding into bowls and serve cold.

Nutrition: calories 262, fat 6.3, fiber 2, carbs 11.5, protein 4.6

Sugary Coconut Parfait

Preparation time: 10 minutes
Cooking time: 15 minutes
Servings: 4
Ingredients:
- 3 eggs, whisked
- 2 cups heavy cream
- 1/3 cup sugar
- 1 tablespoon ghee, melted
- ½ cup coconut cream
- 1 teaspoon turmeric powder
- ½ cup coconut flakes
- 1 teaspoon vanilla extract

Directions:
1. In your instant pot, mix the eggs with the cream and the rest of the ingredients, whisk, put the lid on and cook on High for 15 minutes.
2. Release the pressure naturally for 10 minutes, blend the mix using an immersion blender, divide the mix in bowls and serve.

Nutrition: calories 228, fat 7.5, fiber 3.1, carbs 12.2, protein 1.6

Milky Cardamom Pudding

Preparation time: 10 minutes
Cooking time: 20 minutes
Servings: 4
Ingredients:
- 1 cup quinoa
- 2 cups milk
- 2 eggs, whisked
- 3 tablespoon sugar
- 2 teaspoons vanilla extract
- ½ teaspoon saffron powder
- ¼ teaspoon cardamom, ground

Directions:
1. In your instant pot, combine the quinoa with the milk and the other ingredients, whisk, put the lid on and cook on High for 20 minutes.
2. Release the pressure naturally for 10 minutes, divide the mix into bowls and serve cold.
Nutrition: calories 289, fat 7.3, fiber 3, carbs 42.8, protein 12.8

Dark Chocolate Cream

Preparation time: 10 minutes
Cooking time: 20 minutes
Servings: 4
Ingredients:
- 2 cups milk
- 1 cup heavy cream
- ¼ cup sugar
- 1/3 cup ghee, melted
- ½ teaspoon saffron powder
- 1 teaspoon vanilla extract
- ¼ cup dark chocolate, chopped
- 2 cups water

Directions:
1. In a bowl, combine the milk with the cream and the other ingredients except the water, whisk well and divide into 4 ramekins.
2. Put the water in the instant pot, add the steamer basket, add the ramekins, put the lid on and cook on High for 20 minutes.
3. Release the pressure naturally for 10 minutes, and serve the cream cold.
Nutrition: calories 420, fat 33.7, fiber 0.4, carbs 25.7, protein 5.5

Rhubarb Milky Quinoa

Preparation time: 10 minutes
Cooking time: 15 minutes
Servings: 4
Ingredients:
- 1 cup milk
- ½ cup quinoa
- ½ teaspoon saffron powder
- 2 tablespoons sugar
- ½ teaspoon cardamom powder
- 2 cups rhubarb, chopped
- 1 teaspoon vanilla extract

Directions:
1. In your instant pot, combine the milk with the quinoa and the other ingredients, whisk, put the lid on and cook on High for 15 minutes.
2. Release the pressure naturally for 10 minutes, divide into bows and serve cold.
Nutrition: calories 148, fat 2.7, fiber 2.7, carbs 25.7, protein 5.6

Cardamom Mango and Banana

Preparation time: 10 minutes
Cooking time: 10 minutes
Servings: 4
Ingredients:
- 1 cup mango, peeled and cubed
- 2 bananas, peeled and sliced
- 1 tablespoon lime juice
- ½ teaspoon cardamom powder
- ½ teaspoon dry mango powder
- ½ teaspoon cinnamon powder
- 1 cup milk
- 2 tablespoons sugar

Directions:
1. In your instant pot, combine the mango with the bananas, lime juice and the other ingredients, toss gently, put the lid on and cook on High for 10 minutes.
2. Release the pressure naturally for 10 minutes, divide the mix into bowls and serve cold.
Nutrition: calories 134, fat 1.6, fiber 2.3, carbs 29.8, protein 3.1

Sugary Pumpkin Mix

Preparation time: 10 minutes
Cooking time: 15 minutes
Servings: 4
Ingredients:
- 1 cup milk
- ½ cup sugar
- 1 cup heavy cream
- ½ teaspoon saffron powder
- 1 teaspoon nutmeg, ground
- 2 tablespoons ghee, melted
- 2 cups pumpkin flesh

Directions:
1. In your instant pot, combine the milk with the pumpkin and the other ingredients, toss gently, put the lid on and cook on High for 15 minutes.
2. Release the pressure naturally for 10 minutes, cool the mix down, divide into bowls and serve.
Nutrition: calories 311, fat 19, fiber 1.5, carbs 35.1, protein 3.6

Conclusion

Instant Pot is an essential kitchen appliance for those seeking a way to prepare their meals quickly and healthy. Indian cuisine is believed to be one of the most popular of a kind. To get these two together means make it simple and make it tasty with your everyday cooking. The flavorful diversity of Indian cuisine made right is that this cookbook offers to its readers. Best way to cook rice? Simplest Indian dessert? Both of them in here!

This Indian Instant Pot is a game-changer to Indian cooking. Indian ingredients and Instant Pot sensibilities are blended on these pages creating the ultimate mix of simplicity and authenticity for any home cook. Designed to work well for any experience level this cookbook is a smart and creative choice for Indian cooking novices and experts alike.

It will take you through cooking all the meals of the day and indulge you in the best Indian desserts. Creating everyday cooking staples out of the country's classic is a mastery. This cookbook is a work of culinary art that's ready to deliver bold flavors and colors whenever you need it.

Appendix : Recipes Index

Cocoa Pork Chops and Green Beans 96
Cocoa Turkey and Kidney Beans 78
Cocoa Zucchinis 110
Coconut and White Cinnamon Rice 116
Coconut Banana Pot 120
Coconut Beans and Peppers 36
Coconut Cauliflower Dip 57
Coconut Cauliflower Mix 43
Coconut Cauliflower Soup 30
Coconut Chili Beets 103
Coconut Cod Curry 61
Coconut Cod Mix 62
Coconut Creamy Endives Dip 55
Coconut Curry 38
Coconut Lamb with Carrots 93
Coconut Lentils Stew 34
Coconut Masala Beef 90
Coconut Masala Tomatoes 109
Coconut Meatballs 100
Coconut Onion Dip 56
Coconut Peas Curry 29
Coconut Ribs Curry 87
Coconut Shrimp and Zucchinis 67
Coconut Spiced Chicken 75
Coconut Strawberry Mix 120
Coconut Thoran 40
Coconut Turkey & Carrots 86
Coconut Turkey Soup 32
Coconut Turkey with Chili Beans 82
Cod and Garam Masala Sauce 63
Cod and Mint Chutney 71
Cod and Pepper Paste 71
Cod and Tomato Bowls 61
Coriander Artichokes 102
Coriander Broccoli and Onions 106
Coriander Cabbage Soup 31
Coriander Chicken 81
Coriander Chicken and Mango 75
Coriander Chicken Meatballs 78
Coriander Cod 62
Coriander Lamb with Beets 95
Coriander Okra Mix 36
Coriander Pork with Potatoes 98
Coriander Zucchinis and Eggplants 109
Crab and Shrimp Salad 62
Crab Tamarind Curry 70
Cranberries with Milky Pistachios 115
Cream Cheese Dip 55
Cream Cheese Turkey and Rice 79
Creamy Artichokes and Coconut 102
Creamy Beans and Rice 47
Creamy Beef and Rice 91
Creamy Brussels Sprouts 104
Creamy Coconut Pork 87
Creamy Cod Tikka 60
Creamy Eggplants 109
Creamy Lamb with Green Beans 93
Creamy Mango Salad 54
Creamy Masala Cauliflower 107
Creamy Mushrooms 59

Creamy Potato and Apples Mix 108
Creamy Potato Mushrooms 19
Creamy Potatoes 105
Creamy Salmon and Saffron Asparagus 63
Creamy Turkey and Peas Mix 85
Creamy Wheat Upma 10
Creamy White Fish Mix 60
Cucumber and Mango Salad 55
Cumin Beef 90
Cumin Cod and Rice 61
Cumin Eggplant and Tomato Bowls 53
Cumin Potato and Cream 112
Cumin Quinoa 38
Cumin Spinach and Potato 107
Cumin Turkey and Asparagus 75
Curd & Spinach Chicken Salad 54
Curry Beet Rice 39
Curry Cabbage Thoran 37
Curry Carrot Poriyal 40
Curry Coconut Clams 69
Curry Pork with Lentils 89
Curry Quinoa 18
Curry Rava Upma 16
Curry Shrimp Biryani 27

D

Dark Chocolate Cream 121
Dates Quinoa 119
Dill Potatoes 105
Dum Potatoes 23

E

Eggplant Cumin Bhurtha 42
Eggplant Ka Bharta 42
Eggplant Masala 108
Endives and Cumin Walnuts Pot 49
Endives with Orange Mix 49

F

Farro Corn Masala 17
Fenugreek Beans & Orange Sauce 103
Fenugreek Beets and Onions 112
Fenugreek Peppers Mix 104
Fenugreek Trout 64
Fenugreek Wheat Paratha 9
Fenugreek Zucchini 105
Figs and Spinach Salad 21
Flattened Rice Poha 11
French-styled Oats Upma 10

G

Garam Masala Asparagus 103
Garam Masala Capsicum 13
Garam Masala Shrimp and Okra 66
Garlic Chili Dip 51
Garlic Pork 100
Garlic Rice Mix 46
Garlic Turkey and Cauliflower Rice 82
Garlicky Broccoli Junka 33
Ghee Carrot Pudding 33
Ginger Asparagus 103
Ginger Beef Curry 88
Ginger Beef Mix 88
Ginger Broccoli and Orange Mix 47

Ginger Carrots Chicken Soup 29
Ginger Coconut Tuna 64
Ginger Cod Masala 64
Ginger Peas Pot 40
Ginger Pork with Bamboo 99
Ginger Potato 37
Ginger Zucchinis and Carrots 111
Goat Peppercorn Curry 25
Gold Potato Masala 10
Gold Potato Masala 105
Green Beans Cumin Curry 35
Green Cauliflower Dosa 15
Green Peas Basmati Rice 16
Green Peas Matar 41
Ground Beef Masala 89

H

Herbed Beef Stew 32
Herbed Salmon and Broccoli 61
Hot Coconut Clams 70
Hot Shrimp and Peppers Salad 53

I

Indian Almond Kulfi 113
Indian Coconut Soup 30
Indian Fennel Halibut 63
Indian Spicy Asparagus 49
Indian Tomato Soup 31

J

Jeera Potatoes 13

K

Kale and Dates Salad 44
Keema Beef Peas 26
Khara Wheat and Curry Biscuits 50

L

Lamb Roghan Ghosht 25
Lemongrass Yogurt Turkey 72
Lime Spinach and Okra 108

M

Madras Tomato Beef 87
Mahi Mahi Yogurt Tikka 71
Mango and Kale Mix 45
Mango Beans Dal 14
Mango Broccoli Spread 57
Mango Turmeric Kale 109
Masala & Coconut Fennel Pot 107
Masala Artichokes and Rice 102
Masala Beans Spread 54
Masala Bell Chicken 73
Masala Chicken and Broccoli 81
Masala Chicken and Zucchini 77
Masala Chickpeas Hummus 51
Masala Cinnamon Beef 92
Masala Curry Endives 107
Masala Grapes and Bananas 117
Masala Lamb with Corn 93
Masala Macaroni 28
Masala Pork Chops and Cauliflower 97
Masala Potato 36
Masala Potato Stew 32
Masala Tomato Beans Curry 28
Milky Apricots Rice 119

Milky Cardamom Dalia 11
Milky Cardamom Pudding 121
Milky Grated Paneer Spread 15
Milky Oats Porridge 12
Milky Payasam 113
Milky Pistachios Halwa 113
Milky Raisins Pudding 116
Milky Rice Bowls 20
Milky Spinach Spread 53
Millet Malt Java 22
Millet Uppittu 17
Minty Masala Lamb 94
Minty Masala Tomatoes 111
Minty Yogurt Dip 51
Mulligatawny Tomato Soup 30
Mung and Potato Khichuri 24
Mung Dal Pongal 21
Mung Khichdi 12
Mung Pongal 11
Mushroom and Paneer Dip 59
Mushroom Curd Dip 59
Mustard Mahi Mahi 70
Mustard Pork Chops 95
Mustard Potato Curry 8

N

Narangi Rice Pulao 46
Nutmeg Asparagus 102
Nutmeg Masala Turkey 85
Nutmeg Mutton Stew 33
Nutmeg Okra 106
Nutmeg Pork Chops 97

O

Okra Masala 12
Onion Beef in Yogurt 88
Onion Brussels Sprouts 44
Onion Chicken and Artichokes 73
Onion Langar Dal 28
Onion Pork Chops 96
Onion Pork with Almonds 97
Onion Potato and Carrots 111
Onion Spinach and Broccoli 112
Onion Turkey Yogurt Mix 72
Orange Fenugreek Pork Mix 99
Orange Masala Zucchinis 110
Orange Pulao 45
Orange Turkey and Herbed Broccoli 72
Oregano Chicken and Eggplants 74

P

Pandan Crab and Eggplants 70
Pandi Onion Stew 98
Paneer Cashew Cheese Masala 12
Paneer Fenugreek Masala 23
Paneer Peas 40
Paprika BBQ Ribs 101
Paprika Bean Stew 35
Paprika Chicken and Pineapple 77
Paprika Chicken Pot 77
Paprika Pork Mix 98
Paprika Shrimp Salad 54
Paprika Tuna Curry 65

Paprika Turkey Mix 78
Parsley Endives and Tomatoes 48
Parsnips and Carrots Mix 42
Peach and Mango Lassi 18
Peas and Fennel Mix 49
Peas Pulao 41
Pepper Shrimp Mix 52
Pepper Turkey Mix 74
Pineapple Masala 20
Pineapple Pudding 120
Pistachio Parfait 114
Pistachio Phirni 113
Pomegranate Chicken with Cauliflower 82
Pork and Tomato Chutney 96
Pork Chili Cheese Soup 99
Pork Chops with Spinach 95
Pork Indaad 98
Pork Kaleez Ankiti 100
Pork Potatoes Mix 100
Pork with Cinnamon Carrots Mix 96
Potato and Broccoli Cream 29
Potato Baingan Masala 23
Potato Coconut Dip 55
Potato Egg Curry 18
Potato Ki Kadhi 31
Potato Radish Pods Ki Sabzi 13
Potato Sabjee 37
Punjabi Potato Paratha 8
Pyaaz Onion Chutney 50

Q

Quinoa Curry Mix 39
Quinoa Pilaf 38
Quinoa, Mango and Avocado Salad 58

R

Radish Sea Bass 65
Ragi and Urad Dal Idli 19
Ragi Halwa 22
Raisins Rice 115
Raspberries and Milky Rice 118
Rhubarb Milky Quinoa 121
Rice Ada Pradhaman 114
Rice and Kale 46
Rice Bowls with Masala Sprouts 19
Rice Chicken Biryani 24
Rice Kanda Poha 9
Rice Poha 9
Rice Salad 20
Rice Turkey and Brussels Sprouts 84

S

Saag and Paprika Beef Gosht 90
Saffron Avocado Cream 119
Saffron Cauliflower Rice 118
Saffron Cauliflower Rice Pudding 117
Saffron Coconut Cream 116
Saffron Cumin Shrimp 56
Saffron Red Cabbage 47
Saffron Zucchini Pudding 114
Salmon and Chili Sauce 63
Salmon and Radish Coconut Mix 65
Sea Bass and Cumin Lentils 69

Serrano Potato and Pea Curry 27
Shallot Chicken Wings 84
Shallot Salmon Curry 60
Shrimp and Creamy Beans Appetizer 59
Shrimp and Creamy Corn 67
Shrimp and Radish Coconut Curry 66
Shrimp and Sweet Potatoes Pot 66
Shrimp and White Rice 62
Shrimp Bowls 52
Shrimp Tomato Chili Curry 26
Soupy Peas Ka Nimona 42
Spiced Cauliflower Gobi 43
Spiced Eggplant Mix 108
Spiced Kale and Brussels Sprouts 45
Spiced Lamb & Brussels Sprouts 94
Spicy Artichokes and Rice 48
Spicy Coconut Tilapia 68
Spicy Cumin Tomatoes 48
Spicy Eggplant Mix 46
Spicy Okra Fry 14
Spicy Paprika Cauliflower 43
Spicy Pork and Artichokes 101
Spinach and Chana Dal Rice 16
Spinach and Coconut Avocado Dip 53
Spinach Paneer 23
Spinach Potatoes Kabab 41
Spinach Soup 30
Spinach Turkey Bowls 55
Spinach Turmeric Mix 106
Stuffed Bitter Melon 13
Sugary Coconut Parfait 120
Sugary Orange Cream 118
Sugary Pumpkin Mix 121
Sweet Paprika and Peas Curry 34
Sweet Potato and Zucchini 106
Sweet Potato Cream Soup 14
Sweet Potatoes Vanilla Pudding 117
Sweet Wheat Bowls 117

T

Tamarind Yogurt Dip 51
Tapioca Pearls Knichdi 17
Thyme Lentils and Tomatoes Bowls 59
Tilapia and Radish Saad 65
Tilapia Cardamom Masala 68
Tilapia Curry 68
Toast Chili Upumavu 17
Tomato Chicken and Mushrooms 79
Tomato Chili Chutney 50
Tomato Cod Pot 71
Tomato Cucumber Salad 57
Tomato Omelet 21
Tomato Rice 15
Tomato Salad 48
Trout and Cardamom Tomatoes 62
Tuna and Avocado Mix 66
Tuna and Green Beans 67
Turkey and Curried Lentils 80
Turkey and Fenugreek Chickpeas 80
Turkey and Masala Asparagus 83
Turkey and Masala Sauce 77

CPSIA information can be obtained
at www.ICGtesting.com
Printed in the USA
LVHW020940150723
752576LV00008B/162